FREUD'S LITERARY CULTURE

This original study investigates the role played by literature in Sigmund Freud's creation and development of psychoanalysis. Graham Frankland analyses the whole range of Freud's own texts from a literary-critical perspective, providing a fresh and comprehensive reappraisal of his life's work. Freud was steeped in classical European literature but seems initially to have repressed all literary influences on his scientific work. Frankland traces their reemergence, examining in detail Freud's many literary allusions and quotations as well as the rhetoric and imagery of his writing. He explores Freud's own attempts at analysing literature, the influence of literary criticism on his approach to analysing patients, and his creation of psychoanalytical 'novels', quasi-literary fictions fraught with profoundly personal subtexts. *Freud's Literary Culture* sheds new light on a multi-faceted, contradictory writer who continues to have an unparalleled impact on our postmodern culture precisely because he was so deeply rooted in European literary tradition.

GRAHAM FRANKLAND is Research Fellow in German at the University of Liverpool. He is currently translating Freud's 'The Unconscious' for Penguin Modern Classics.

CAMBRIDGE STUDIES IN GERMAN

General editors
H.B. Nisbet, University of Cambridge
Martin Swales, University of London
Advisory editor
Theodore J. Ziolkowski, Princeton University

Also in the series

FREUD'S LITERARY CULTURE

GRAHAM FRANKLAND

CAMBRIDGE
UNIVERSITY PRESS

PUBLISHED BY THE PRESS SYNDICATE OF THE UNIVERSITY OF CAMBRIDGE
The Pitt Building, Trumpington Street, Cambridge, United Kingdom

CAMBRIDGE UNIVERSITY PRESS
The Edinburgh Building, Cambridge CB2 2RU, UK   www.cup.cam.ac.uk
40 West 20th Street, New York, NY 10011-4211, USA   www.cup.org
10 Stamford Road, Oakleigh, Melbourne 3166, Australia
Ruiz de Alarcón 13, 28014 Madrid, Spain

© Graham Frankland 2000

First published 2000

Printed in the United Kingdom at the University Press, Cambridge

Typeface Monotype Baskerville 11/12½pt   *System* QuarkXpress™ [SE]

A catalogue record for this book is available from the British Library

Library of Congress Cataloguing in Publication data
Frankland, Graham.
Freud's literary culture / Graham Frankland.
p.   cm. – (Cambridge studies in German)
Includes bibliographical references and index.
ISBN 0 521 66316 4 (hardback)
1. Psychoanalysis and literature.   2. Freud, Sigmund, 1856–1939 –
Views on literature.   3. Freud, Sigmund, 1856–1939 – Knowledge –
Literature.   4. Literature – History and criticism – Theory, etc.
PN56.P92F66   2000
150.19′52–dc21   00-38041 CIP

ISBN 0 521 66316 4 hardback

For Janet

Contents

Preface

Throughout this book, the intention of which is to examine the role played by literature in Freud's creation, presentation, and development of psychoanalysis, my approach to his works will essentially be that of a literary critic. For this reason I shall not be aiming to make definitive pronouncements on the truth value of psychoanalysis, nor shall I address – at least, not explicitly – the various contemporary debates about the scientific and philosophical credentials of psychoanalysis, such as the feminist critique of Freud's patriarchal and phallocentric assumptions, for example, or the contentious issues involving memories of abuse recovered during therapy. Such omissions do not, of course, imply an imperious rejection on my part of the validity of these debates. In one respect, they correspond merely to a narrowing of *focus* that is essential when dealing with such a wide – and heavily trod – field as psychoanalysis. More importantly, they are a necessary corollary of my treatment of Freud's work not as a body of knowledge, but as a body of *writing*. I shall concentrate on analysing Freud's texts *as* texts – their rhetoric and imagery, their inner tensions and subtexts, their sources, their cultural background, and so on. Indeed, it is by focusing so intensively on the precise texture of Freud's works and, in particular, on his literary preoccupations and assumptions, that I hope to shed light on his creation of a new 'science' from some unexpected angles.

It should already be clear from this qualification that my own recourse to Freudian ideas – a recurrent theme of this book – does not constitute any endorsement of the absolute validity of those ideas. My work should leave the reader with not so much a new set of conclusions about psychoanalysis as a fresh sensitivity towards Freud's writing, an alertness to its rich contexts and fraught subtexts which, in the best literary-critical tradition, should ambiguate rather than definitively categorize his work. And yet the perspectives opened up by this 'literary-critical' approach are by no means without relevance to the current controversies and debates about psychoanalysis. For example, my focus on the question of how profoundly Freud's literary culture contextualizes psychoanalysis and reveals its essentially subjective origins in his own culturally acquired assumptions may subtly enrich – if only by the force of analogy – a feminist critique, say, of Freud's assumptions about gender. Similarly, and again only implicitly, it could be seen to go to the heart of the controversy about the scientific status of psychoanalysis. My findings could, for example, easily be appropriated by a strident critic of Freud's fundamentally unscientific methodology; equally, though, they could be invoked to question the whole relevance of the debate about his scientific credentials by revealing this to be based on too limited a critical paradigm with which to evaluate such a complex writer. Such issues are not conclusively resolved by this book. However, as commentators on Freud – and, for that matter, Freud himself – are generally at their weakest when trying to develop their sharpest insights into systematic theories or definitive, totalizing critiques, this irresolution may prove a fruitful one.

Acknowledgements

This book is based on the thesis for which I was awarded a PhD at the University of Liverpool in 1996. For help throughout its writing I am indebted above all to Dr Jim Simpson, whose course at the University of Liverpool first encouraged me to investigate Freud's works further, and who then provided invaluable assistance as my doctoral supervisor. I should also like to thank Dr Helena Kirkby for kindly reading through the early drafts of this book.

Introduction

It was primarily due to the traditional humanist education he received at the Sperl *Gymnasium* in Vienna that Sigmund Freud was so steeped in classical European literature. Here he was exposed to Homer and Sophocles, Shakespeare and Milton, and, of course, Goethe and Schiller, amongst many others. An equally important factor, though, was his own life-long passion for books. He was reading Goethe and even Shakespeare well before he went to secondary school, and his veneration of these authors was certainly more intense than that of most of his contemporaries who enjoyed a similar education. Although on leaving school he chose a career as a scientist, this by no means indicates that his literary interests had somehow waned. Not only was he fond of claiming that his inspiration to study medicine came from the public reading of an – albeit apocryphal – Goethe essay, 'Nature', his most enduring role models were men who, like Goethe and Leonardo da Vinci, excelled in both scientific and artistic fields of endeavour.

Freud certainly began his medical career as a strict materialist and empiricist, and he never relinquished his faith in nineteenth-century scientific values. It would be easy to surmise that the stern discipline of his medical training, received under the aegis of the pioneering 'Helmholtzian' Ernst von Brücke, stifled his youthful literary interests and thwarted forever his ambitions to emulate the Renaissance men he so admired. There is, however, a broad consensus amongst critics – the pioneers include Lionel Trilling, Philip Rieff, and Paul Ricoeur – that nothing quite so straightforward occurred.[1] Indeed, of the Freud commentators writing today, those concerned with the scientific or therapeutic credentials of psychoanalysis tend to be far less interesting than those who concentrate on the literary dimensions of Freud's texts, for example postmodernist critics such as Harold Bloom and those influenced by Jacques Lacan.[2] Whilst Freud would no doubt be aggrieved at this fundamental shift in the reception of his works, it does amount to a recognition of what he occasionally admitted were secret life-long aspirations. By various means – some overt, some surreptitious – Freud managed to reconcile his passion for literature with his scientific ambitions, and the result was a 'science' which simply cannot be properly understood or appreciated without reference to its creator's literary culture.

In the popular imagination, at least, Freud is more commonly viewed as a representative product of *fin-de-siècle* Vienna, or as a typically Jewish thinker. When his writing is analysed more carefully, however, it becomes evident that he is far more deeply rooted in the tradition of European literature than in, say, contemporary Austrian culture or any specifically Jewish tradition. Indeed, he is typical of the bourgeoisie of his era primarily because of his highly literary German education and culture; and, similarly, he is most typically Jewish, if such a designation means anything at all, in that this *Bildung* – personified in the towering figures of Goethe and Schiller – represented something of an *ersatz* religion to so many liberal, secularized German Jews. Freud's intimate acquaintance with classical literature is fundamental not only to his make-up as a writer, but to his very sense of his own identity, and a detailed study of his literary culture promises to shed more light on his work than any other socio-historical factor.

There is certainly no shortage of studies devoted to examining the various interfaces between psychoanalysis and literature. An analysis of Freud's own literary background, however, is already quite distinct from the vast majority of such studies, which tend to treat psychoanalysis as a static, *a priori* body of insights and techniques to be – more or less judiciously – applied to literary texts.[3] Whilst a number of critics, such as Gunnar Brandell and Steven Marcus, have addressed the very different question of humanist influences on Freudian theory itself,[4] few attempt to synthesize what is known about Freud's literary culture into a coherent account of its role in the development of psychoanalysis, and even fewer try to integrate the whole range of Freud's texts into such a framework. It should be borne in mind that Freud wrote a great variety of psychoanalytical works. Many are essentially clinical, such as his case histories and his guides to conducting therapeutic sessions; others concentrate on non-pathological objects of interpretation, most famously dreams, parapraxes, and jokes. Quite distinct again are Freud's various theoretical works, tackling such meta-psychological questions as the structure of the human psyche and the nature of the instincts; furthermore, he wrote many works of 'applied' analysis, addressing cultural phenomena ranging from religion to works of art and literature. Although Freud critics tend to emphasize a particular text or group of texts in their attempt to define the nature of his undertaking, my own central hypothesis – concerning the pervasive and dynamic nature of his literary influences – encompasses the entire range of his works.

The most obvious clue that Freud's literary interests penetrate the whole range of his written output is the fact that, regardless of their subject matter, his texts are replete with allusions to European literature. Whilst critics have drawn attention to individual quotations used by Freud, none has attempted to produce an account of their various functions within his texts. This is unfortunate as these allusions raise a crucial question, namely the possibility of 'unconscious' literary influences on Freud's actual formulation of theory. His gradually evolving theory of the instincts is a particularly germane area in this respect. My attempt at a coherent historical account of its development, structured entirely in terms of Freud's use of literary references, reveals much that is new about his susceptibility to sources of literary influence, not least the fact that these seem to acquire particular resonance during the periodic crises from which were born his most fundamental revisions of theory.

It is more difficult to make an original contribution regarding Freud's pieces of literary criticism. The emotional ambivalence which governs his writings on literature is widely acknowledged by critics such as Sarah Kofman.[5] Nevertheless, its subtle shifts and manoeuvres within his texts tend to be oversimplified by even the most careful of them, and this complex issue is often treated as nothing more than evidence of Freud's putative lack of literary sensitivity and his 'reductionism'. This is regrettable, for Freud was possessed of a sophisticated – not to mention, drastically original – understanding of literary meaning, as well as a healthy respect for *Dichter*[6] as pioneering psychoanalysts. The vehemence of his ambivalence points, rather, to the emotional intensity of his relations with poets, and the mercurial oscillations in his attitude to them, which shape his literary-critical texts, can be appreciated only in this dynamic context.

The question of Freud's competence as a literary critic bears on issues much more fundamental than just that of psychoanalytical literary criticism. With my third hypothesis I seek to re-evaluate Freud's entire hermeneutic – that is, his mode of interpreting dreams, symptoms, jokes, slips, screen memories, and so on – and I do this by viewing his interpretation of these 'texts' as the substitute gratification, so to speak, of a frustrated literary critic. I examine the traces this covert paradigm of literary response leaves on his attempts to *read* meaning in an unprecedented variety of psychic phenomena, with a view to shedding new light on the dynamic nature of this literary source of influence. The hypothesis of a 'repressed' literary-critical paradigm then proves particularly helpful in elucidating the relationship between psychoanalysis and postmodernist criticism.

My parallel argument, that Freud can also usefully be viewed as something of a thwarted *Dichter*, has been anticipated by a handful of critics, most notably Patrick Mahony.[7] Nevertheless, my own approach to this question is quite distinct in that I base my analysis on Freud's own conception of the process of literary creation. He considers literary narratives to be fantastical, essentially aesthetic, but also self-analytical and even therapeutic reworkings of what is, fundamentally, the author's own autobiography. Thus I read some of Freud's more problematical texts as psychoanalytical 'novels', quasi-literary attempts to work through and achieve critical and aesthetic distance from his own most personal conflicts.

Despite the radical nature of this re-evaluation of Freud – as a 'repressed' literary critic, even a *Dichter*, in the thrall, both intellectually and emotionally, of his literary forebears – I do not intend to question (or advocate) the truth value of psychoanalytical doctrine itself. My principal aim is to resituate Freud's work in the context of various literary traditions, and to demonstrate the active role these play within his texts. Far from denigrating Freud's achievements, this should allow for a more nuanced appreciation of his contribution to twentieth-century culture. Although critics are still as fascinated as ever by the overlap between psychoanalysis and literature, most seem to underestimate the sheer scale of the literary dimensions of psychoanalysis itself. Conversely, however, it would be a mistake to overemphasize these literary aspects. Many of the most important critics attempt to reclaim Freud for some or other discipline: Frank Sulloway sees Freud essentially as a biologist, Paul Ricoeur reads him as a philosopher, whilst Harold Bloom describes him as nothing less (or more) than a 'strong' poet. Yet it is precisely the cross-fertilization between scientific and literary cultures which makes of Freud a writer *sui generis*, undermining all such attempts to categorize his work. He is certainly more than a nineteenth-century mechanist, but, equally, he is not merely an unwitting philosopher, a deconstructionist *manqué*, or an anxious poet. Such contradictory readings can be reconciled, often in unexpected and intriguing ways, when his works are viewed in their proper literary context. Admittedly, Freud's own sustained hostility towards any suggestion of non-scientific influences on his work usually causes him to attempt to screen off this context, but on closer analysis his literary culture clearly emerges as a sufficiently rich and subtle source of influence to illuminate many of the confusions, enigmas, and paradoxes of psychoanalysis.

CHAPTER ONE

The unconscious of psychoanalysis:
Freud's literary allusions

FUNCTION AND FORM

In a letter written in 1906 Freud answers a publisher's request to name
ten 'good' books. As he openly declares he has deliberately excluded
books of purely aesthetic value, the list offers only a limited insight into
his literary tastes. He cannot, however, resist mentioning some works he
would have included in a list of the very greatest works of literature:
Sophocles' tragedies, Goethe's *Faust*, and Shakespeare's *Hamlet* and
Macbeth.[1] Anyone familiar with Freud's own writings will immediately
recognize that these are, by far, the works to which he most commonly
alludes. The author he most frequently refers to is undoubtedly Goethe.
Although over half of these references are to *Faust*, only one is to the
second part of that tragedy, and this – the epigraph to *The
Psychopathology of Everyday Life* – was suggested by his friend Fliess. (Freud
did not usually need such prompting; indeed, Fliess had to dissuade him
from using a Goethe quotation as the epigraph to *The Interpretation of
Dreams*.) Only Shakespeare comes close to Goethe as a source of allusions, and, although Freud refers to about fifteen of his plays, again half
of the references are to one work, *Hamlet*. Mainly due to *Jokes and their
Relation to the Unconscious*, Heine is the next most quoted author, followed
very closely by Schiller. Goethe, Heine, and Schiller apart, though,
Freud is more likely to refer to classical Greek and Roman literature
than to any other German author. Most of these references are again
to a single play, this time Sophocles' *Oedipus*. Even this brief survey
reveals that there is nothing eccentric about the kind of works to which
Freud tends to allude; they are all absolutely central to the literary
canon of his age.

When referring to works by Goethe, Shakespeare, and so on, Freud
rarely identifies the source. Nor does he tend to give German translations of passages quoted in English, French, Italian, Latin, and even
Greek. He clearly assumes his reader shares his own highly literary

Bildung and can automatically understand quotations and place allusions. To an important extent, his literary culture was the common property of the well-educated German bourgeoisie of his age. It is often remarked that his tastes were far more conservative than his literary criticism, but the question of 'taste' is less significant here than the consideration that Freud was influenced most powerfully by the canonical works on which he was raised in *childhood*. For example, the intriguing discrepancy between the number of allusions to the two parts of *Faust* may simply be the result of his having read the first part at a more impressionable age. In relaxed letters he clearly enjoys referring to *Faust II*; it is just that he never does so during the intensely creative bursts in which he produced his psychoanalytical texts.

Although his tastes were conditioned by social factors, above all his classical German *Bildung*, the extent to which he was imbued with literature was also the result of certain idiosyncratic character traits. From the age of seven, books were Freud's passion and his only indulgence. His appetite for reading remained voracious and extended far beyond his clinical field. Furthermore, it was in his youth that his extraordinary powers of memory were at their height: he could quote verbatim long passages from books he had only skimmed through (VI, 135).[2] Of course, Freud read a great deal of contemporary literature, and the fact that he rarely mentions it in his own texts indicates a strong personal inclination towards classical literature. By alluding to the classics in the context of his scientific theories he can suggest a universality and a timelessness which modern literature would fail to evoke. His tendency to reach back to works from his childhood may be 'preconscious', then, but it is also most expedient.

Even in non-literary analyses Freud makes allusions with the same unerring frequency. Clearly literature is more than just an object of analysis for him, it is a key feature of his thought processes. He wrote at great speed, intensely and erratically, and the presence of small inaccuracies in some of his quotations indicates not a lack of sensitivity, but rather the immediacy with which the lines suggest themselves to him. Of course, many quotations are the result of some deliberation. A letter to his fiancée, Martha Bernays, reveals how methodically he developed his literary cultivation: he tells her of a play he has seen in Paris which he despises because it contains 'hardly a word anyone would want to commit to memory'.[3] Nevertheless, his predilection for quoting the works he first explored in his youth suggests that his allusions are drawn from sources beyond his conscious control. He imputes a special degree of 'truth' to these works, and again this may be attributed to the impressionable age at which he encountered them. They were received by a mind still evolving from what Freud himself calls a 'primary' mode of thinking, in which there is little or no distinction between truth and emotionally charged fiction. Such assertions are rather speculative, but there can be no doubt that an analysis of Freud's use of allusions would offer an excellent initial orientation in a study of his literary culture.

Freud integrates quotations from his favourite works of literature into his own texts with great ease; indeed, his use of certain allusions seems to be almost automatic. Not surprisingly, then, many of these are used with little regard for their literary context or their specifically aesthetic qualities. Freud often simply takes advantage of his rich literary culture to express his own ideas more impressively. The very first literary allusion in his psychological works appears in the *Studies on Hysteria*, published in 1895, where he claims phobias commonly involve 'all the vermin of which Mephistopheles boasted himself master' (II, 87). Clearly this allusion to *Faust* is little more than an ornate circumlocution. And yet even the most cursory analysis reveals that Freud's literary references serve a wide variety of important functions. One more substantial use he makes of certain literary passages is to provide an analogy to some aspect of his theory, as in *The Interpretation of Dreams* when he claims that absurdity in a dream often signifies a disdainful judgement in the dream-thoughts. The dream, then, is parodying the absurdity of whoever is targeted by this criticism, and as an analogy of this mode of expression Freud quotes four lines of poetry in which Heine heightens his mockery of King Ludwig's dreadful poetry by expressing it in even poorer verse (V, 435n.). Here the use of a quotation is really more felicitous than Freud's original idea. The presence of intractable absurdity in dreams is perfectly understandable as the result of highly complex processes of condensation, displacement, and so on. Freud's need to view it as a deliberate, self-contained, and coherent expression such as is found in conscious thought seems to be related to a mania for interpretation which was no doubt an element of his genius but which could also lead him astray. It could be argued that the parallel between an absurd dream and the work of a poet as sophisticated and self-conscious as Heine is singularly inappropriate, but it is so cleverly drawn that it helps suspend potential criticism. This is reminiscent of the mechanism Freud describes in his theory of 'harmless' wit, whereby a weak idea can be made to seem inherently impressive solely by virtue of its witty formulation. In *Jokes and their Relation to the Unconscious* he claims: 'The thought seeks to wrap itself in a joke ... because this wrapping bribes our powers of criticism and confuses them' (VIII, 132). Something analogous is clearly at work in some of Freud's wittier uses of literary quotation. To support the same theory about absurd dreams he goes on to quote from *Hamlet*, tempting us to surmise that he is more likely to have recourse to this kind of literary stratagem when he needs to shore up a more vulnerable piece of theory.

Such references are used by Freud largely independently of their literary context, but many of his more interesting allusions seem to invoke the texts from which they are taken. In 1923 Freud, enthusiastic about applying the nomenclature established in *The Ego and the Id* to clinical observation, writes in a passage in his very next paper, 'Neurosis and Psychosis':

Such an application of the hypothesis might also bring with it a profitable return from grey theory to the perpetual green of experience. (XIX, 149)

This allusion to Mephistopheles' advice to the student in *Faust* demands, by its very indirectness, some work on the part of the reader to place it. This helps establish a deeper literary communion between Freud and his reader, no doubt enhancing the effectiveness of an allusion whatever its function is intended to be. Some quotations, moreover, seem to evoke important subtexts independently of Freud's conscious rhetorical intent. To exemplify the concept of ambivalence, for example, Freud often quotes Brutus' famous speech from *Julius Caesar* in which he justifies killing the friend he loved. This would seem to be an inaccurate analogy: in Brutus both emotions are fully conscious and rationally justified, that is, they modify rather than contradict each other. However, there is little doubt that Freud's choice of Brutus to illustrate ambivalence is overdetermined by a deeply personal factor. At the age of fourteen he gave a performance of the Brutus–Caesar dialogue from Schiller's first version of *The Robbers*, and the part of Caesar was played by his nephew John. In *The Interpretation of Dreams* Freud admits that the most deeply ambivalent of his adult friendships were modelled on John, 'this first figure who "früh sich einst dem trüben Blick gezeigt" (long since appeared before my troubled gaze)' (V, 483).[4] Brutus' ambivalent feelings, then, are Freud's own towards his nephew – his quotation from the Dedication of *Faust* here only confirms the depths to which this identification can be traced in him.

This well-documented example of the personal determinants of an apparently superficial reference provides some justification for looking at the literary context of other allusions. At one point in his paper on the 'demonological' neurosis Freud admits that this text will not convince non-analysts, and he claims this does not concern him. The only proof which he believes is necessary is the fact that psychoanalysis alone can improve the condition of neurotic patients, and, with Odysseus in Sophocles' *Philoctetes*, he claims: '"These shafts can conquer Troy, these shafts alone"' (XIX, 84). This quotation appears to be used in a superficial and merely tendentious fashion; however, if the character of Philoctetes is considered more carefully, then a deeper determinant begins to reveal itself. Due to his terrible wound Philoctetes aroused such revulsion that his Greek comrades forced him to live on an uninhabited island. His wretched isolation there continued for ten years until it was revealed that only he possessed the invincible arrows needed to take Troy. In his own 'splendid isolation' – which he claimed lasted ten years – it is not unlikely that Freud identified himself with this classical hero, a man who suffered at the hands of his intolerant comrades, but who was ultimately vindicated when the power which he alone possessed was recognized for its unique practical value. Such speculation may be idle, but it is at least clear, if only from the many literary 'free associations' in the analyses of his own dreams, that characters and situations from literature exercised a deep influence on Freud independently of his conscious awareness.

With this reflection in mind, one of the most intriguing aspects of Freud's literary allusions is the fact that most of his quotations from *Faust* can be traced back to the character of Mephistopheles. This can, in part, be attributed to a certain carelessness, as in *The Interpretation of Dreams* when, regarding distortion in dreams, he offers one of his favourite quotations:

> Das Beste, was du wissen kannst,
> darfst du den Buben doch nicht sagen.
>
> (After all, the best of what you know
> may not be told to boys.)   IV, 142

Freud claims this complaint is made by 'the poet', whereas it is, strictly speaking, made by Goethe's devil, Mephistopheles. Occasionally, this imprecision works against Freud, as in his Dora analysis when, apologizing for the long duration of a psychoanalysis, he quotes the following lines:

> Nicht Kunst und Wissenschaft allein,
> Geduld will bei dem Werke sein!
>
> (Not Art and Science serve, alone;
> Patience must in the work be shown.) VII, 16

Clearly Freud again believes he is speaking with Goethe, but, given the already formidable resistances aroused by psychoanalysis, the context of these lines is particularly unfortunate. Not only are they, again, spoken by Mephistopheles, the work the devil refers to here is witchcraft.

Although these examples appear to belong to the category of allusions made independently of their context, Goethe's Mephistopheles actually represents much more than any narrowly conceived archetype of evil, and Freud's predilection for speaking with his voice should not be explained away as carelessness. Mephistopheles exposes hypocritical pretensions and reveals the sensual roots of that which the pious consider to be sublime. No doubt Freud relished such a character – the scene he quotes from most often is the one between Mephistopheles and the student, in which the devil's cynicism is at its most outrageous. In *Beyond the Pleasure Principle*, for example, Freud finds himself denying the existence of an instinct for perfection which 'in the poet's words, "ungebändigt immer vorwärts dringt" (presses ever forward unsubdued)' (XVIII, 42). He claims instead that this phenomenon is merely the result of repression. Of course, Faust himself displays very few moral inhibitions, and his striving is certainly not appeased by any of the worldly gratifications offered by Mephistopheles. More important than Faust's character here, though, is the fact that Freud is speaking with Mephistopheles. This subliminally underpins his assertion that the drive for perfection is rooted in erotic instincts.

Privately, Freud indulged in the identification with Mephistopheles more openly. In a letter to Jung, who was becoming uneasy about probing the sexual history of his patients, he quotes: 'In league with the Devil and yet you fear fire?'[5] – a remonstration he repeated to Lou Andreas-Salomé almost a decade later. And in a subsequent letter to Jung, commenting on the need for outside expertise before analysis can be applied to mythology, Freud again quotes from *Faust*: 'Although it was the Devil who taught her, / He cannot do it by himself.'[6]

In fact, some of Freud's most felicitous allusions come from this fondness for speaking with Mephistopheles. Of the various allusions to Goethe's *Faust* made in the paper 'Analysis Terminable and Interminable', one in particular, again some words of Mephistopheles, helps convey a crucial perspective on neurosis. The 'defence mechanisms' are designed to protect the ego, but, because they tend to overreact or to become reactivated when they have outlived their usefulness, they are also instrumental in generating neurotic symptoms. Thus: '"Vernunft wird Unsinn, Wohltat Plage" (Reason becomes unreason, kindness torment) as the poet complains' (XXIII, 238). Mephistopheles is actually satirizing the legal system here, but the analogy is a good one. The defence mechanisms regulate conduct according to socially established decrees of morality, but these decrees quickly become fossilized and out of touch with instinctual needs (as, indeed, Mephistopheles goes on to protest). Thus the quotation Freud uses contains the very kernel of his theory: the torment of neurosis is the result of repression which is initially intended as benevolent; and the unreason of a neurotic symptom is actually meaningful, based on an outdated and decentred 'reason'.

Quotations such as these are undeniably more effective for evoking their original context, but they still represent only a plundering of literary texts for the ideas they contain. Yet, despite Freud's regular protestations to the contrary, he was not insensitive to aesthetic qualities, and this, too, is evident in his use of allusions. The very presence of so many quotations in his works speaks for his appreciation of the literary originals, and within his own texts they lend Freud's ideas a concreteness and an economy of expression that he appreciates for its own sake. They are an essential part of his own style, evincing his characteristically acute sensitivity towards the responses of his reader. This is made explicit in a 1917 introductory lecture when, after a long section of difficult theory on narcissism, Freud reveals his strategy:

You will find it refreshing, I believe, if, after what is the essentially dry imagery of science, I present you with a poetic representation of the economic contrast between narcissism and being in love. (XVI, 418)

He goes on to quote a full twenty lines from Goethe's *West Eastern Divan*. The quotation adds nothing to Freud's own exposition, nor does it necessarily corroborate his theory, but he clearly feels its poetic qualities alone qualify it for inclusion.

Freud does not always merely draw on the aesthetic resources of others, he also uses literary allusions to increase the impact of his own stylistic techniques. In *The Interpretation of Dreams* he uses the following quotation from *Faust* to illustrate overdetermination:

> Ein Tritt tausend Fäden regt,
> Die Schifflein herüber, hinüber schießen,
> Die Fäden ungesehen fließen,
> Ein Schlag tausend Verbindungen schlägt.
>
> (. . . a thousand threads one treadle throws,
> Where fly the shuttles hither and thither,
> Unseen the threads are knit together,
> And an infinite combination grows.) IV, 283

The context of this quotation could again be considered unfortunate: Mephistopheles is satirizing the 'Collegium Logicum' and the kind of rigid determinism that in fact underlies Freud's own theory of overdetermination. He even goes on to attack analysts who destroy that which they wish to describe by taking it to pieces. The quotation, however, works very well *in its own right*. Mephistopheles' intention of confusing the student is very much consonant with one of Freud's own stylistic devices. He would often give a survey of the baffling complexities of a subject in order to make his reader more receptive to his own reassuringly lucid insights. The above quotation works in the same vein by affirming the complexity of overdetermination. More importantly, the rhythm, repetition, alliteration, and rhyme employed in the quotation evoke, by sheer intensity of aesthetic economy, the very process of condensation itself.

Of course, the longer a literary quotation is, the more likely it is to display this kind of intrinsic aesthetic value. Of all the quotations Freud uses from *Faust*, the longest is to be found in his Schreber analysis. Here he quotes eleven lines in which the chorus of spirits laments that Faust, having cursed all things that humans value, has destroyed the world, and it bids him to rebuild it in his own bosom (XII, 70). Freud offers this as a metaphor of paranoia, where the sufferer withdraws all libido from the outside world and inhabits instead a complex delusional system. Again this is not an appropriate 'diagnosis' of Faust; Freud even claims that Faust's character provides evidence that such detachment of the libido does not necessarily lead to paranoia. Nevertheless, the quotation *in itself* expresses the grandiosity, the inwardness, and the dramatic psychogenesis of paranoid delusions so forcefully and with such an economy of means that it remains the most abiding formulation of the illness that the reader is likely to take away from the text. Freud's willingness to devote a dozen lines of his text to quoting poetry at least demonstrates his awareness that literary allusions are integral to the aesthetic dimension of his own writing.

THE POLEMICS OF ALLUSION

Although Freud uses literary quotations for both their content and form, their most important function in his texts is quite independent of this superficial distinction. This function is best explained by extending the analogy with his own theory of wit. His most straightforward allusions resemble the most basic form of wit, where the key factor is the pleasure gained from playing with words and ideas. Freud often simply draws on his literary culture to give himself a pleasure from making connections that is an end in itself. In its next stage of development, wit circumvents our increasingly inhibitive critical judgement by expressing an idea that is of some value. As with Freud's more effective literary quotations, the wit here performs the function of causing the idea to appear more valuable than it actually is. Finally, wit develops still further when it gains access to the deepest sources of pleasure by circumventing resistances and suspending repression, becoming what Freud calls tendentious wit. Similarly, the most important function of Freud's literary allusions is 'tendentious' or polemical; and, by conferring respectability on himself through association with great poets, he is specifically contriving to overcome resistances in his reader by making such allusions.

In the very first paragraph of *Leonardo da Vinci and a Memory of his Childhood* Freud tries to forestall any objections to his producing a pathography of such a great artist by quoting from Schiller. He claims he does not wish 'To blacken the radiant and drag the sublime into the dust' (XI, 63). The quotation itself, however, contains absolutely nothing that justifies Freud. He clearly hopes that simply by knowing his Schiller he can demonstrate his respect for the brilliant and the sublime. Of course, this alone could not remove the odium aroused by his dealing with such subjects as incest and perverse sexuality, but here, too, Freud often seeks help from great authors. References to *Oedipus* and *Hamlet*, for example, tend *immediately* to follow every new exposition of Oedipus-complex theory; Freud's intention of thus encouraging receptivity and deflecting potential indignation is perfectly manifest.

After *The Interpretation of Dreams*, Freud's richest text for literary allusions is *Civilization and its Discontents*. In this book, after a lifetime of dealing with the sore point of sexuality, he opens up a new wound: innate human aggression. Plautus's 'homo homini lupus', Galsworthy's 'The Apple Tree', and a long Heine quotation (in which among the simple pleasures in life the poet numbers a few enemies hanging from a beautiful tree) all help to suspend the possible objection that Freud is once again arbitrarily undermining human dignity. He does not deny that this is his tactic, claiming of the Heine quotation:

A great imaginative writer may permit himself to give expression – jokingly, at all events – to psychological truths that are severely proscribed. (XXI, 110n.)

It has always been Freud's conviction that artists work by presenting primary sexual and aggressive material, but in such a way as to disarm outrage and circumvent revulsion. He keenly regrets his frequent failure to do the same in his capacity as a scientist, and he does not hesitate to enlist the help of poets to do this work for him. After he has triumphantly developed his theory of aggression to its climax – namely, the formula that life consists in the conflict between Eros and Death – he is careful to give the final word to the same poet:

And it is this battle of the giants that our nurse-maids try to appease with their lullaby about Heaven [Eiapopeia vom Himmel]. (XXI, 122)

This reference to Heine's *Deutschland* brings Freud's unrestrainedly philosophical flight of theory back into a world with which his readers are familiar. More importantly, despite the fact that in Heine the battle is socio-political, the reference also seems to help corroborate Freud's bleak philosophical conclusion. Only literature could serve this dual purpose so efficiently.

It was, of course, the odium aroused by the topic of sexuality that Freud most needed to avert, and here no poet stood him in better stead than Goethe, the great apologist for the liberation of elemental nature from conventional moral prejudices. For example, in the analysis of his dream of three women in a kitchen, Freud links the pleasure of university study to that of being fed by his mother. This radical and potentially scandalous association seems more respectable following, as it does, this quotation:

> So wird's Euch an der Weisheit *Brüsten*
> mit jedem Tage mehr gelüsten.
>
> (Thus, at the *breasts* of Wisdom clinging,
> Thou'lt find each day a greater rapture bringing.)
> IV, 206 (original emphasis)

Again there is a deep irony in that Mephistopheles' advice to the student (concerning the study of medicine, no less) is far more shocking than anything in Freud's dream analysis. However, by unmasking sublimation the devil is in possession of an important truth. Incidentally, the objection that this quotation is a free association, not a deliberate allusion, is as weak as the distinction between the two itself. Not only has Freud consciously chosen to present this and not another association, his allusions often themselves appear as if spontaneously, again much like witticisms.

Perverse sexuality is, of course, an even more controversial subject, but in his *Three Essays on Sexuality*, for example, Freud manages to locate fetishism in the realm of normal behaviour by quoting a passage in which Faust demands Gretchen's scarf or garter. In fact, the quotation rather ennobles this perversion – after all, if Freud only wants to exemplify normality, the allusion to Faust, a character both fictional and superhuman, is not ideal. It is, however, not the literary context, but the invocation of *Goethe* that is the keynote here. Shortly after this quotation Freud again tries to suspend moral judgements on sexual perversions by asserting:

The highest and the lowest are always closest to each other in the sphere of sexuality: 'vom Himmel durch die Welt zur Hölle' (From Heaven, across the world, to Hell.) (VII, 161–2)

It is difficult to see why Freud implies that his use of this quotation is self-explanatory here. It may correspond to an interpretation of the whole of *Faust* as an allegory of sublimation. However, many of his readers who are unable to make such a connection will still recognize the words as Goethe's, and this alone is enough to serve Freud's primary purpose of undermining moral objections.

Adverse opinion never caused Freud to falter in his investigations into sexuality. He only ever displays reticence – purely out of practical considerations for the psychoanalytical movement – about publishing his theories on religion, which in the post-Enlightenment age were actually much less explosive. In this and other fields, however, poets could serve even more directly polemical purposes. Tendentious allusions like those cited above work on a mainly subliminal level, merely lending Freud an air of respectability. As far as this is directed towards his potential adversaries, it is intended to create something like a temporary cease-fire during which he can produce his own arguments more freely. Freud is also aware, however, that his knowledge of literature is just as useful in open combat – as a supply of ammunition. When, in *Civilization and its Discontents*, he returns to his argument calling for the removal of religion from modern culture, his first thought is 'the well-known saying of one of our great poets and thinkers', namely Goethe:

Wer Wissenschaft und Kunst besitzt, hat auch Religion;
Wer jene beide [*sic*] nicht besitzt, der habe Religion!

(He who possesses science and art also has religion;
but he who possesses neither of those two, let him have religion!)
XXI, 74

He interprets this as an apology for religion and regrets: 'If we also set out to deprive the common man of his religion, we shall clearly not have the poet's authority on our side.' This statement is in need of interpretation. Firstly, it reveals that, to Freud, a poet does indeed represent an *authority*, but it would also seem to suggest that this authority is not absolute. Freud goes on partly to vindicate the Goethe quotation by pointing out the interchangeability of religion, art, and science, all of which can function as 'auxiliary constructions'. However, Goethe's epigram says far more than this. The poet clearly uses the word 'religion' twice in order to signify two different things. The first usage refers to a pantheistic awe before the beauty of creation, the second to a blind cleaving to doctrine and tradition. It is the latter which Freud is attacking, and he must be aware that in this he does have the 'poet's authority' firmly on his side. It is difficult to imagine him using the quotation otherwise.

A literary quotation he uses in *The Future of an Illusion*, his most direct assault on religion, is more telling. He says 'with one of our fellow-unbelievers':

> Den Himmel überlassen wir
> Den Engeln und den Spatzen.
>
> (We leave Heaven
> to the angels and the sparrows.) XXI, 50

With extreme economy he borrows much of the force of Heine's crusade for sensual emancipation from religious morality. He does not even need to mention the poet's name; the word fellow-unbeliever (Unglaubensgenossen) bears the unmistakeable stamp of Heine's irreverent wit. When criticizing a less formidable 'enemy', abstract philosophy, Freud regularly alludes to the section in Heine's 'Die Heimkehr' about the German professor who finds the world too fragmentary and therefore:

> Mit seinen Nachtmützen und Schlafrockfetzen
> Stopft er die Lücken des Weltenbaus.
>
> (With his nightcaps and the tatters of his dressing-gown
> he patches up the gaps in the structure of the universe.)
> XXII, 161

Again Heine is using the comic technique which Freud calls degradation. The nightcaps and the sparrows are used to deflate grandiose intellectual schemes, philosophical and religious, by juxtaposing them with the banality of everyday reality, a bathetic tendency that Freud especially relished. The latter quotation, however, has a poignancy that is more than just sardonic. In a letter to Jung in 1908 Freud admits that he himself has fought off the temptation to 'fill in the gaps in the universe'.[7] The quotation, then, is aimed primarily at a tendency within himself.

No doubt the materialist doctrine of 'hunger and love' helped Freud to suppress his speculative urge. He sometimes calls this 'popular', but at other times admits it is formulated 'in the words of the poet'. It is actually taken from Schiller's 'Die Weltweisen', and this context is revealing: the poem is another satire against those philosophers abstracted from the sensual reality of nature. If only on a subliminal level, it seems Freud knows how to use the polemical weight of a literary quotation against himself. He would have been the first to admit that a choice of allusion can never be wholly arbitrary. It is likely to be overdetermined by unconscious factors, and sometimes it is the polemic which is latent. In a letter to Werner Achelis Freud denies that there is anything 'Promethean' about his use of the line from Virgil's *Aeneid*, 'Flectere si nequeo superos, Acheronta movebo', as the epigraph to his dream book.[8] He claims it refers only to the dynamics of the dream. There can, however, be no real doubt that it simultaneously expresses his defiance of the authorities in Vienna which he felt were denying him official recognition.

Although Freud will often, implicitly or explicitly, manipulate a poet's words in this fashion to reinforce the impact of his own assertions, the most important category of polemical allusions depends on him remaining, or at least appearing to remain, absolutely faithful to the poet's insight. For example, to support his remarkable theory that the Wolf Man's dream of wolves in a tree is based on a voyeuristic experience of the primal scene, he 'proves' that a tree is a symbol of voyeurism by referring the reader to 'Boccaccio's well-known story' (XVII, 43n.). This presumes not only the existence of universal symbols, but also that a *Dichter* has mysterious access to them, otherwise the tree in Boccaccio's tale would be nothing more than a story device. Here the authority Freud imputes to writers is of a different order; their 'evidence' is sufficient to prove a scientific theory. In his book on parapraxes he uses examples from Schiller's *Piccolomini* and Shakespeare's *Merchant of Venice* to show that these authors actually understand the mechanism of parapraxes. When in 1916 he comes to condense this very long book into brief popular lectures, he retains these lengthy examples in full. Clearly he believes this particular kind of literary sanction to be his most valuable evidence. However, when he claims it represents the 'support of great poets' (Parteinahme der großen Dichter) for the psychoanalytical theory (VI, 98), the phrase is somewhat tendentious, not to mention anachronistic.

Similarly, when referring to the 'correctly' formulated dreams in Jensen's *Gradiva*, Freud claims the agreement between this work and the assumptions of his theory is 'evidence in favour of the correctness of my analysis of dreams' (IV, 97n.). In his essay on the novella he once again speaks of the 'support given by writers' (IX, 8), and, although he has now omitted the word 'great', he does not admit, as he does elsewhere, that he considers Jensen to be a poor novelist. Indeed, on the very next page he simply refers to poets as 'the deepest observers [tiefste Kenner] of the human mind'. It seems that even a second-rate literary authority can satisfy his need for prestigious sanction. And yet Freud is disregarding a serious problem which arises, however 'great' the author. Details in plays and novels are overdetermined in accordance not with observations from actual experience, but rather with established literary conventions. Novellas in particular condense 'meaning' with great intensity, and this is excessively evident in Jensen's *Gradiva*, marred as it is by contrived coincidences and a general lack of subtlety. This consideration does not necessarily harm Freud's theories of parapraxes or dreams, but it makes questionable his use of literature as a source of direct evidence for them.

Other attempts by Freud to find 'evidence' in literature are equally problematical. To corroborate his ingenious theory that Moses actually gave the Jews the Egyptian monotheism of his pharaoh, he cites a line of poetry in which Heine describes Judaism as 'the unhealthy beliefs of Ancient Egypt' (XXIII, 30n.). There is, in fact, no reason whatsoever to believe that Heine's wording implies any contradiction of the biblical narrative, and Freud fails, furthermore, to see any irony in his looking to Heine for objective evidence about the history of Judaism. More controversially, his hypothesis depends on the Jews having murdered Moses. He claims that his source for this was Sellin, and Ernest Jones confirms that it was indeed this Hebrew scholar's thesis that sparked off the writing of *Moses and Monotheism*. However, Freud remarks that the idea of Moses' murder had already been postulated 'by the young Goethe without any evidence', and he gives an unusually detailed reference to the whereabouts of the passage in 'Israel in the Wilderness' (XXIII, 89). Generally he does not even mention an author's name; here he gives the edition, the volume, and the page number, revealing, perhaps, how much prestige he believes the passage can lend to his own hypothesis. It is only after the mention of Goethe that Freud admits the murder of Moses is now 'an indispensable part of our construction'. Indeed, it is particularly revealing that this admission is made in the very same *sentence* as the reference to Goethe. Freud himself would grant that this kind of temporal contiguity often signifies a more profound – and unconscious – causal connection. The corroboration from Goethe is clearly instrumental in encouraging Freud to create this bronze statue on feet of clay.

Literature can supply Freud with more convincing evidence if it is used not as an oracle, but as the raw material from which theories are inferred. This approach is strikingly evident in his 1918 paper 'The Taboo of Virginity', where his analysis of this archaic phenomenon as it occurs in various guises in modern German literature – in Schnitzler, Hebbel, and so on – is almost as detailed as his study of the anthropological material itself. Indeed, in his 'Some Character-Types Met with in Psycho-Analytic Work' Freud eventually forgets the title of his essay and produces protracted analyses of characters met with in *literature*; his fullest illustration of 'the exception', for example, is Shakespeare's Richard III. Despite the obvious problem of Richard being fully conscious of how the bitterness caused by his deformity fuels his motivation to 'prove a villain', he is presented as a paradigm of this character type. Freud's justification for this choice is that discretion prevents him from using real case histories. Not only is this claim patently belied by his own publication of full case histories, Freud positively relishes the literary substitute – and he goes on to make a specifically literary analysis of the way in which Shakespeare subtly facilitates our identification with Richard. When he comes on to 'those wrecked by success', he actually produces the Macbeth essay he has long wanted to write, and his allusions have developed into literary criticism proper. To justify this he now merely tries to blur the distinction between clinical cases and literary characters 'which great writers have created from the wealth of their knowledge of the mind' (XIV, 318). He does return to clinical experience, albeit five lines from the end of his analysis, almost as if he has to apologize for indulging in pure literary criticism. Even in the final section, 'Criminals from a Sense of Guilt', the only example offered comes from 'Zarathustra's sayings "On the Pale Criminal"' (XIV, 332). Freud would, of course, have vigorously denied that any of his original sources were literary. Accordingly, he is careful to attribute the discovery of the passage in Nietzsche to 'a friend', a tactic he commonly employed in his attempt to keep any suggestion of literary influence at arm's length. In the first edition Freud actually wrote 'Zarathustra's obscure sayings', but in 1924 he took the trouble of having the word *dunklen* struck out, thus removing any taint of a personal encounter with this particular author.

Even apart from the question of Freud's sources, there is no doubt that in this essay, ostensibly on characterology, literary references alter the very course of the text. The importance of literary allusions in Freud's works is nowhere better demonstrated than in those passages which appear to have been written for the sole purpose of making an allusion possible. The most striking example of this is to be found at the end of the last essay of *Totem and Taboo*. After relating the dramatic hypothesis of 'The Return of Totemism in Childhood' he concludes by discussing its weaknesses. As a rhetorical strategy this would seem to be rather anti-climactic, or even positively detrimental. To believe this, however, would be seriously to underestimate Freud's polemical skill. He is, as always, fully aware of the overriding importance of his readers' objections. His tactic is deliberately to highlight them, then turn them dramatically to his own advantage. This he achieves with the help of two quotations from *Faust*. He first tackles the formidable problem of his assumption of an inherited sense of guilt. He counters it with the suggestion that only dispositions are inherited, and that these are then reactivated by individual experiences. This is hardly less problematical than the initial assumption, but he adds:

This may be the meaning of the poet's words:

> Was du ererbt von deinen Vätern hast,
> Erwirb es, um es zu besitzen.
>
> (What thou hast inherited from thy fathers,
> acquire it to make it thine.)   XIII, 158

Now, this clearly is not Faust's meaning; he is rather cursing the ineffectualness of all that he has inherited. However, torn from its context, the quotation helps Freud to bridge the theoretical gap between ontogenetic experience and phylogenetic inheritance. The rhetorical effect is, in fact, heightened by the obscurity and ambiguity of the line.

His use of a second quotation is more strategic and decidedly more effective. It is employed to counter a second, equally justified objection, namely that there is no need to assume the murder of the primal father was actual, especially in the light of Freud's own discoveries about the decisive significance of wishes in primary thought processes. He responds by pointing out that, to primitive man, action stands in the place of thought. This retort works well at the end of a text full of tenuous and selective argumentation – above all because he consolidates it with Faust's famous: 'Im Anfang war die Tat (In the beginning was the Deed)' (XIII, 161). In fact, the line is so appropriate and effective that its use demands closer inspection. It can then be seen that Freud's desire to make use of this quotation has determined the direction of the entire passage and, to some extent, the structure of the whole essay. I have already suggested that Freud has deliberately raised these particular objections at the end of his text precisely because he knows how to dismiss them with the aid of two of his favourite lines from Goethe. However, the manipulation goes even further. The initial objection is that primitives may have *wished* to kill the primal father without having done so. Freud deliberately confuses this distinction with the one between *thought* and action. The line from Goethe, then, is used to make the claim that primitives do not 'think', this being rather more convincing than the one he would actually need to make: that primitives have no thwarted wishes. Even more deliberate is his placing of the *Faust* quotation at the very end of the essay; indeed, these are the final words of the entire book. In this way their dramatic force and resonance is cunningly conferred onto the hypothesis of the primal parricide as a whole. Again this seems to be a deliberate manipulation. Why else would Freud deal with this somewhat extraneous objection so prominently, at the very end of his text? The line itself is quite divorced from its original context. Faust is expressing his dissatisfaction with language and, in attempting a translation, is actually rewriting St John's Gospel to correspond with his own needs. It is ironic rather than appropriate that Freud uses a fictional character's conception of creation to assert the reality of an act of destruction. Due to this loss of context, Goethe cannot stand as an authority here. However, Freud's brilliantly strategic use of the quotation, the most striking line from Goethe's greatest work, conveys the impression that the poet is indeed championing Freud's entire hypothesis.

*

Although Freud uses allusions very deliberately to serve manifold polemical purposes, and although they convey a general impression of great cultivation very much consonant with his desire to be seen to transcend pathology, all the evidence suggests that there was no affectation in his habit of making literary references. His conversation and his private correspondence were similarly replete with them, regardless of whether he was making jokes or revealing his most intimate concerns. A week after the death of his daughter Sophie, in a letter to his closest friend Ferenczi, he quotes both Goethe's *Egmont* and Schiller's *Piccolomini*.[9] There is no cleverness in his use of quotations such as these, they clearly give Freud moral support in his grief. Even on his death-bed literary quotations helped him to express what may otherwise have remained inexpressible for him. His doctor reports that, when close to death, he quoted these lines from Goethe's 'Wandrers Nachtlied':

> Süßer Friede,
> Komm, ach komm in meine Brust!
>
> (Sweet peace,
> Come, oh come into my heart!)[10]

Although these quotations demonstrate the point most unequivocally, it is actually unlikely that any of his literary allusions, even those whose effect he calculated most carefully, were ever merely ostentatious.

Nevertheless, Freud is fully aware of the effect these references have on his reader. Great writers were father-figures to him and his attitude towards them involves a particular kind of highly sublimated ambivalence. In his use of literary allusions, however, he tends to display only the most humbly reverential aspect of this ambivalence, often causing him to present the *Dichter* as some kind of oracular authority. His respect for this mysterious, inspired genius is the closest Freud comes to having religion, or at least a kind of *ersatz* totem – something to be consulted and revered but not interfered with. Of course, this quasi-theological conception of the artist was endemic in his culture. It is only surprising that Freud, the thinker who contributed so substantially to the overthrow of such unquestioningly patriarchal and mystical attitudes, should himself ostensibly share this conception. There is clearly a polemical motive underlying his deference to the literary ideology of his projected reader. The contrast between this and his controversial ventures into literary criticism is indeed striking, but his professed reverence for the *Dichter* is not dishonest. It is more a case of a safe manifest truth screening a latent 'threat'.

Given the polemical aspect of Freud's literary allusions, it is not surprising that when he makes them he tends to mask more radical psychoanalytical attitudes towards literature with a piety which he assumes he shares with his reader. This establishing of a cultural common ground can only further serve the fundamental purpose of all these allusions: to facilitate the reception of his own texts. The advantages he gains range from mere ornamentation and aesthetic relief to a much fuller literary communion with his reader. All of these vitally increase the accessibility of his own texts. Even more importantly, the allusions can disarm potential outrage and offer the prestigious sanction of a literary authority. This polemical support is only rarely available, but its source makes it particularly valuable to Freud. It represents corroboration from a non-pathological sphere, helping to extend the realm of psychoanalysis far beyond mental illness. Indeed, references to the canon of classical authors are the single most effective means of suggesting the universal validity of psychoanalysis.

Although any association with the *Dichter* is most welcome to Freud, he is always at pains to distance himself from any suggestion of dependence on them. In his *Gradiva* analysis he claims it 'certainly never . . . occurred to me to look for a confirmation of my findings in imaginative writings' (IX, 54), one of several unprovoked denials which reveal just how sensitive the issue is for him. He is usually careful to attribute striking finds in literature to other analysts, hence it is Rank who discovered the letter in which Schiller prefigures free-association technique, and most of the examples from literature given in his book on parapraxes are similarly attributed to pupils. The same is true even of much of Freud's literary criticism: it is Jung who prompts the study of *Gradiva*, Jentsch who causes him to analyse 'The Sand-Man', and Rank who suggests the *Rosmersholm* analysis. He feels a strong need to assert that his own sources are empirical, not literary. Nevertheless, the most revealing allusions in Freud's texts clearly belong to a study of literary influences on the actual *formulation* of psychoanalytical theory. For example, his speech in acceptance of the Goethe prize in 1930 contains a wealth of allusions. They are offered as insights, treated by Goethe as self-evident, which support Freud's relatively innocuous hypothesis that, if the poet were alive, he would be receptive to psychoanalysis. Here Freud is blithely disregarding the fact that Goethe preceded him, and that he himself was raised knowing much of the poet's work by heart. Whatever was 'self-evident' to the great man was equally so for his youthful admirer. With this consideration in mind, the references to Goethe's work made in this speech shed light on a much more important issue than any idle hypothesis about how Goethe would have responded to psychoanalysis. Along with many of the most resonant literary allusions in Freud's own texts, they raise the highly problematical but crucial question of the unconscious sources of Freudian theory itself.

DEFERRED ACTION: FROM SEDUCTION TO OEDIPUS

Freud's references to literature clearly demonstrate the abiding presence of authors such as Goethe, Sophocles, and Shakespeare within his texts, to the extent that they sometimes determine the very structure of his own works. Perhaps the most remarkable aspect of these allusions, however, is not that they serve such varied and pervasive functions, but that they so overwhelmingly outnumber his references to any scientific authors. Their sheer frequency calls for a far more radical evaluation of the role played by literature in Freud's development of psychoanalysis. Many allusions are, of course, made with the implicit assumption that poets have substantially anticipated psychoanalytical theory. The critic Leo Bersani argues, therefore, that Freud prefers 'an art of secure statement' and quotes, say, Goethe for 'a kind of versified confirmation of certain doctrinal points'.[11] Although Freud himself would probably have concurred with this description, I would question whether this process is as superficial and as one-sided as Bersani implies. For this purpose I shall focus attention on Freud's emergence from certain theoretical crises, such as the collapse of his 'seduction theory' and his postulation of primary narcissism. During such crises literary influences can most clearly be seen to affect – perhaps unconsciously – the very *formulation* of psychoanalytical theory.

In the speech he wrote for Freud's eightieth birthday Thomas Mann praises Freud precisely because he has *not* drawn on great literature for the creation of psychoanalysis. Such a problematic declaration from so formidable a figure deserves quoting in full:

Indeed we know that the genius in whose honour we are gathered here, Sigmund Freud, . . . trod the difficult path of his discoveries quite alone, quite independently, solely as a doctor and scientist, unaware of the comfort and reinforcement which great literature would have been able to provide for him. He did not know Nietzsche, whose works abound with anticipatory flashes of Freudian insight; nor Novalis, whose Romantic-biological day-dreams and inspirations so often come astonishingly close to psychoanalytical ideas; nor Kierkegaard, whose Christian courage to explore psychological extremes would have spoken so profoundly and so beneficially to him; nor, to be sure, did he know Schopenhauer, that melancholy symphonist of a philosophy of instincts striving for transformation and redemption . . . Indeed it had to be this way.[12]

When Mann delivered his address in person at Berggasse 19, Freud was delighted by it. Despite this apparent sanction, however, the above statement must be at least heavily qualified. The contention, for example, that Freud was unaware of Novalis is easily refuted. Apart from his intimate knowledge of the German Romantics in general, Freud actually quotes Novalis approvingly in the opening chapter of *The Interpretation of Dreams* (IV, 83).[13] In the same chapter he also commends Schopenhauer's assertion in *Parerga und Paralipomena* that impulses which remain unconscious during waking hours are registered during dreams (IV, 36). Even if Freud had at that time read no other works by Schopenhauer, he was still aware of central tenets of his thought through, for example, the intermediacy of Eduard von Hartmann's *Philosophie des Unbewußten* of 1869, a work which, in a 1914 addition to *The Interpretation of Dreams*, he belatedly acknowledges as anticipating his own thinking (V, 528n.).

My own aim, however, is not to establish intellectual 'priority' as such, but rather to examine various modes of *intertextuality*, whereby the influence of Freud's reading can be discerned at the very heart of even his most original writing. Freud need not even have read certain authors in order to have been exposed to their influence. Philip Rieff, for example, points out that Freud existed in 'a *Zeitgeist* thoroughly saturated with Schopenhauer and Nietzsche',[14] whilst Lionel Trilling claims that literary influences – he mentions Novalis, Schopenhauer, Nietzsche, and Ibsen – can be taken for granted, even though it is not clear whether the influence derives from Freud's reading or from the late-nineteenth-century *Zeitgeist*.[15] It is true, for example, that when Freud acquired Nietzsche's works in 1900, he already knew enough about the philosopher to confide to Fliess that he was expecting to find 'words for much that remains mute in me'.[16] In 1914 he claims:

In later years I have denied myself the very great pleasure of reading the works of Nietzsche, with the deliberate object of not being hampered in working out the impressions received in psycho-analysis by any sort of anticipatory ideas. (XIV, 15–16)

This assertion reveals more than Freud may have wished, not least that he was conversant enough with Nietzschean thought to fear its proximity to his own ideas. More importantly, Freud reveals his anxiety about – and, therefore, fundamental receptiveness towards – non-scientific influences. Earlier on the same page he admits that the concept of repression can be found in Schopenhauer, yet he claims priority on account of his 'not being well-read'. Although Freud, fearing unconscious influences on his nascent science, may indeed have avoided philosophy as such, imaginative literature was never the object of any such abstinence. On the contrary, Freud's knowledge of European literature is admired by even his harshest critics. The sheer breadth of his reading ensured that, despite Mann's – and Freud's own – heroic image of the lone explorer, psychoanalysis was not and could not have been conceived in any splendid isolation.

Only in 1920, in 'A Note on the Prehistory of the Technique of Analysis', does Freud acknowledge that he may have absorbed a key idea, namely the technique of free association, from a literary source. He attributes the possibility to 'the fragment of cryptomnesia which in so many cases may be suspected to lie behind apparent originality' (XVIII, 265). Cryptomnesia, whereby the source of an idea is forgotten and the idea is subsequently experienced not as a memory, but as an original conception, may indeed be more widespread in Freud's development of psychoanalysis than even he appreciated. He is well known for his capacity to 'forget' suggestive ideas – innate bisexuality, for example, or destructive drives – which then germinate unconsciously within him only to bear fruit much later. In the case of literary influences, though, this mechanism places too heavy an emphasis on the question of priority. Perhaps a more useful concept is that of deferred action (Nachträglichkeit), whereby powerful impressions are stored unconsciously until, in later stages of development, they are reworked and invested with new meaning. A possible example of this mechanism was touched on earlier in this chapter. Freud's reference to Goethe's account of Moses' death was first made in a 1937 draft of *Moses and Monotheism*. Nevertheless, it is highly probable that Freud was acquainted with 'Israel in the Wilderness' long before he knew of Sellin's hypothesis of Moses' murder. Freud's remark that Goethe's account is offered 'without any evidence' does not amount to an expression of reservation, rather it appears to be an affirmation of his faith in the poet's powers of insight. He must have been deeply struck by the mighty Goethe's suggestion that the 'father' of the Jews was ultimately killed by his own followers, even if he was not yet ready to develop the suggestion into a sustained account. The case for *Moses and Monotheism* having been sparked by the deferred action of Goethe's suggestion, then, is at least plausible.

Due to Freud's powerful resistances against any suggestion of unscientific elements in the development of psychoanalytical theory, literary influences on his thinking must be considered quite distinctly from the 'respectable' influence of scientists such as Darwin, Brücke, and Charcot. Freud's claims that psychoanalytical ideas have been significantly anticipated by poets are always made with the tacit assumption that direct influence is not even an issue. As he sees it, the conclusions he has reached by arduous and scrupulous clinical work can, retrospectively, be compared to the insights evinced in great works of literature and the broad similarity appreciated. Nevertheless, for such a feat as the single-handed creation of a new science, Freud must have drawn upon many sources. Clinical experience and theoretical knowledge from his medical training are, of course, foremost amongst these.

Nowadays, however, even the most orthodox psychoanalysts do not deny
that social and cultural prejudices peculiar to Freud himself also affected
his thinking. As Freud was particularly steeped in literary culture, it
would be perverse to discount this as one such influence. At school his
passions had been not the sciences, but literature, languages, and, to
some extent, philosophy. If, as he acknowledges, his science brings him
to conclusions similar to those to be found in the works of poets and philosophers, the question of influence from these humanist spheres
becomes particularly pressing. If literature was an early passion which
was then suppressed in later life, it could be argued that literary
influences are, therefore, all the more 'dynamic'. Psychoanalysis itself
resembles one of those unconsciously overdetermined compromise-for-
mations, such as neurotic illnesses or works of art, which Freud devoted
his life to studying, and it would be reasonable to expect analogies drawn
from psychoanalytical theory to be, at least, illuminating.

It may be 1930 before Freud, in his Goethe Prize speech, produces a
substantial account of the various ways in which he has been anticipated
by Goethe, but careful study reveals that the list he produces is no mere
retrospective comparison of one independent body of thought with
another. His first reference, for example, is to Goethe's awareness of 'the
incomparable strength of the first affective ties of human creatures', to
which end he cites five lines from the Dedication of *Faust*, including the
line about nebulous figures who 'long since appeared before my troubled
gaze' (XXI, 209). It will be remembered that the very same line is quoted
over thirty years earlier in *The Interpretation of Dreams*. In the dream book,
moreover, the line appears in relation to a memory of his nephew John,
revealing that this passage from *Faust* – or, more probably, the entire play
– was foremost in Freud's mind during the critical phase of his self-analysis. Norman Brown is just one critic who highlights the Faustian vein
which can then be seen to run through the whole of psychoanalysis. He
claims, for example, that Freud's image of man – as constituted by the
very renunciation of those instincts which he most urgently strives to
satisfy – is a genuinely Faustian vision,[17] almost as if such concepts as the
pleasure principle and repression had been developed primarily to
explain Faust's striving.

Brown's account of Faust's character, a man striving for the one unat-
tainable object, the mother, may be one-sided, but even when other
dimensions of Faust's character are sketched in, the pervasive influence
of Goethe's masterpiece remains conspicuous. When, for example, in
1933 Freud describes psychoanalysis as 'a work of culture – not unlike

the draining of the Zuider Zee' (XXII, 80), Thomas Mann is only the first of many to hear the literary echo: 'Thus, at the end, the traits of this venerable man whom we are honouring merge into those of the aged Faust.'[18] Bruno Bettelheim, who convincingly argues that much is lost when we overlook Freud's literary allusions, also points to this passage when he pictures Freud as a mature Faust reclaiming the soul from threatening instinctual forces.[19] Ironically, Bettelheim himself, perhaps in his concern to champion Freud as a humanist, appears to be overlooking the majority of his allusions to *Faust*, which clearly demonstrate that Freud is at least equally inspired by the character of Mephistopheles. Either way, psychoanalysis is demonstrably the product of a man both intimately acquainted with and profoundly affected by *Faust*, to the extent that the play could be said to constitute a leitmotif throughout his textual elaboration of psychoanalysis. Whether Freud took insights directly from Goethe or merely retraced his own ideas in Goethe's texts, the poet was clearly never far from his mind. Fritz Wittels's account of a meeting with Freud bears this out eloquently:

One evening as I was reading out an essay to Freud, he suddenly leapt up, shouted: 'Let's see what the old man says about this', and fetched *Faust II* from his book-case. When I saw how lovingly he caressed the volume and buried himself in it, to find a quotation which to me did not seem urgently necessary, I realized that he had a special relationship with Goethe.[20]

Of course, *Faust* is not the only play of Goethe's which gripped Freud and from which he could quote almost without thinking. Furthermore, it is perhaps misleading to separate direct literary influences on Freud too rigidly from, say, his clinical experience. Some critics have suggested that Freud derived much of his therapeutic approach itself from literary precursors. Alfred von Berger, the theatre critic who gave *Studies on Hysteria* its most sympathetic review in 1895, was the first to point out the resemblance between Freud's cures and the one portrayed in Goethe's *Iphigenie*.[21] Freud himself sanctions this comparison some thirty-five years later in his Goethe Prize speech, where he writes:

In what is perhaps his most sublime poetical creation, *Iphigenie*, Goethe shows us a striking instance of expiation, of the freeing of a suffering mind from the burden of guilt, and he makes this catharsis come about through a passionate outburst of feeling under the beneficent influence of loving sympathy. (XXI, 210)

He actually goes on to give even fuller examples of similar 'psychotherapy' rendered by Goethe himself, familiar to Freud from the poet's

Campaign in France and his letters. Freud thus places most emphasis on Goethe as a precursor not in theory, but in therapy.[22]

Several critics have used Freud's literary allusions to point to unconscious literary influences on his creation of psychoanalysis. Jean Starobinski provides the most sustained analysis, concentrating, perhaps surprisingly, on Virgil's *Aeneid*. He suggests that the epigraph to *The Interpretation of Dreams*, 'Flectere si nequeo superos, Acheronta movebo', was 'predestined to serve as the model upon which Freud was to construct or fortify his theory of the repressed'. He points, for example, to the mention of the river Acheron to explain Freud's persistent use of the imagery of fluidity for instinctual energies, and he even claims that the work of analysis in general may have been 'sustained by the model of Virgilian catabasis'.[23] The enormous influence he thus attributes to an apparently secondary element of Freud's text is debatable, but it seems to be at least partly vindicated by a remark Freud himself makes in the 1907 work 'Delusions and Dreams in Jensen's *Gradiva*'. Here, having pointed out that a poet incorporates the laws of the unconscious in his works, he continues: 'We discover these laws by analysing his writings just as we find them from cases of real illness' (IX, 92). Again Freud believes he is referring only to the way his independently developed theories appear, in hindsight, to be corroborated in works of literature. Nevertheless, the ambiguity of his wording appears to point to the potentially functional role played by works of literature in the elaboration of psychoanalytical theory. If Starobinski appears to overinterpret Freud's literary allusion, it is not because he ascribes too much influence to a literary source, but because he has not singled out the most appropriate work of literature.

Although Freud knew his Virgil well, his fame actually rests on a theory named after a character from Greek literature – Sophocles' Oedipus. Although Oedipus is primarily a mythological figure, there is no doubt that Sophocles' tragedy represents to Freud the authoritative version of this myth. In any case, the extent to which Sophocles' play is bound up with Freud's discovery of the Oedipus complex goes far beyond mere nomenclature. In *The Interpretation of Dreams* Freud makes his first published reference to the complex, and he also discusses *Oedipus* and *Hamlet* for the first time. He justifies turning to literature by pointing out that for such a contentious theory he must base his evidence 'on the broadest possible foundation' (IV, 249). Nevertheless, Freud actually first mentions the complex in a letter to Fliess written in October 1897.[24] Here he relates both that he has discovered the complex within himself and that it is universal. Again he immediately begins a discussion of both *Oedipus* and *Hamlet*. In the context of a letter to his closest confidant, Freud hardly needs to mention these works for any polemical purposes. His justification for turning to them in *The Interpretation of Dreams*, then, is something of a rationalization. It seems that he does not need to 'turn to' these literary works, they are, rather, already immanent in his theory, having actually helped him to crystallize this theory as it emerged from his self-analysis. Equally importantly, the authority of Sophocles and Shakespeare has enabled Freud to make the enormous leap from intimate self-discovery to general theory, the literary works forming a bridge between the individual and the universal dimension. Freud appears to admit as much in *The Interpretation of Dreams* when he refers to the ancient legend 'whose profound and universal power to move can only be understood if the hypothesis I have put forward in regard to the psychology of children has an equally universal validity' (IV, 261). His reference to the legend's 'power to move' here indicates that he has Sophocles' literary treatment of the theme in mind.

For the rest of Freud's life this play, along with *Hamlet*, remains at the very heart of a theory which was to become the shibboleth of the psychoanalytical movement. For example, the instant he mentions that Dora is in love with her father he turns to the 'poetical rendering of what is typical in these relations' (VII, 56); and he uses precisely the same strategy in the *Introductory Lectures on Psycho-Analysis*, written a full twenty years after the celebrated letter to Fliess. Another general account of his theories, the fragment *An Outline of Psycho-Analysis*, written no less than forty years after *The Interpretation of Dreams*, is even broader in scope than the introductory lectures and is much more highly condensed, yet here Freud again introduces the Oedipus complex with a discussion of *Oedipus* and *Hamlet*. There is no doubt that these plays are inextricably bound up with his theory of the complex, and it is certainly possible that they are somehow involved with its very formulation, as opposed to just its expedient presentation. Freud commonly refers to Sophocles' text not merely for purposes of demonstration, but also as a source of evidence. Jocasta's remark that men commonly dream of incest is, for example, taken as corroboration that the Oedipus myth itself stems from dream material (IV, 264); and as late as 1938, in his *Outline of Psycho-Analysis*, Freud provides 'evidence' for his contention that the super-ego is the 'heir to the Oedipus complex' by referring to the fact that Sophocles has Oedipus punish himself even though he also portrays him as an innocent victim of a preordained fate (XXIII, 205). Freud actually comes closest to admitting that Sophocles' play has helped him to formulate the Oedipus complex in his *Autobiographical Study* of 1925. Here he writes that the 'overwhelming effect of its dramatic treatment' helped him to recognize 'a universal law of mental life' (XX, 63). Freud does indeed seem to imply that Sophocles has already performed a sophisticated psychological analysis and then communicated the results to his audience:

[The spectator] understands the dramatist's voice as though it were saying to him: 'You are struggling in vain against your responsibility and are protesting in vain of what you have done in opposition to these criminal intentions. You are guilty, for you have not been able to destroy them; they still persist in you unconsciously.' (XVI, 331)

If Freud really does believe that Sophocles spoke so eloquently to him, then it could be argued that the Greek poet has provided him with the cornerstone of his entire science. It is perhaps worth remembering here that Freud often fantasized about emulating Heinrich Schliemann, the archaeologist who realized his childhood ambition of discovering the city of Troy. Like Freud, he demonstrated the factual basis of a Greek myth – and, moreover, his breakthrough was due, at least in part, to the fact that he took a Greek poet, Homer, at his word.

Other critics have recognized the importance of literary sources in the theory of the Oedipus complex. Kurt Eissler fleetingly suggests that Freud may have discovered the complex from his study of Shakespeare's tragedy and then 'applied his insights about Hamlet to his self-analysis, rather than vice versa'.[25] This is indeed a radical assessment of the literary contribution to Freud's theory, but there is some evidence to support it. For example, just three weeks before Freud first proposed the Oedipus theory in October 1897, he wrote another letter to Fliess telling him that his 'seduction theory' of neurotic aetiology had collapsed. He no longer believed his patients' accounts of seduction and abuse in early childhood, which, until then, he had considered to be the primary cause of their neuroses. He now badly needed an equally powerful aetiological factor rooted in infantile sexuality, and it was this theoretical crisis which was soon to result in his momentous Oedipus theory. However, even in this earlier letter, which merely announces his abandonment of the seduction theory, Freud already has the play *Hamlet* in mind. He is remarkably calm about the collapse of his 'neurotica'; indeed, he alludes to *Hamlet* in order to console himself: 'I vary Hamlet's saying, "To be in readiness": to be cheerful is everything!'[26] It may well be that a reference to Shakespeare's masterpiece was so consoling to him because this very play was already indicating an escape from his theoretical impasse.

Gilles Deleuze goes even further when he suggests that the oedipal constellation was not even present in Freud's 'unconscious', but was derived entirely from his Goethean classical culture.[27] It must indeed be noted that Freud's preoccupation with Sophocles' play long predates his self-analysis, indicating the primacy of the literary dimension. When only seventeen years old he wrote a letter to his schoolfriend Emil Fluss in which he mentions his Greek paper in the *Matura* examinations. This consisted of a long passage from Sophocles' *Oedipus*, and Freud scored the highest mark in the class because, he claims, he had already read it for his own pleasure and had made this clear in his script.[28] It is safe to assume that the Greek passages remained with him throughout his life. Over sixty years after his *Matura* he wrote to Arnold Zweig: 'Incidentally, I have always been proud of the substantial remains of Greek in my memory (Sophocles' choruses, passages from Homer).'[29] It even seems that Freud knew his fame would one day be connected with Sophocles' play, long before he knew precisely how. As a student walking through the great court of Vienna University, he fantasized about having his bust installed here inscribed with a passage from *Oedipus*. When, in 1906, his Viennese pupils, unaware of this fantasy, presented him with a medallion inscribed with the very same Greek quotation, Freud paled at the uncanny wish-fulfilment. It seems, however, that this coincidence was determined less by fate than by Freud's unconscious determination to emulate Oedipus' defeat of the Theban sphinx. Long before he knew that his own great riddle would be the aetiology of neurosis, he seems to have known his answer would involve Oedipus.

NATURPHILOSOPHIE AND THE 'SCHOOL OF HELMHOLTZ'

Perhaps due to the breakdown of a theory constructed entirely on the basis of clinical observations, Freud, in his elaboration of the Oedipus complex, appears to fall back on insights and expectations engendered in him by a literary culture to which he was exposed long before his scientific training. If influences from literary sources are to be elucidated any further, it will first be necessary to establish a more precise context for this 'regression' from a later stage in Freud's intellectual development to one which had ostensibly been superseded. The case of the Oedipus complex suggests that Freud's alternative intellectual approach places a greater emphasis not only on literature and myth, but also on the development of radical, universal theories by means of a form of speculation independent of biological doctrine and even clinical observation. Particularly germane to this discussion, then, is one of the central questions which Peter Gay poses in his biography of Freud, namely: 'Was Freud the scientific positivist he claimed to be, or was he, rather, principally indebted to the cloudy speculations of the romantics . . .?'[30] Jones relates that Freud began his intellectual life as an adherent of something other than empirical materialism: 'Freud himself, inspired by Goethe, who was one of the first pioneers, passed through a brief period of the pantheistic *Naturphilosophie*.'[31] This latter, a profoundly speculative, idealist philosophy, both grew out of and then itself influenced German Romanticism. It held that Nature could not be reduced to its mechanical components and was, rather, the manifestation of certain eternal and universal spiritual principles. *Naturphilosophie* is closely associated with the philosopher Friedrich Schelling, an acquaintance of Goethe, who criticized post-Enlightenment positivism and advocated instead a vitalistic, even pantheistic vision of Nature.

Jones implies that Freud's adherence to this Romantic philosophy was a youthful aberration which was soon corrected by the rigours of his medical training. Nevertheless, if Freud was indeed exposed to this tradition through his love of Goethe, then it would be unwise to presume that the influence was so easily shed. It should be remembered here that on four separate occasions Freud claims it was an essay on 'Nature' written, he believed, by Goethe, which inspired him to become a scientist in the first place. In *The Interpretation of Dreams*, for example, he writes:

when at the end of my school-days I was hesitating in my choice of career, it was hearing that essay read aloud at a public lecture that decided me to take up the study of natural science. (V, 441)

Gay's scepticism towards Freud's anecdote – he finds it almost mythopoeic in its compression[32] – may well be in order, but the fact that, a whole quarter of a century later, this essay, which Freud still describes as incomparably beautiful, is a key free association to his dream about Goethe suggests that it was a significant source of stimulation for him.[33] The young Freud was passionately stirred by what may be termed a Romantic philosophy of Nature. The 'Goethe' essay is a mystical and pantheistic account of the omnipotence of Nature, profoundly at odds with the strict positivism which Freud encountered in his university training. That Freud should even claim to have been moved to study science not by the hard-headed materialism of the latter part of the nineteenth century, but by such a rhapsodic paean to eternal mysteries should be borne in mind throughout the following discussion.

Jones astutely qualifies the 'Goethe' anecdote by pointing out that Freud also hoped medical studies would provide him with an opportunity to solve some of the world's riddles whilst simultaneously holding in check his youthful attraction to speculation.[34] The period of radical materialism which Freud passed through during his medical degree was, indeed, partly a reaction against his adolescent passion for a Romantic vision of Nature. It is important to point out, however, that Goethe himself was never implicated in this reaction; Freud would have been aware that the poet himself later came to regard the pantheistic sentiments of the fragment on 'Nature' as immature. Nevertheless, Freud's initial materialism was extreme indeed. In *The Interpretation of Dreams* he relates that, during a student debate about the relationship of philosophy to the natural sciences, he almost came to fight a duel, so forcefully did he express his new convictions (VI, 212–13). Admittedly, in this passage Freud refers to himself as 'a green youngster, full of materialistic theories'. Clearly, his violence towards mystical vitalism was soon muted. Nevertheless, it is still in evidence decades later, for example in his overreaction to Jung's postulation of a monistic libido, an apparent regression to vitalism. In *Totem and Taboo* Freud, perhaps in response to Jung's apostasy, aims a direct blow at *Naturphilosophie* by characterizing it as a descendant of the primitive world-view of savages who believe all things are inhabited by spirits and demons (XIII, 76). Freud's positivistic vehemence is, however, most in evidence earliest in his career, for example in his unpublished 'Project for a Scientific Psychology' of 1895. His attempt here to establish a quantitative framework for all neurological processes is described by Ricoeur as a conscious refutation of the vitalism associated with *Naturphilosophie*.[35]

The main influence at work in Freud's acquired hostility towards Romantic philosophies was the mid-nineteenth-century biophysics movement usually associated with the name of Hermann von Helmholtz. His 'school' sought to establish a wholly materialistic biology by means of an extremely strict empirical methodology. It was, therefore, implacably hostile towards metaphysical speculation and mystical vitalism, or, as Gay puts it, all 'loose, poetic talk of mysterious innate powers'.[36] Both before and after graduation Freud studied in Ernst von Brücke's Physiological Institute, which was considered a stronghold of Helmholtzian science, Brücke having been a founding member of the biophysics movement. In the 1840s Brücke had even sworn something

like an oath to remain faithful to the movement's endeavour to reduce
all forces present in the organism to the chemical and physical forces of
attraction and repulsion. The positivistic vocabulary evident in Freud's
1895 project – and, to some extent, throughout his later elaboration of
psychoanalysis – demonstrates the profound influence this current of
thought had on him. Not surprisingly, Freud's exposure to such extreme
materialism coincided with a suppression of his tendency towards speculation and, therefore, of many sources of literary influence on his thinking. Thus, despite Freud's prolific literary allusions, a critic as judicious
as Rieff can claim that 'in his major works he kept his humanist literacy
under wraps'. Rieff, of course, understands that his primary motives
were strategic: Freud hoped 'his ideas would be more attractive coming
from a dogged insular scientist than from the voracious book-browser
and idea-fancier he also was'.[37]

Several critics have devoted entire studies to demonstrating that the
'School of Helmholtz' never really existed, or at least that its influence
has been overestimated by Freud scholars. Paul Cranefield, for example,
convincingly points out that Brücke and Helmholtz had both softened
their strict biophysical line of 1847 by the time Freud came under their
influence. He even claims that the *Naturphilosophie* which Helmholtzians
attempted to eradicate was, by antithesis, present in their doctrines, thus
he cites the 'school' as one of the sources of Freud's familiarity with this
Romantic philosophy.[38] Many Freud scholars have undoubtedly overlooked the complexity of such scientific influences. Nevertheless, during
his medical training Freud did indeed pass through a phase of fervent
materialism, and at this time Brücke and Helmholtz represented
significant authority-figures to him. Even as late as 1920, in a letter to
Stefan Zweig, he describes Helmholtz as 'an intellectual giant',[39] but it
is a passage in *The Interpretation of Dreams* which best reveals something of
the awe in which Freud held the man. Here, addressing the question of
the 'creativity' of the unconscious, he writes:

We are probably inclined greatly to over-estimate the conscious character of
intellectual and artistic production as well. Accounts given us by some of the
most highly productive men, such as Goethe and Helmholtz, show rather that
what is essential and new in their creations came to them without premedita-
tion and as an almost ready-made whole. (V, 613)

Thus it appears that, for brilliance and originality, Freud ranks the professor of physiology not far behind Goethe himself. It is worth remembering that Freud's study contained not only his massive Weimar edition

of Goethe's collected works, but also an engraving of Helmholtz which remained on display throughout his life.

Brücke, after whom Freud named one of his sons, was, of course, an even greater influence. On the very page on which he refers to the *Naturphilosophie* mediated to Freud by Goethe, Jones also relates that Brücke became a father-figure to Freud.[40] Scientific discipline was, it seems, Freud's chosen repressive moment of his tendency to indulge in philosophical speculation; thus his father worship of Brücke was, in fact, essential in order to supplant the influence of a mentor of Goethe's stature. However, if Freud really did ruthlessly suppress his speculative tendencies, and with them many literary influences on theory formulation, then not only does the severity of this 'repression' reflect the potency of his initial desire, it is also reasonable to expect that the repressed should, in some guise, eventually return within Freud's science.

It is certainly true that Freud did not adhere for long to the positivistic rigour of the biophysics movement. Perhaps for this reason the attack on some of his less scientific practices is as virulent today as it has ever been. Wilfred Trotter offers a typical opinion when he complains of the 'odour of humanity' which pervades psychoanalysis and which is so oppressive to anyone trained in the 'bracing atmosphere of the biological sciences'.[41] Of course, Freud was himself trained in this very atmosphere. Henri Ellenberger claims that the turning point came in 1897 when Freud 'emancipated himself from the influence of Brücke and Charcot, and identified himself with Goethe'.[42] Certainly by the time he came to write *The Interpretation of Dreams* he felt confident enough to make the following attack on contemporary psychiatry:

It is true that the dominance of the brain over the organism is asserted with apparent confidence. Nevertheless, anything that might indicate that mental life is in any way independent of demonstrable organic changes or that its manifestations are in any way spontaneous alarms the modern psychiatrist, as though a recognition of such things would inevitably bring back the days of the Philosophy of Nature, and of the metaphysical view of the nature of mind. The suspicions of the psychiatrists have put the mind, as it were, under tutelage. . . . (IV, 41)

Freud's persistent emphasis on desire, and, therefore, on the spontaneous intentionality and autonomy of the mind, would indeed have been regarded by the strictest materialists as a lapse into vitalism. Freud's speculations about human drives, derivatives of an unconscious and physically unspecifiable Will, do, in fact, place him in a broadly Romantic tradition which includes Schelling, Schopenhauer, and Nietzsche.

Freud's respect for the Romantic and philosophical conceptions of dreams dismissed by contemporary materialists is actually a recurrent theme in *The Interpretation of Dreams*. For example, he claims:

There can be no doubt that the psychical achievements of dreams received readier and warmer recognition during the intellectual period which has now been left behind, when the human mind was dominated by philosophy and not by the exact natural sciences. (IV, 63)

Although Freud often sides with the philosophers and the Romantics against the materialists, he does, of course, continue to use a vocabulary drawn from the exact sciences, just as he continues to hope that one day his psychological findings will be substantiated by physiological data. Even as late as 1933, when writing to Albert Einstein, he justifies his essentially speculative and mythopoeic forces of Eros and Death as a theoretical transfiguration of the basic polarity of attraction and repulsion, no doubt an allusion to Brücke's 'oath' to reduce all vital phenomena to these basic physical forces (XXII, 209). Nevertheless, as Rieff points out, Freud's Helmholtzian vocabulary soon becomes 'merely metaphoric'[43] as Freud leaves his radical materialism behind.

It was Freud's increasing interest in what he called his metapsychology which marked his most decisive shift away from Helmholtzian materialism and, to some extent, back to the Romantic speculations which stirred him in his youth. In *The Psychopathology of Everyday Life*, written in 1901, he admits his metapsychology at least shares the same universal scope as any metaphysical system when he describes his task as 'to transform *metaphysics* into *metapsychology*' (VI, 259). His most radical metapsychological speculations, furthermore, have little to do with any such coolly scientific process of translation. As he admits in a letter to Fliess, his goal of a universal psychology became his dominating passion or, speaking with Schiller, his tyrant,[44] and its development required that Freud unleash his 'daemon of creative speculation'.[45] Perhaps it is not surprising, then, that rather than reducing metaphysics to metapsychology, Freud's attempt to produce a universal theory of vital forces irreducible to mechanical processes actually appears to introduce a subjective and metaphysical dimension into psychoanalytical theory. Ricoeur says of this process that 'under the coating of a scientific mythology, there arises the *Naturphilosophie* which the young Freud admired in Goethe'.[46]

Freud's constant emphasis on the dynamic interplay of antagonistic forces about which no physical data is available was almost bound to activate his underlying fascination with Romantic philosophy. The similarities between this philosophy and Freudian theory are well documented, hence Trilling's description of psychoanalysis as 'one of the culminations of the Romanticist literature of the nineteenth century'.[47] Ellenberger studies the correspondences in most detail and also makes the most sweeping claim, namely that Freud had 'hardly a single concept . . . that had not been anticipated by the philosophy of nature and Romantic medicine'.[48] The present study, of course, is less concerned with priority than it is with Freud's texts in their own right. Perry Meisel penetratingly comments that Freud's anecdote about the 'Goethe' essay 'situates his work from the start within a nexus of overtly literary traditions that rival the scientific ones, and eventually overpower them, in their relative contribution to the texture of his writing'.[49] The remainder of the present chapter will be devoted to following the literary threads which appear to hold some of his texts together. As there is hardly a single area of psychoanalytical theory that remains unaffected by this literary and philosophical substratum, it will for present purposes be necessary to single out one aspect of theory whose textual elaboration may be examined in detail. Freud's theory of the instincts, which culminates in his postulation of two primal drives, Eros and Thanatos, is a singularly appropriate object for such an examination. Here Freud's speculative attempts to locate meaning in the very structure of nature causes the mask of scientific exactitude, donned under the aegis of Brücke and Helmholtz, to slip and to reveal the legacy of his literary culture functioning at the very heart of his formulation of psychoanalytical theory.

INSTINCT THEORY IN CRISIS: NARCISSUS AND EROS

Although in the preceding discussion I have implied that Freud embarked on the creation of psychoanalysis as a rational empiricist who was then gradually overwhelmed by the literary and speculative leanings he had suppressed, it should not be overlooked that Freud's earliest theory of the instincts was always couched in literary terms. As early as 1898, for example, he refers to 'the influence of the two most powerful motive forces – hunger and love' (III, 316), the first of about ten published allusions he makes to Schiller's poem 'Die Weltweisen'. Schiller's pair of terms corresponds with Freud's initial instinctual dualism of self-preservation drives and sexual drives, the conflict between which Freud regarded as the cause of neurotic illness. In his earliest allusions, however, Freud never ascribes the term 'hunger and love' to its literary source, insisting it is merely a popular saying which he uses as shorthand for the fundamental biological instincts. It is 1910 before he admits that this central psychic conflict is formulated in the words of a poet, although he still does not mention Schiller by name:

As the poet has said, all the organic instincts that operate in our mind may be classified as 'hunger' or 'love'. (XI, 214–15)

When in *Beyond the Pleasure Principle*, published in 1920, he offers an overview of his instinct theory, he also admits that the saying provided him with not just a verbal formulation, but also a conceptual model:

Psycho-analysis, which could not escape making *some* assumption about the instincts, kept at first to the popular division of instincts typified in the phrase 'hunger and love' [für die das Wort von 'Hunger und Liebe' vorbildlich ist]. (XVIII, 51)

Finally, in 1930, Freud reveals not only the source of the phrase, but also the extent to which it played a constructive role in his development of a theory of the drives. In *Civilization and its Discontents* he writes:

In what was at first my utter perplexity, I took as my starting-point [Anhalt] a saying of the poet-philosopher, Schiller, that 'hunger and love are what moves the world'. (XXI, 117)

Over the course of thirty years, then, Freud becomes less anxious about the fact that this formulation of drive theory derives from a literary source. Given that since the early 1890s he had observed the fundamental conflict between sexual impulses and ego-preservation in his patients, it may be argued that Schiller's 'hunger and love' is less an influence than merely a felicitous expression. Nevertheless, in a letter written to Martha in 1884, long before his clinical observation of the distinction between self-preservation and sexuality, Freud describes 'hunger and love' as the true philosophy.[50] As this basic dualism contributed significantly to Freud's elaboration of such key concepts as the pleasure and reality principles, it may well be that the long-term impact of this line of poetry has been unjustly overlooked. I have already mentioned that the poetic context of the line – Schiller's satire on barren philosophical speculation – touched a particular nerve in Freud, who was struggling to discipline his own speculative bent. It should also be remembered that, in Freud's estimation, Schiller ranks not far behind Goethe as an intellectual authority. Whenever Freud mentions the poet he usually includes a reference to his powers as a thinker, thus he is a 'poet-philosopher' or 'the great poet and thinker' (XVIII, 264). When in 1926 Freud writes: 'You will recollect the words of our poet-philosopher: "Hunger and love". Incidentally, quite a formidable pair of forces! [ein ganz respektables Kräftepaar!]' (XX, 200), much of the respectability appears to be conferred by the poet himself. Schiller's authority did indeed play something of an instrumental role in Freud's initial assumption of an instinctual dualism.

The sanction of a poet was particularly important to Freud here because he was aware that the drives, existing on the boundary between the physical and the mental, were one of the most problematical areas of psychoanalytical theory. He did not want to deduce his theory of the instincts from any *a priori* assumptions, but he astutely recognized that pure induction from clinical observation was also impossible. In his 1915 paper 'Instincts and their Vicissitudes' he writes:

Even at the stage of description it is not possible to avoid applying certain abstract ideas to the material in hand, ideas derived from somewhere or other but certainly not from the new observations alone. (XIV, 117)

Schiller's 'hunger and love', which for decades served Freud as a working hypothesis, seems to be one of these unspecified 'abstract ideas', and there are others to be found in Freud's development of a theory of the drives.

A possible objection to the claim that Schiller's poetic antithesis was a primary influence on Freud would be the contention that the instincts of self-preservation and reproduction had long been recognized by biologists as fundamental. Freud himself, for example in his 1914 text 'On Narcissism: an Introduction', claims the antithesis is essentially biological. Nevertheless, on the same page he insists he would prefer 'to keep psychology clear from everything that is different in nature from it, even biological lines of thought', and later in the same paragraph he declares that psychoanalysts 'cannot wait for another science to present us with the final conclusions on the theory of instincts' (XIV, 78–9). Freud makes this bold declaration of independence from biology in a text which introduces a Greek myth, that of Narcissus, into the very heart of his theory of the drives, thus inaugurating, moreover, an upheaval which would culminate in his postulation of the fundamental drives Eros and Thanatos. If he does indeed hold biological doctrine at bay from his theory of the instincts, which by his own admission cannot be elaborated in an intellectual vacuum, then it is reasonable to suggest that his intimate familiarity with classical literature and mythology at least partially helps him to fill the void. In a 1933 lecture Freud seems to point to this possibility when he claims: 'The theory of the instincts is so to say our mythology. Instincts are mythical entities, magnificent in their indefiniteness' (XXII, 95).

It would be unwise to look for a single turning-point in Freud's shift from biophysical empiricism to quasi-mythopoeic speculation. His gradually evolving series of theoretical compromises hardly lends itself to precise dating. Nevertheless, it is significant that in 1910, in his study of Leonardo, Freud not only offers his first published definition of the term narcissism, but also makes his first published reference to 'Eros . . ., the preserver of all living things' (XI, 100 and 70). It is also in a 1910 addition to his *Three Essays on Sexuality* that the term Oedipus complex makes its published debut. The terms Oedipus complex, narcissism, and Eros would, of course, go on to enjoy ever-increasing significance in Freudian theory. Although it may be a coincidence that they all first appear as official psychoanalytical terminology in the same year, it is worth noting that Oedipus, Narcissus, and Eros were all familiar to Freud from the solid classical education he enjoyed at his *Gymnasium*, and it was this humanist culture which came decisively to the fore amidst the upheaval caused by a complication he uncovered around 1910.

The problem arose as Freud came to view the instincts of self-preservation in terms of libido invested in the subject's own ego. The distinction between ego drives and sexual drives then became wholly secondary, and both 'hunger and love' had to be considered as primarily libidinal. Naturally, purely biological notions about drives were now more irrelevant than ever, and Freud was left with a theoretical crisis. Just as he emerged from the 1897 'seduction theory' crisis with the assistance of the Oedipus myth, this time the myth of Narcissus helped him to reformulate an essential area of psychoanalytical theory. Admittedly, the term narcissism existed before Freud, and it may appear, therefore, that Freud's own *Bildung* has little to do with this particular innovation. The essential difference is that Freud postulates narcissism not as some curious perversion, but rather as a *universal* libidinal phase. The pattern is remarkably similar to that of his development of the theory of the Oedipus complex. Here Freud asserted the radical universality of what was previously considered only an aberration, and it was Greek mythology which helped him to bridge the gap between the individual and the universal. In 'On Narcissism: an Introduction', written in 1913, Freud speaks of the concept as a medical term introduced by Näcke and Havelock Ellis. Nevertheless, when he actually introduces the term three years earlier, in *Leonardo da Vinci and a Memory of his Childhood*, it is the Greek myth which is foremost in his mind:

He finds the objects of his love along the path of *narcissism*, as we say; for Narcissus, according to the Greek legend, was a youth who preferred his own reflection to everything else and who was changed into the lovely flower of that name. (XI, 100)

Not long afterwards Freud comes to believe that the narcissistic phase is, in fact, universal. His boldness here is not limited to his according a universal status to an ostensibly marginal perversion. Much more significantly, his concept of narcissism necessitates a radical revision of his theory of the instincts which takes him at least a decade to complete. Freud dares to place the myth of Narcissus at the heart of this upheaval, and it is clearly the timeless appeal of classical literature which gives him the courage to recognize a theoretically awkward phenomenon as universal, and to prosecute the enormous revisions this necessitates.

Freud knew the myth of Narcissus primarily through his study of Ovid's *Metamorphoses* in the original Latin, a compulsory text on his *Gymnasium* syllabus.[51] The extent to which his theory depends on the literary elaboration of a myth is examined by Mark Edmundson, who, somewhat speculatively, traces this elaboration through Ovid, Shakespeare, and Milton.[52] Although Freud had read all the works Edmundson refers to, he alludes to none of them in his own textual exposition of narcissism theory. Nevertheless, Freud is indeed particularly given to making literary allusions in works dealing with narcissism. One of the earliest such texts is his 1911 case history of Schreber, in which much of the evidence he provides for his contention that the self-preservation drives are libidinal is literary. For example, he quotes two lines from the Persian poet Jalaludin Rumi:

> For when the flames of love arise,
> Then Self, the gloomy tyrant, dies. XII, 65

He goes on to mention what he believes is a related phenomenon in Wagner's *Tristan und Isolde*, and even his quotation of eleven lines from *Faust* concerning the hero's detachment of libido serves a similar function of illustrating and corroborating his theory of narcissistic libidinal investment (XII, 69n., and 70). Most strikingly, it will be remembered that, in a 1917 introductory lecture, Freud concludes his description of narcissism theory with a 'poetic representation of the economic contrast between narcissism and being in love', namely, a full twenty lines of verse from Goethe's *West Eastern Divan* (XVI, 418).

However, the most significant literary reference concerning narcissism is made in 'On Narcissism: an Introduction' itself. Here, having established that a subject's libido is initially invested entirely in the ego, Freud has to explain why this libido should ever then be transferred onto external objects. His rather cryptic answer is that we must love in order not to become ill:

This follows somewhat on the lines of Heine's picture of the psychogenesis of Creation:

> Krankheit ist wohl der letzte Grund
> Des ganzen Schöpferdrangs gewesen;
> Erschaffend konnte ich genesen,
> Erschaffend wurde ich gesund.

> (Illness was no doubt the final cause
> of the whole urge to create.
> By creating, I could recover;
> by creating, I became healthy.) XIV, 85

This rather opaque reference to one of Heine's *New Poems* is made at a point when Freud is being forced to address the problem that narcissism has undermined his old instinctual dualism. Heine offers a kind of indirect authority for the postulation not only of primary narcissism itself, but also of a new opposition between ego-libido and object-libido. It is significant that Freud should make such complex use of a quotation precisely when his instinct theory is emerging from a state of violent flux. In fact, his assumption that we must love in order not to become ill is already implicit in Ovid's account of Narcissus pining to death for his hopeless self-love. That the myth of Narcissus in particular, and Freud's literary culture in general, should come to the fore when biological 'certainties' concerning the drives are breaking down does at least tend to suggest that this alternative culture is playing an active role during a critical phase of theory formulation.

*

The revisions which ensued from the theory of narcissism gradually caused Freud to regard libido, previously a quantitative psychic energy analogous to electricity, more in terms of a manifestation of a cosmological drive which he eventually named after the Greek god of love, Eros. This nomenclature is one of the key indications that the theory of narcissism does indeed mark a decisive shift in Freud from the influence of his scientific training back to his classical *Bildung*. Freud's Eros is far more fundamental than sexuality, comprising not only both object-love and self-preservation, but also crucial micro- and macrocosmic functions. His Eros is active not only psychologically, but also both biologically, in every cell of organic matter, and socially, in every variety of human collective. Freud tends, therefore, to describe the drive in vast, universal terms. For example, he speaks in 1923 of 'the efforts of Eros to combine organic substances into ever larger unities' (XVIII, 42–3), or in 1921 of 'Eros, which holds together everything in the world' (XVIII, 92). He is quite aware that such bold formulations are more akin to metaphysical speculation than to empirical biology and, correspondingly, he chooses to justify his new conception with references to non-scientific authorities. Even the *Three Essays on Sexuality*, initially written in 1905 and one of the fundamental empirical texts of psychoanalytical theory, does not escape this new emphasis. Freud chooses to preface the 1920 edition of this work with an attack on critics of his extension of the concept of sexuality:

For it is some time since Arthur Schopenhauer, the philosopher, showed mankind the extent to which their activities are determined by sexual impulses – in the ordinary sense of the word. It should surely have been impossible for a whole world of readers to banish such a startling piece of information so completely from their minds. (VII, 134)

Thomas Mann would, incidentally, have done well to note Freud's implicit assumption here that Schopenhauer's ideas are familiar to any well-read German.

After invoking Schopenhauer's authority, Freud immediately goes on to point out 'how closely the enlarged sexuality of psycho-analysis coincides with the Eros of the divine Plato'. This is a particularly interesting reference, not least because the 1905 text to which it is appended actually opens with what Freud imagined was a refutation of Plato's Eros. Freud writes:

The popular view of the sexual instinct is beautifully reflected in the poetic fable which tells how the original human beings were cut up into two halves – man and woman – and how these are always striving to unite again in love. (VII, 136)

Despite his aesthetic approval of this passage in Plato's *Symposium*, Freud goes on, he believes, to undermine it completely by beginning his essay with a discussion of homosexuality. In 1905, then, Freud is glad to distance himself, by means of hard clinical fact, from a philosophical or poetic conception of sexuality. Nevertheless, Aristophanes' fable of mythical primal genders in the *Symposium* does, in fact, fully account for homosexuality – Freud merely reveals that his Plato has become rusty.

Freud certainly was not ignorant of this philosopher's work; in fact, he had studied some Plato in the original Greek during his *Gymnasium* days.[53] In his 1921 book *Group Psychology and the Analysis of the Ego* he even makes a full concession of priority to the philosopher:

Yet [psycho-analysis] has done nothing original in taking love in this 'wider' sense. In its origin, function, and relation to sexual love, the 'Eros' of the philosopher Plato coincides exactly with the love-force, the libido of psycho-analysis. (XVIII, 91)

Gerasimos Santas argues at length that Freud's comparison here is extremely problematical.[54] He points out, amongst other things, that Plato actually contrasts 'eros' with 'philia', a non-sexual love, and, more damningly, that Freud has misunderstood the basic nature of Plato's dialogues. In the *Symposium*, for example, Aristophanes no more gives Plato's view of Eros than does Erixymachus, who advocates the Empedoclean view of Eros as a cosmic force of unity and harmony. The positions of both speakers are ultimately refuted by Plato's actual spokesman, Socrates. Santas is no doubt correct in concluding that Freud has relied not on Plato's own texts, but instead on inadequate studies by his pupils Pfister and Nachmansohn. Both in 1905 and 1921, then, Freud appears to have misunderstood Plato. The crucial difference is that the younger Freud more or less attempts to refute the philosopher, whereas the older Freud invokes him as an intellectual authority to underpin his rapidly developing new instinct theory. This reflects the underlying shift in Freud's approach from positivist empiricism to a kind of mythopoeic speculation shot through with literary culture. Freud's choice of the Greek word 'Eros' for his newly developed notion of 'life instincts' certainly derives from his classical training, even if not directly from Plato. Admittedly, in 1921 he still uses the term in quotation marks. He claims he could have used the more genteel expressions 'Eros' and 'erotic' from the outset, but he refuses such a concession to pusillanimity, his fear being: 'one gives way first in words, and then little by little in substance too' (XVIII, 91). Freud did indeed resist the term 'Eros' with its poetic and philosophical connotations, but by the mid-1920s it has completely overwhelmed his sexual theory. He has yielded, furthermore, not just to the word, but also to his long suppressed urge for metaphysical speculation. Santas may provide a detailed account of the inadequacy of Freud's invocations of Plato, but he also consistently fails to recognize the essentially cosmological dimension of the later Freud's Eros.

Although Plato may not have been his primary source, Freud's preoccupation with a notion of 'Eros' certainly marks a regression from his positivistic approach back to broader cultural influences. The most important amongst these are not philosophical, but literary. In 1920, shortly before making the term his own, Freud claims it is 'the Eros of poets and philosophers' (XVIII, 50), and it is indeed the literary dimension of this term which primarily appealed to him. Even in 'Die Weltweisen' Schiller's 'love' implies something of the universal cohesive function of Freud's Eros, but the concept was more probably mediated to Freud by Goethe, a poet celebrated both for his classical erudition and his erotic frankness. Freud himself makes the connection in his Goethe Prize speech:

Goethe always rated Eros high, never tried to belittle its power, followed its primitive and even wanton expressions with no less attentiveness than its highly sublimated ones and has, as it seems to me, expounded its essential unity throughout all its manifestations no less decisively than Plato did in the remote past. (XXI, 210)

Already in the Goethe-inspired paean 'Nature' Freud had been told: 'Her crown is love. Only through love can she be approached. . . . She has separated everything in order to reunite it all.'[55] As for the term itself, Freud would have known it from a variety of works by Goethe, for example the poem 'Primal Words. Orphic' in which Eros features as one of the five primal words. Freud alludes to four of the five at some time or other. Of course, the word also occurs in *Faust*, and Freud's reference to 'Eros, which holds together everything in the world' (Eros, der alles in der Welt zusammenhält) (XVIII, 92) is almost certainly an allusion to the opening monologue of *Faust* in which the hero expresses his yearning to know 'what holds the world together in its innermost depths' (was die Welt/ Im Innersten zusammenhält). Whatever the precise source of the concept of Eros, clearly Freud's classical humanist culture has again provided him with an authority which underwrites the radical universality of the results of his more abstract speculation. Of course, despite his great love and respect for ancient literature and for Goethe, Freud would never have accepted that these played any such active role, even in his most speculative theories. In *The Question of Lay Analysis*, written in 1926, he has his imaginary interlocutor suggest that mythology is the source of one of his theories primarily, it seems, so that he can respond with a particularly resounding 'Oh, by no means' (XX, 214). Whilst it is certainly true that his main test-bed was, as ever, clinical experience, Freud was more aware than most that such experience must be shaped by certain *a priori* 'abstract ideas'. Evidence abounds that his own observations were filtered through a grid of ideas and assumptions which were inculcated in him by his literary culture and which increasingly leave their mark on the resulting theories.

INSTINCT THEORY IN CRISIS: THANATOS

The revisions resulting from Freud's discovery of primary narcissism certainly do not end with his postulation of a 'life' drive. Eros is, if anything, too all-embracing for Freud. Ego-libido and object-libido may offer him a new conception of psychic conflict, but these drive energies, both being erotic in nature, are too fundamentally similar to sustain the dualism he insists on. It is with his most wildly speculative text *Beyond the Pleasure Principle*, published in 1920, that Freud formulates the theory of a drive worthy of standing in opposition to Eros – the death instinct. Having done so, he claims with curious pride: 'Our views have from the very first been *dualistic*, and to-day they are even more definitely dualistic than before' (XVIII, 53). Initially, Freud is himself wary of his own conclusions, and he admits that his new dualism is essentially the result of having 'given free rein to the inclination, which I kept down for so long, to speculation' (XX, 57). Such speculation, he admits in *Beyond the Pleasure Principle* itself, can never be objective: 'Each of us is governed in such cases by deep-rooted internal prejudices, into whose hands our speculation unwittingly plays' (XVIII, 59).

Clearly one such prejudice in Freud is his need to think in terms of two fundamental and antagonistic forces. He is himself aware that he holds this particular conviction in advance of its actually being substantiated by evidence. When reviewing his theory of the instincts in 1930, he writes of the breakdown of his initial dualism:

Nevertheless, there still remained in me a kind of conviction, for which I was not as yet able to find reasons [eine noch nicht zu begründende Gewißheit], that the instincts could not all be of the same kind. (XXI, 118)

Clearly, Freud's postulation of the death instinct and thereby of a new instinctual dualism is very much the result of speculation drawing on obscurely subjective prejudices and predilections.[56] Although he insists he is merely following a train of thought out of curiosity and is not even convinced by his own ideas, by the time he comes to write *The Ego and the Id* in 1923, the instinctual dualism of Eros and Death is established as psychoanalytical doctrine. In this text Freud admits that hate, a libidinal affect which aims to destroy its object, appears to undermine his new polarity. However, by twists and turns involving fusions and defusions he manages, in what appears primarily to be an act of faith, to sustain this polarity. By 1930, instead of trying to justify his instinctual dualism, Freud simply becomes more vociferous in his support for it. In so doing, he inadvertently betrays its profoundly subjective dimension:

To begin with it was only tentatively that I put forward the views that I have developed here, but in the course of time they have gained such a hold upon me that I can no longer think in any other way. (XXI, 119)

It is not only the subjective nature of Freud's later theory of the drives that seems to call for an examination of the contribution made to it by literary culture, but also its increasingly 'metaphysical' bias. Many psychoanalysts refused to adopt the death instinct primarily because it was so far removed from biological principles. In the same way that Freud's Eros goes beyond the reproductive instinct, the death instinct is much more than any innate, survival-orientated aggressive instinct. It is essentially a desire for self-annihilation, or, rather, it transcends any individual urge and appears to serve a cosmological tendency towards disintegration which exists even prior to life itself. Although Freud scrupulously avoids mysticism with regard to this drive, he cannot deny that such attributes are, in the broadest sense of the word, metaphysical. His most overt concession to its cosmological nature is that he names it after a god: Thanatos, the Greek god of death.[57]

The quasi-Romantic tendencies of the younger Freud are quite manifest in this new theory. It is essentially philosophical in that it attempts to account not just for individual behaviour, but for the whole of life. In fact, Freud now actually dares to define life as the 'conflict and compromise between these two trends' (XIX, 41). Furthermore, it is both mythopoeic, in that it posits physically unspecifiable, superhuman forces, personified in the guise of Greek gods, and resolutely dualistic, a mode of thinking which Ellenberger for one describes as 'typically Romantic'.[58] The critic who shows the greatest awareness of the layers of literary culture which erupt to the surface in the later Freud's instinct theory is Ricoeur, who writes, for example: 'by contrasting Eros with death, Freud recaptured a certain mythical basis preserved by the German romantic tradition; through the latter he was able to go back to Plato and Empedocles'.[59]

Ricoeur is correct to point to the philosophical influences mediated to Freud by his literary cultivation. It is 1937 before Freud finally acknowledges, at a safe distance of two and a half millennia, as Bloom caustically notes,[60] that his theory of the drives does indeed correspond to the cosmological theory of the pre-Socratic poet-philosopher Empedocles. Now, though, Freud is actually willing to concede that this may be a case of direct influence:

I am very ready to give up the prestige of originality for the sake of such a confirmation, especially as I can never be certain, in view of the wide extent of my reading in early years, whether what I took for a new creation might not be an effect of cryptomnesia. (XXIII, 245)

This admission reveals not only that Freud's appetite for books was indeed voracious, but also that his interests certainly ranged as far as the literary end of the philosophy spectrum and, most importantly, that he considers himself to be unconsciously receptive to such non-scientific influences. It was his postulation of the death instinct in 1920 that first caused him to revise his attitude to the mythopoeic passage about primal genders in Plato's *Symposium*. Freud's ideas about a tendency existing beyond the pleasure principle are largely based on an assumption that drives are conservative in nature, that is, they seek to restore an earlier state. At the zenith of his speculative flight in *Beyond the Pleasure Principle* he suddenly needs evidence that even the sexual drives are conservative. Instantly, he turns to Plato:

In quite a different region, it is true, we *do* meet with such a hypothesis; but it is of so fantastic a kind – a myth rather than a scientific explanation – that I should not venture to produce it here, were it not that it fulfils precisely the one condition whose fulfilment we desire. . . . What I have in mind is, of course, the theory which Plato put into the mouth of Aristophanes in the *Symposium*, and which deals not only with the *origin* of the sexual instinct but also with the most important of its variations in relation to its object. (XVIII, 57)

Not only does he now concede that this 'theory' of sexuality does, in fact, fully account for homosexuality, he actually quotes ten lines from Plato and, in a footnote added to the text about a year later, he discusses at some length Plato's oriental sources for the myth. This fantastic passage, which Freud had once admired as literature but essentially sought to dismiss, now actually seems to be fuelling his speculation. He continues:

Shall we follow the hint given us by the poet-philosopher, and venture upon the hypothesis that living substance at the time of its coming to life was torn apart into small particles, which have ever since endeavoured to reunite through the sexual instincts? (XVIII, 58)

Admittedly, it is this final move which causes Freud to come to his senses, and he ends the paragraph: 'But here, I think, the moment has come for breaking off.' Indeed, he never does go any further, and when encapsulating his theory of the drives in 1938 in *An Outline of Psycho-Analysis*, he concedes that Eros, striving as it does for ever-increasing unity, cannot be a conservative drive unless all living substance was originally a single whole. Even here, though, he cannot resist the following footnote: 'Creative writers have imagined something of the sort, but nothing like it is known to us from the actual history of living substance' (XXIII, 149n.). Although his biological training is working hard to maintain Freud's sobriety, his literary interests continue to pull in the opposite direction.

As well as Plato and Empedocles, the German philosophers Nietzsche and Schopenhauer take on a new lease of life within Freud's texts around the time of his postulation of a death instinct. Echoes of Nietzsche are most evident in the very titles of two works from this era: *Beyond the Pleasure Principle* and *The Ego and the Id*. The id (das Es) is a term which Freud acknowledges derives from Nietzsche, and whilst Freud's elaboration of this psychic agency is certainly his own, his definition of it as 'whatever in our nature is impersonal and, so to speak, subject to natural law' (das Unpersönliche und sozusagen Naturnotwendige in unserem Wesen) (XIX, 23n.) seems calculated to justify the increasingly metaphysical emphasis of his theoretical texts. In *Beyond the Pleasure Principle* he even quotes Nietzsche directly when he describes the compulsion to repeat – the phenomenon which prompts him to conceive of the death instinct – as the '"perpetual recurrence of the same thing"' (ewige Wiederkehr des Gleichen) (XVIII, 22). In this text, however, it is Schopenhauer who receives Freud's most explicit acknowledgement. Shortly after having first suggested the death instinct, Freud writes:

There is something else, at any rate, that we cannot remain blind to. We have unwittingly steered our course into the harbour of Schopenhauer's philosophy. For him death is the 'true result and to that extent the purpose of life', while the sexual instinct is the embodiment of the will to live. (XVIII, 49–50)

Telling here is Freud's use of the image of a harbour. It is not surprising that without a fundamental instinctual dualism he should feel adrift, but his open admission that a philosopher now represents a haven to him reveals an important shift in his attitude. Whereas previously he had feared and avoided speculative philosophy, he now increasingly finds it pertinent to his new theory of the instincts, a strong indication that his earliest humanist influences are decisively reasserting themselves.

It should be noted that in *Beyond the Pleasure Principle* itself Freud is more concerned to find corroboration for the death instinct from biology than from philosophy. Nevertheless, the biological evidence turns out to be singularly inconclusive, and this in no way deters Freud. He does, of course, offer much empirical evidence in the form of a series of examples of a compulsion to repeat which appears to function prior to the pleasure principle. His most detailed example of a compulsive repetition, however, is taken not from clinical practice, but from literature:

> The most moving poetic picture of a fate such as this is given by Tasso in his romantic epic *Gerusalemme Liberata*. Its hero, Tancred, unwittingly kills his beloved Clorinda in a duel while she is disguised in the armour of an enemy knight. After her burial he makes his way into a strange magic forest which strikes the Crusaders' army with terror. He slashes with his sword at a tall tree; but blood streams from the cut and the voice of Clorinda, whose soul is imprisoned in the tree, is heard complaining that he has wounded his beloved again.
>
> If we take into account observations such as these, based upon behaviour in the transference and upon the life-histories of men and women, we shall find courage to assume that there really does exist in the mind a compulsion to repeat which overrides the pleasure principle. (XVIII, 22)

Freud, then, uses this literary episode as epistemologically valid empirical evidence. Moreover, he chooses to make his most forceful assertion of the existence of the compulsion to repeat immediately after producing this excessive narrative detail of what is, after all, an example not of a neurotic, but of a romantic, literary fate. Bloom certainly has grounds for claiming that Freud has here 'abandoned the empirical for . . . the literary authority of the daemonic'.[61] The passage from Tasso does not merely provide Freud with an illustration of an already established theory, but also with some degree of speculative impetus. As with so many of his more significant allusions, Freud's interest in the literary passage *precedes* the theory in support of which it is subsequently invoked. In his Wolf Man case history, published over a year before *Beyond the Pleasure Principle* was written, he refers to precisely the same passage in which Tancred cuts down the tree inhabited by Clorinda (XVII, 86). Here it is only a passing allusion, but it demonstrates that the passage occupied his mind while his theory of the death instinct was still evolving.

Freud's recourse to evidence from a romantic epic in *Beyond the Pleasure Principle* is only the most overt literary element of his formulation of the death instinct. In fact, this theory may owe more to his literary culture than any other he ever developed. Initially he admits that the idea of a death instinct may be entirely subjective:

It may be, however, that this belief in the internal necessity of dying is only another of those illusions which we have created 'um die Schwere des Daseins zu ertragen' ('To bear the burden of existence'). (XVIII, 45)

Thus, even when Freud is trying to caution himself about the dangers of subjectivity he cannot help but quote from literature, in this instance Schiller's *Die Braut von Messina*. Furthermore, it is certainly more likely that poets are unconsciously fuelling rather than checking his speculative urges. In a 1933 lecture he has to admit that science has not yet vindicated his self-destruction instinct: 'Poets, it is true, talk of such things; but poets are irresponsible people and enjoy the privilege of poetic licence' (XXII, 106). By this Freud does not mean to cast doubt on poetic insights; he simply means that the literary evidence alone is not sufficient to prove his hypothesis. Nevertheless, that Freud should cling to such a questionable and unpopular theory so tenaciously tends to suggest that *for him* literary evidence is indeed good enough.

In his article on the relationship between Freud and Goethe, Uwe Peters points out that the idea of a natural death from an inherent life-span derives from Romanticism.[62] Certainly, in the essay 'Nature', for example, Freud had heard: 'She continually creates and continually destroys', and: 'Life is her most beautiful creation, and death is the ploy by which she creates life in more abundance.'[63] In this essay Nature is spoken of in terms of a creative-destructive maternal deity similar to those Freud refers to in 1913 in 'The Theme of the Three Caskets':

The great Mother-goddesses of the oriental peoples, however, all seem to have been both creators and destroyers – both goddesses of life and fertility and goddesses of death. (XII, 299)

In fact, in this essay Freud refers to the 'ancient ambivalence' between love and death a full six years *before* he developed his own polarity of Eros and Thanatos. When, in 1922, he praises the dramatist and novelist Arthur Schnitzler for the way his work centres on the polarity of love and death, he claims: 'all this moves me with an uncanny feeling of familiarity'.[64] Clearly, Freud was aware of this commonplace literary opposition long before his own instinct theory came to corroborate its validity. His admission that he finds the literary polarity *unheimlich* merely tends to suggest that its influence on him has been largely subliminal. In all, it seems Trilling is well justified in his claim that the scientifically unverifiable death instinct confirms 'our sense of Freud's oneness with the tradition of literature'. He points out that something like a death instinct recurs throughout classical European literature, and as one particularly pertinent example he cites Sophocles' *Oedipus*.[65]

The claim that Freud has simply taken the idea of a fundamental death instinct from literature is, however, too crude. It oversimplifies the complex process by which Freud actually fills the vacuum left by his postulation of primary narcissism. It would be misguided to speak of 'priority' in this case, when Freud has clearly beaten out his own path to a highly original conception of death. This does not, however, reduce the functional role played by literature to that of providing prestigious illustrations. Its most important role may actually be that it *emboldens* Freud in the creative process of theory formulation itself. One of the most revealing statements he makes in *Beyond the Pleasure Principle* concerns the assumption of a natural death. Here he writes:

We are accustomed to think that such is the fact, and we are strengthened in our thought by the writings of our poets. (XVIII, 44–5)

Freud's use of the word 'strengthened' is most interesting here. It implies that poets are not just the source of particular unchallenged assumptions of his own, but also of a general speculative boldness. It is worth remembering that Freud was fond of attributing his life's achievements to no other special talent than courage.

Freud was particularly in need of such courage for this theoretical innovation. In the following sentence from *Beyond the Pleasure Principle* the term death instinct (Todestrieb) makes what must be the most hesitant published debut of any psychoanalytical term:

The opposition between the ego or death instincts [Ich(Todes-)trieben] and the sexual or life instincts would then cease to hold and the compulsion to repeat would no longer possess the importance we have ascribed to it. (XVIII, 45)

The uncomfortable parenthetical construction, subjunctively negated, reflects Freud's apprehensiveness towards his own demonic creation. Even the compulsion to repeat is an awkward concept for Freud. Having amassed a series of examples of its apparent functioning, he then explains how weak all this evidence is, because his examples of repetition in child's play, therapeutic transference, and traumatic dreams are all capable of alternative interpretations. Clearly, he is still plagued with doubts, and yet he continues: 'Enough is left unexplained to justify the hypothesis of a compulsion to repeat' (XVIII, 23). Indeed, this apparently weak assumption leads him to qualify what he considers to be his single greatest insight, namely that a dream represents a fulfilled wish. It is only to be expected, then, that Freud should be singularly uncomfortable about the fact that 'often far-fetched speculation' as he calls it (XVIII, 24), is having such an impact on his science. His repeated use of words such as 'courage', 'dare', and 'boldly' reveals his constant need to steel himself against his own doubts. Literature is an important source of this critical courage; for example, it will be remembered that Freud speaks of his 'courage to assume that there really does exist in the mind a compulsion to repeat' immediately after his long reference to Tasso's *Gerusalemme Liberata* (XVIII, 22). It may be that he would simply have lacked the nerve to base a new dualism of Eros and Thanatos on such problematical speculation were it not for the fact that the polarity of Love and Death already had such a distinguished literary pedigree.

Thomas Mann's statement that Freud ploughed his own furrow without the help of poets and philosophers proves to have been singularly inappropriate. Nevertheless, it should be granted that Mann's emphasis on great literature as a 'comfort and reinforcement' penetrates to the crux of the matter. In *Beyond the Pleasure Principle*, at least, Freud has indeed drawn reinforcement from great literature, and this perhaps sheds light on the fact that, with the very last line of this text, Freud should turn to a poet, Friedrich Rückert, for consolation that his science is making such unsatisfactory progress:

> Was man nicht erfliegen kann, muß man erhinken . . .
> Die Schrift sagt, es ist keine Sünde zu hinken.

> (What we cannot reach flying we must reach limping . . .
> The Book tells us it is no sin to limp.)   XVIII, 64

CIVILIZATION AND ITS DISCONTENTS: THE GOETHEAN SUBTEXT

The final major text in Freud's development of a theory of the instincts is *Civilization and its Discontents* of 1930. It is based entirely on his Eros–Death dualism, and in it Freud significantly elaborates his concept of the death instinct. One of the earliest literary quotations in this work appears to be another example of Freud using Schiller to warn himself against the temptations of metaphysics. With regard to those who believe they can gain access to mystical wisdom, Freud quotes: 'Es freue sich,/ Wer da atmet im rosigen Licht (Let him rejoice who breathes up here in the roseate light)' (XXI, 73). Despite this, Freud actually goes on to strike his most cosmological tone yet. For example, he defines civilization as 'a process in the service of Eros', and he describes its development as 'the struggle between Eros and Death' (XXI, 122). Then he elaborates on this cosmic struggle for civilization with an allusion to Greek mythology, underscored by the lines from Heine about the 'battle of the giants' (quoted above, p. 15). Later he speaks of 'the eternal Eros' as one of the '"Heavenly Powers"' (XXI, 133), a reference to Goethe's *Wilhelm Meister*. All this tends to suggest that, despite the sobering quotation from Schiller, Freud's new cosmological emphasis is, in fact, saturated with literary influences.

Eros and Death are not the only supra-personal forces referred to by Freud in *Civilization and its Discontents*. Ananke – another term which made its Freudian debut in 1910 – also features in the dramatis personae, and again it has strong poetic connotations. It is related to the concept of destiny in Greek tragedy, but it probably carries most authority for Freud because, like Eros, it features in Goethe's 'Primal Words. Orphic'. Freud himself cites as his source Multatuli, the Dutch novelist whose *Letters* appear in Freud's 1906 list of ten good books. In *Beyond the Pleasure Principle*, when Freud is still coming to terms with the metaphysical implications of his instinct theory, he openly disapproves of any attempt to mythologize the laws of nature. Here he even suggests of his own proposition of a natural death:

Perhaps we have adopted the belief because there is some comfort in it. If we are to die ourselves . . ., it is easier to submit to a remorseless law of nature, to the sublime Ἀνάγκη [Necessity], than to a chance which might perhaps have been escaped. (XVIII, 45)

In 1920, then, Freud relates the mythical Ananke to a wishful illusion which masks uncomfortable truths. By 1924, though, in the essay 'The Economic Problem of Masochism', Freud ventures to say that he does not object to Multatuli's claim that the modern equivalents of Greek Fate are the forces of Λόγος and Ἀνάγκη. Nevertheless, he does go on to qualify this approval:

but all who transfer the guidance of the world to Providence, to God, or to God and Nature, arouse a suspicion that they still look upon these ultimate and remotest powers as a parental couple, in a mythological sense. (XIX, 168)

Freud is still uncomfortable with any mythologizing tendencies, then, and he warns himself against his own inclination towards the kind of metaphysical speculation to be found in the Goethe-inspired fragment 'Nature'. By the time he comes to write *Civilization and its Discontents*, however, such scruples have been overcome to the extent that he can even write: 'Eros and Ananke have become the parents of human civilization' (XXI, 101). In the face of the quasi-mythical Thanatos, not only has sexuality become Eros, but even Freud's highest instance, implacable external reality, has now become Ananke. His increasingly speculative use of such terms draws together the threads of myth, literature, and philosophy which have, in fact, always contributed to the fabric of his science. Freud now speaks of material life as if it were merely the reflection of a more fundamental reality of eternal, universal, and antagonistic forces. It appears, then, that something of the vitalistic essentialism which had once attracted him to Romantic philosophy has finally erupted to the surface of psychoanalytical theory. Again Ricoeur offers the most succinct appraisal of this process:

Having reached this ultimate phase of the metapsychology, one may then wonder whether the Freudian theory has not restored the *Naturphilosophie* which the school of Helmholtz endeavoured to overthrow, and Goethe's *Weltanschauung* which the young Freud had admired so much.[66]

In *Civilization and its Discontents* Goethe is certainly the most important literary figure associated with this process. Freud quotes Goethe at some of the essay's key junctures, and the poet often appears to be playing a much more significant role than that of mere ornamentation or strategic sanction. Freud actually opens the essay with a discussion of religion in which, by tracing Romain Rolland's subjective and vaguely metaphysical 'oceanic feeling' back to a specific phase in the development of the infantile ego, he seeks firmly to disassociate himself from this writer's mysticism. In a text so richly laced with literary allusions, however, it is perhaps not surprising that Freud should ultimately fail to maintain this strictly positivistic and reductive approach. In fact, he leads on from the discussion of religion to his central question, the function of human culture, with a paragraph in which he quotes not only Voltaire and Theodor Fontane, but also 'the well-known saying of one of our great poets and thinkers', namely Goethe's epigram about science, art, and religion (XXI, 74). Freud, then, has Goethe in mind from the very outset of his discussion of human civilization.

By far the most interesting reference to Goethe in *Civilization and its Discontents* actually occurs in a footnote. Freud is addressing the question of human aggression and for this purpose he needs to introduce the still relatively new idea of a destruction drive. He begins to speak of the devil as an embodiment of this inherent human 'evil', obviously using such terms ironically, not least because he will go on to demonstrate that humans owe their most powerful moral impulses to this destructive energy. Nevertheless, for Freud, a devout atheist to whom world literature represents something of an *ersatz* religion, there really is only one devil: Goethe's Mephistopheles. Fascinatingly, this character does indeed seem to be closely bound up with his conception of a destructive drive. The footnote made by Freud at this juncture deserves quoting in full:

In Goethe's Mephistopheles we have a quite exceptionally convincing identification of the principle of evil with the destructive instinct:

> Denn alles, was entsteht,
> Ist wert, daß es zugrunde geht . . .
> So ist denn alles, was Ihr Sünde,
> Zerstörung, kurz das Böse nennt,
> Mein eigentliches Element.

> (For all things, from the Void
> Called forth, deserve to be destroyed . . .
> Thus, all which you as Sin have rated –
> Destruction, – aught with Evil blent, –
> That is my proper element.)

The Devil himself names as his adversary, not what is holy and good, but Nature's power to create, to multiply life – that is, Eros:

> Der Luft, dem Wasser, wie der Erden
> Entwinden tausend Keime sich,
> Im Trocknen, Feuchten, Warmen, Kalten!
> Hätt' ich mir nicht die Flamme vorbehalten,
> Ich hätte nichts Aparts für mich.

> (From Water, Earth, and Air unfolding,
> A thousand germs break forth and grow,
> In dry, and wet, and warm, and chilly:
> And had I not the Flame reserved, why, really,
> There's nothing special of my own to show.) XXI, 120n.

The correspondence in aims between Freud's death instinct and Goethe's Mephistopheles is even more far-reaching than Freud admits. The instinct certainly has little to do with any Christian conception of evil. It is actually related to the primal drive for a final extinction of tension in absolute gratification, precisely the state which Mephistopheles seeks to induce in Faust. In Freud's scheme, Faust may stand for the erotic drives which strive onwards towards absolute union, and perhaps for all instinctual sublimation, which creates a semblance of an eternal upward striving for perfection. It will be remembered that when Freud explained, in *Beyond the Pleasure Principle*, that a traditionally conceived 'instinct for perfection' is illusory and actually results from repression, he describes it as a drive which 'ungebändigt immer vorwärts dringt (presses ever forward unsubdued)', that is, by quoting Mephistopheles' description of Faust's spirit (XVIII, 42). This suggests both that Freud did indeed view *Faust* in terms of an instinctual polarity between Mephistopheles and Faust, and, most significantly of all, that Mephistopheles was in his thoughts precisely at the point when the postulation of a death instinct became necessary – a full ten *years* before the footnote in *Civilization and its Discontents*. Evidence is hardly needed that the relevant passages in *Faust* were, in fact, always close to Freud's mind. Mephistopheles' lament about proliferating 'germs of life' had, for example, already been alluded to by Freud over thirty years earlier in *The Interpretation of Dreams* (IV, 78).

When the persistent power of Goethe's masterpiece over Freud's mind is taken into account, it looks increasingly unlikely that the footnote in *Civilization and its Discontents* amounts to a mere illustration of the death instinct hit upon by Freud long after he has independently developed this theory. It is more plausible that *Faust* played a salient role not only in Freud's 'conviction, for which I was not as yet able to find reasons' that the drives are fundamentally dualistic in nature, but, more importantly, in the increasing influence that the polarity of Love and Death came to have on his elaboration of this dualism. Although it is only in a footnote, ostensibly as an afterthought, that Freud has Mephistopheles provide the otherwise silent death instinct with a voice, this appears to be one of those Freudian footnotes which Hélène Cixous describes as a 'typographical metaphor of repression'.[67] Telling here is the fact that in the body of the text immediately before he inserts the footnote about Mephistopheles, Freud already speaks with Goethe's voice. The note is appended to a paragraph in which he describes having to overcome his own resistance to the idea of a destructive drive, and he reflects that he is now facing similar resistance from his own supporters:

For 'little children do not like it' [die Kindlein, sie hören es nicht gerne] when there is talk of the inborn human inclination to 'badness', to aggressiveness, and so to cruelty as well. (XXI, 120)

The allusion here to Goethe's ballad about the homecoming of the exiled Count is so subtle as to be almost subliminal, but it strongly indicates that Freud feels Goethe to be on his side in this latest controversy, and that his unshakeable faith in Goethe underlies his own new-found faith in Thanatos.

Freud's boldness in *Civilization and its Discontents* is not limited to his
addressing such a vast question as the purpose of human culture, nor to
the sweeping use he makes of his polarity of Eros and Thanatos.
Perhaps the most radical section of the essay is his attempt to trace
human morality back to internalized aggressive impulses, a major metapsychological innovation which implies that the super-ego is fuelled by
the energy of the death instinct. His startlingly deconstructive conclusion is that instinctual renunciation actually leads to an ineradicable
sense of guilt, and that this latter is, therefore, endemic in human
culture. Although Freud claims absolute originality for the paradoxical
insight that renunciation leads to bad conscience – an idea 'which
belongs entirely to psycho-analysis and which is foreign to people's ordinary way of thinking' (XXI, 128) – again his boldness is demonstrably
and inextricably linked with the strong literary undercurrents at work in
this text. Jones is just one of many who point to the similarity between
Freud's argument and that of Nietzsche in *The Genealogy of Morals*. He
even suggests a possible element of 'deferred action', Nietzsche's genealogy of morality having been familiar to Freud at least as early as 1908,
when it was explained to him by his pupil Hitschmann.[68] Trilling actually speaks of a 'will' in the Nietzschean sense of the term underlying
Freud's reasoning in this section of *Civilization and its Discontents*. He
detects Freud's determination to explain suffering in terms of original
sin, and he traces this back to a literary influence, namely, the young
Freud's devotion to Milton's *Paradise Lost*.[69] An English poet who more
obviously appears to underwrite Freud's assumption of innate human
guilt, however, is Shakespeare. Again it is only in a footnote, appended
to his diagnosis of guilt as the central problem of human culture, that
Freud quotes Hamlet: 'Thus conscience does make cowards of us all'
(XXI, 134n.). Yet again, though, this line can hardly be described as a
mere afterthought: Freud had already quoted it over thirty years earlier.
It sprang to his mind as he wrote the momentous letter to Fliess in which
he first outlined the Oedipus complex,[70] demonstrating just how important the line had always been for him.

Although such authors as Shakespeare, Milton, and Nietzsche certainly had an impact on Freud to an extent rarely appreciated by critics,
again, at least with regard to his new aetiology of guilt, it is Goethe who
plays the dominant role. Freud ends the paragraph in which he discusses
'the fatal inevitability of the sense of guilt' by citing an instance in which
Goethe's Harp-player in *Wilhelm Meister* refers to an endemic, universal
guilt:

One is reminded of the great poet's moving arraignment of the 'Heavenly Powers':–

> Ihr führt in's Leben uns hinein.
> Ihr laßt den Armen schuldig werden,
> Dann überlaßt Ihr ihn den Pein,
> Denn jede Schuld rächt sich auf Erden.

> (To earth, this weary earth, ye bring us
> To guilt ye let us heedless go,
> Then leave repentance fierce to wring us:
> A moment's guilt, an age of woe!) XXI, 133

With such an authoritative source Freud can quell any fears he may have about how far his speculation is leading him away from common sense. Goethe here sanctions the idea that something about the most fundamental vital forces – Eros who urges for gratification, Ananke who forbids this desire, and Thanatos whose destructive energy is harnessed to enforce this prohibition – inevitably leads to neurotic guilt. As with so many literary passages which appear to influence and reinforce Freud's formulation of theory, the quotation from *Wilhelm Meister* occupied his mind for most of his adult life. As early as 1901, in the summary of his dream theory 'On Dreams', Freud's initial association to the opening dream consists of the first two lines of the above stanza (V, 637). Here the exact relevance of the quotation is not quite clear. Indeed, it appears that it took Freud half a lifetime to make sense of his own literary free association to the concept of guilt. Having finally done so, he quite uncharacteristically admits the extent to which he is indebted to Goethe. His quotation from *Wilhelm Meister* in *Civilization and its Discontents* is followed by this paragraph:

And we may well heave a sigh of relief at the thought that it is nevertheless vouchsafed to a few to salvage without effort from the whirlpool of their own feelings the deepest truths, towards which the rest of us have to find our way through tormenting uncertainty and with restless groping. (XXI, 133)

Freud parades rather than hides his intimate knowledge of Goethe's works, but he usually endeavours to conceal the ways in which this knowledge provides him with key points of orientation during his more groping speculations. In *Civilization and its Discontents* quotations from Goethe help Freud to broach the subject of the purpose of human culture, to underpin his postulation of innate aggression, and, finally, to authorize his theory about the inherence of human guilt. His hypotheses about the instinctual dualism of Eros and Thanatos or about the inevitability of neurotic guilt are not simply lifted from literary sources. Rather the literary corroboration, especially from a poet of Goethe's stature, fuels Freud's radical, speculative impetus, thus inevitably colouring and shaping the results. Perhaps the primary advantage of this process for Freud is that it allows for a *dialogic* development of his more abstract theories. A poet, even when he does not surface in the form of an allusion, often provides Freud with an inner second voice, enabling him to avoid the purely subjective, monologic speculation which he feared most.

This process is certainly not limited to *Civilization and its Discontents*, nor even to Freud's theory of the instincts. The great works of classical literature constitute a fertile substratum which underlies the whole body of psychoanalysis. This may, at least in part, be what Shoshana Felman has in mind with her suggestive comment: 'in the same way that psychoanalysis points to the unconscious of literature, *literature, in its turn, is the unconscious of psychoanalysis*'.[71] The metaphor of unconsciousness is indeed apt. In the earliest stages of psychoanalysis this literary substratum is hardly detectable. By *The Interpretation of Dreams*, however, in which Freud, with great reluctance, is forced publicly to explore his own unconscious, the literary currents are already becoming overt. Of course, right up until Freud's death they continue to be partially obscured by his scrupulously empirical scientific training and aspirations. Nevertheless, the products of his bolder speculative and universalizing tendencies are demonstrably rooted in the rich undersoil of his literary culture. Although he continued to believe that his vocation was hard science, it is tempting to read an alternative meaning into Freud's own quotation, in his autobiography, of Mephistopheles' advice to the student:

> Vergebens, daß Ihr ringsum wissenschaftlich schweift,
> Ein jeder lernt nur, was er lernen kann.

> (It is in vain that you range around from science to science:
> each man learns only what he can learn.)   XX, 9

CHAPTER TWO

A sublime ambivalence:
Freud as literary critic

FREUD, FORMALISM, AND THE *ARS POETICA*

In the previous chapter I sought to establish that literature far transcends the status of a mere object of psychoanalysis. It should therefore be clear that the present chapter is not intended simply to constitute a psychoanalytical theory of literature, which, anyway, would not properly belong to a study of Freud's own literary culture. Nevertheless, a critique of the texts in which he attempts to put literature on the couch is essential to any account of his own complex relationships with *Dichter*. It is important, first of all, to point out that Freud's literary criticism is not some misguided secondary application of a medical technique to an inappropriate object. Psychoanalysis was always intended to be a general theory of the mind, and literature belonged within its compass from its very inception. Although it was not until 1907 that Freud published a primarily literary study, his letters to Fliess clearly illustrate that the germ of psychoanalytical literary criticism was present from the beginning. Detailed sketches of the analyses of *Oedipus* and *Hamlet* appear simultaneously with Freud's very first declaration of the ubiquity of the Oedipus complex in the letter to Fliess of 1897.[1] Secondly, far from viewing them as mere caricatures of genuine psychoanalytical studies, Freud was himself particularly proud of his works of art criticism. His 1910 book on Leonardo was his own personal favourite, but his specifically literary studies, such as the 1907 paper on Jensen's *Gradiva* and the 1913 essay 'The Theme of the Three Caskets', also gave him a pleasure all the more striking when contrasted with the customary depressions which followed the publication of major works such as *The Interpretation of Dreams* and *Civilization and its Discontents*. To Jung Freud wrote of his *Gradiva* essay:

This time I knew my little work deserved praise; it was written during sunny days and I derived great pleasure from doing it. Of course it doesn't contain anything new for us, but it allows us to enjoy our wealth.[2]

He implies here that a literary study is the most pleasurable form of psychoanalysis, the ultimate reward for long hours spent developing theory. Moreover, he explicitly acknowledges that such a study entails nothing new for his analytical method, psychoanalysis having always, potentially, been a method of literary criticism.

It may, of course, be argued that Freud considered literary criticism to be nothing new because he merely 'treated' works of literature as if they were symptoms, dreams, or fantasies. Critics often misconstrue and oversimplify Freud's literary analyses in this way. Modern 'literary' readings of Freud, from Trilling to Bloom, tend to dismiss them entirely as examples of mere psychobiographical reductionism which fail to explore the more radical implications of psychoanalytical theory. This dismissal is itself somewhat reductive. Although there is no doubt that Freud was capable of degrading literature, this degradation was usually motivated not by his lack of literary appreciation, but rather by his strikingly ambivalent attitudes towards creative writers. In order to understand how this ambivalence manifests itself within Freud's own texts, it will first be necessary to elucidate the sophistication of Freud's readings of literature and to establish the extent of his genuine reverence towards poets. Only in this context, one which fully acknowledges Freud's high degree of literary cultivation, can the subtle nature of his ambivalence towards *Dichter* be adequately evaluated.

The most common questionable assumption made about Freud's attempts to analyse art was to some extent shared by Freud himself. It concerns his perceived prioritization of content to the exclusion of form. Peter Fuller, for example, states that Freud not only ignored form, but actually projected it beyond the realm of his science because he was not moved by it, viewing it as mere sugar-coating on the all important content.[3] This and similar comments will be refuted at length in Chapter 3, which deals with Freud's hermeneutic. For the present it suffices to say that Freud's interpretative approach focuses on form in several specific ways. His central emphasis in analysing symptoms, dreams, fantasies, jokes, and even parapraxes is usually on a language-specific *close reading*. For example, Freud reads dream-texts above all for traces of what he calls dream-work. This causes him to focus on rhetorical figures, imagery, text-immanent structural relations, and, most importantly, linguistic ambiguities.[4]

It is worth remembering that Freud had no detailed theory of literature. No doubt, had his magnum opus addressed the interpretation not of dreams, but of literature, his emphasis would similarly have been on close reading, and his appreciation of formal devices would have been, if anything, even more sophisticated in response to the sophistication of the object of analysis. This speculative assertion is borne out by Freud's own sporadic analyses of literary texts. His elucidation of motif patterns in *The Merchant of Venice* and *King Lear* in the essay 'The Theme of the Three Caskets', for instance, remains true to the text-specific proto-structuralism of *The Interpretation of Dreams*. His sensitivity to formal concerns is not based on a crude equation of poet and dreamer. In his study of *Gradiva* Freud's interest can be seen to be sparked by the intensity of Jensen's *conscious* formal elaboration of certain passages. For example, he defends the effort spent on interpreting the passage about Hanold's journey because 'the author has taken so much trouble over describing the journey' (IX, 65). Freud considers Jensen to be in full semantic control here. Regarding Zoë's ambiguous dialogue he writes: 'It is a triumph of ingenuity and wit to be able to express the delusion and the truth in the same turn of words' (IX, 84). Clearly, this is a triumph of conscious insight, of language, and of form.

Of course, Freud believes that, like dreams, all works of art derive ultimately from disguised wish-fulfilments. Nevertheless, his salient interest is in the complex modes of distortion via which this desire becomes inscribed in a text. In dreams these displacements take place due to censorship, whereas in art, as Freud explicitly points out in 'The Claims of Psycho-Analysis to Scientific Interest' (1913), they conform to 'laws of beauty' (XIII, 187). He recognizes, then, that there exists a whole realm of specifically aesthetic modes of distortion. He also distinguishes between the pleasure generated by the subject matter of literature and a wholly aesthetic pleasure which can exist as an end in itself. This abstract theoretical awareness of purely formal considerations is present in his treatment of actual literary texts. For example, at the end of 'The "Uncanny"' he comments that, although they deal with uncanny material, there is no uncanny effect in the Rhampsinitus story because of the way Herodotus presents it to the reader, and there is no uncanny effect in 'The Canterville Ghost' because of Wilde's use of irony. When it is appropriate to do so, Freud prioritizes style, perspective, and tone over content, causing him explicitly to acknowledge: 'Thus we see how independent emotional effects can be of the actual subject-matter in the world of fiction' (XVII, 252).

When Freud does concentrate solely on the content of a piece of literature, it is not because he lacks aesthetic appreciation, he simply chooses to ignore his own sensitivity to form. When reading Jensen's 'The

Red Umbrella', he confesses to Jung that, although the content is most meaningful, the writing is 'hideously insensitive'.[5] Admittedly, in his essay 'The Moses of Michelangelo' he claims 'that the subject-matter of works of art has a stronger attraction for me than their formal and technical qualities' (XIII, 211). Whilst this statement is undoubtedly true, it is far from a confession of aesthetic insensitivity. Freud's interest in form is only *relatively* overshadowed by his powerful and highly sophisticated fascination with content. 'The Theme of the Three Caskets', for example, may only deal with a motif, but there can be no doubt that Freud's subtle and penetrating evaluation of this motif enriches rather than impoverishes *The Merchant of Venice* and, especially, *King Lear*. An interest in literary 'content' does not, by itself, imply a lack of respect for the literariness of fiction. In the final section of 'The "Uncanny"' Freud fully acknowledges the fictional and aesthetic specificities of 'poetic reality' which make of it a realm of experience equal in status to, yet fundamentally distinct from, lived reality (XVII, 249–51). In fact, literature escapes the scorn which Freud reserves for religious illusions precisely because of its self-conscious fictionality: 'Art is almost always harmless and beneficent; it does not seek to be anything but an illusion' (XXII, 160).

In his reading of literary texts Freud's respect for the demarcated, self-sufficient 'otherness' of literature is manifest. One consequence is that his interpretations depend overwhelmingly on strictly textual evidence. Invocations of psychoanalytical theory constitute only a minute proportion of his analysis of Ibsen's *Rosmersholm*, for example, or Stefan Zweig's 'Four-and-Twenty Hours in a Woman's Life'. In his study of *Macbeth* they are essentially absent, their place being taken by relevant information about the play's historical background. Freud's energy is more often devoted to a reconstruction of the story. The selectivity of his plot synopses is often criticized, but it is actually less an abuse than a traditional privilege of literary criticism. Although his reading of Hoffmann's Sand-Man as a castrating father is often disparaged, it does make sense of a wealth of story details, whilst his equally contentious marginalization of Olympia is justified by his observation that 'the author himself treats the episode of Olympia with a faint touch of satire' (XVII, 227). Similarly, Freud uses Shakespeare's play itself to refute both the 'diagnosis' of Hamlet as neurasthenic and the Goethean interpretation of the tragedy: 'The plot of the drama shows us, however, that Hamlet is far from being represented as a person incapable of taking any action' (IV, 265). His literary analyses are redeemed again and again by the systematically story-specific nature of his approach. In his *Gradiva* essay he calls his 'dissecting

[of] the whole story' an 'essential preliminary', and, having accomplished this task over the course of more than twenty pages, he insists: 'we must linger a little more over the story itself' (IX, 41). Consequently, the standard reproach that Freud treats Hanold as if he were a patient suffering from real reminiscences can easily be countered by the observation that in the text itself Jensen's Zoë does exactly the same.

Although Freud studies *Gradiva* for its dream passages, he only broaches the subject of disguised wish-fulfilments on the very last of the essay's seventy pages. The charge that Freud reduces texts to instinctual urges is, in fact, inappropriate even when levelled at his treatment of dream-texts, let alone his literary analyses. Freud's interest in content tends to increase the complexity of a text rather than reveal its 'essence'. In his Michelangelo article he speaks of art studies which disregard the overt 'general effect', concentrating instead on minute individual characteristics, and he claims that such studies possess 'something extraordinarily attractive' (XIII, 219). His own literary analyses follow this pattern and are thus able to circumvent traditional preoccupations with the moral tendencies of a work and gain access to more complex and ambiguous elements of its content. Thus Freud does not, for example, contest the 'two wise lessons' demonstrated by *King Lear*, concerning the follies of executing one's last will whilst still alive and being duped by flattery. He simply chooses to look beyond (or, rather, behind) this banal, utilitarian dimension of the play for a deeper source of its 'overpowering effect' (XII, 300).

Rather than simply debunking them, Freud's technique usually enriches or ambiguates the moral or other 'intentional' elements of a work's content. After mentioning the ostensible subject matter of 'Four-and-Twenty Hours in a Woman's Life', Freud goes on: 'But the story tells far more than this . . ., something quite different, something universally human' (XXI, 191). Freud demands not morality, but humanity from a work's content, a traditional but creditable literary-critical approach. In 'Creative Writers and Day-Dreaming', written in 1907, he explains that a simplistic division of good and evil characters smacks of unadulterated fantasy and defies 'the variety of human characters that are to be observed in real life' (IX, 150). Freud's discrimination in this respect is demonstrably not the result of his psychoanalytical insight, but rather of his literary cultivation. As early as 1883 he was complaining to Martha about Dickens's crude distinctions between virtuous and vicious characters, adding that the novelist had transcended these in *David Copperfield*, a novel in which the characters are sinful in a human way.[6]

Occasionally, Freud will completely overturn the moral tendency of a work of literature, as in the case of *Oedipus*. Of Sophocles' didactic theme of submission to the will of the gods, Freud claims: 'I cannot think that this morality is a strong point of the play.' In fact, due to this attempted displacement of responsibility, Freud says that 'fundamentally it is an amoral work' (XVI, 331). Nevertheless, he does admire the play *as* a tragedy. The tragic inevitability in the story is not a didactic device, but stems rather from a powerful latent theme, again concerning 'something universally human'. For this reason the protagonist's fate is not 'arbitrary' as it is in Grillparzer's *Die Ahnfrau*. Arbitrariness here does not, as some would suspect, simply denote a failure to conform to the doctrine of the Oedipus complex. Freud goes to great lengths to prove that *Gradiva*, a story which receives no oedipal reading, contains not a single arbitrary story element. Every ambiguity, for example, is a 'necessary consequence of the premisses of the story' (IX, 85). The story, then, is true neither to psychoanalytical orthodoxy nor to Jensen's intentions, but to *itself*. It is by relentlessly trusting not the teller, but the tale that Freud's conception of literary content transcends mere intentionality or moral tendency and achieves a sophistication worthy of a professional literary critic.

Astute critics acknowledge the subtlety of Freud's literary criticism in this respect, but continue to reproach him for dismissing preoccupations with the author's moralizing intentions only then to replace them with a crude fixation on his private life. This reproach is relatively well grounded, but the nature and extent of Freud's biographical interests is not usually adequately recognized. In his acceptance speech for the Goethe Prize Freud defends his biographical approach with an allusion to *Faust*, claiming that psychoanalysis can elucidate 'new connecting threads in the "weaver's masterpiece" spread between the instinctual endowments, the experiences and the works of an artist' (XXI, 212). Despite the order in which he places these three elements, in practice he actually neglects the instinctual endowments and privileges the works. He was perfectly capable of distinguishing between a study of art and a study of the artist. It is, rather, his critics who fail to recognize that Freud's works on Dostoevsky, Leonardo, and Goethe are primarily biographical, whereas his pieces on Shakespeare, Michelangelo, Hoffmann, Ibsen, Zweig, and so on centre overwhelmingly on their works. Freud happily interprets *Gradiva* knowing nothing of Jensen. He does ultimately indulge in biographical *speculation*, but he never uses biographical information as a premise from which he can draw conclusions. For him such information offers entirely supplementary means of confirming already established conclusions. If he does speculate about a writer's desires, this is always deduced from *textual* traces. Indeed, he takes this approach to dubious extremes, most strikingly when he substantiates the biographical 'fact' of Dostoevsky's compulsive masturbation by means of an analysis of compulsive gambling in a Stefan Zweig novella (XXI, 191–4).

In addition to this misunderstanding of its epistemological status, the subtlety and complexity of the biographical element in Freud's literary-critical approach is also usually underestimated. His hypothesis in 'Creative Writers and Day-Dreaming' – that fiction is a wish-fulfilling realm of illusion in which the artist, disguised as the hero, achieves wealth, power, fame, and love – does reduce writing to the life of the writer, but this conception is only as crude as the pulp fiction to which Freud specifically restricts himself. Even when analysing dreams, Freud is aware of how complex the relations between dreamer and dream-protagonists can be. The dreamer's ego is always present, but it can be a mere observer, or present only via identification with another person, or split into two characters, or dissipated amongst several. Freud is also aware that in literary fiction the situation is far more complex. In 'Creative Writers and Day-Dreaming' he writes: 'often the connection [between the life of the writer and his works] has been thought of in much too simple terms'. He demands, for example, that 'the work itself' must be searched for traces of not only a powerful, present experience, but also a related infantile experience and a projected future scenario of wish-fulfilment before a biographical reading can even begin. And, despite the complexity of this triple chronological determination, Freud immediately adds that it is 'too exiguous a pattern' and only 'a first approach to the true state of affairs' (IX, 151).

Freud does not believe that a biographical hypothesis alone can account for the effect of a work of literature. This explains why he needs to read *King Lear* as something more than just the poet's reaction to his own bitter experience of ingratitude (XII, 300–1). For him the ego of the *reader* (or spectator) is at least as essential an object of study as the ego of the poet. This emphasis on reception is fundamental to Freud's study of literary texts. His first text to deal explicitly with literature, 'Psychopathic Characters on the Stage', only published posthumously but written between 1905 and 1906, has the dynamics of reception as its central theme. For Freud, art is an essentially social act, and form is crucial because it is the means by which an author adapts his material for an audience. Art cannot be reduced to its content, as Freud acknowledges in his Michelangelo study:

> I realize that this cannot be merely a matter of *intellectual* comprehension; what he aims at is to awaken in us the same emotional attitude, the same mental constitution as that which in him produced the impetus to create. (XIII, 212)

Freud's key concept here is identification; without it, literary effects are all but impossible. With regard to *Richard III* he writes:

> the writer must know how to furnish us with a secret background of sympathy for his hero, . . . and such sympathy can only be based on understanding or on a sense of possible inner fellow-feeling for him. (XIV, 314)

Aesthetic pleasure can only be generated when audience, character, and dramatist share desires, fantasies, inhibitions, and conflicts. In 'Psychopathic Characters on the Stage' he even claims of one reception constellation: 'Here the precondition of enjoyment is that the spectator should himself be a neurotic' (VII, 308).

The element of reception theory in Freud's literary studies consists of much more than just the notion of identification. Some critics so disastrously missed the point of Freud's analysis of *Oedipus* that they believed they could dismiss it simply by pointing out, for example, that Oedipus does not marry Jocasta out of any sexual attraction and is not even aware that she is his mother. Obviously such critics failed to recognize that Freud implicitly attributes an Oedipus complex not to Oedipus, but to the unknown creator of the legend and, furthermore, to the *audience*, thus: 'His destiny moves us only because it might have been ours' (IV, 262). In 1938 when countering such critics, however, Freud chooses not to refer to this element of identification which alone would annihilate their objections. Instead he makes the more subtle point that not only is Oedipus' lack of awareness of the identity of his mother and father a metaphor for the unconsciousness of the complex, but also 'that a distortion of this kind is inevitable if an attempt is made at a poetic handling of the material' (XXIII, 191). This statement takes us to the heart of his preoccupation with reception and his conception of aesthetics as a whole.

Due to the fact that it involves shared repressions, the very material which is capable of generating pleasure in an audience is also that most likely to arouse resistance. For Freud, the *ars poetica* consists in the manipulation of this resistance. Thus *Hamlet* is a successful play because the hero only becomes neurotic in the course of the action, and his complex is universal, yet 'is never given a definite name' (VII, 309). In his study of *Richard III* Freud explains the mechanism at length:

It is, however, a subtle economy of art in the poet that he does not permit his hero to give open and complete expression to all his secret motives. By this means he obliges us to supplement them; he engages our intellectual activity, diverts it from critical reflection and keeps us firmly identified with his hero. (XIV, 315)

The poet's specific skill, then, is in 'avoiding resistances and offering fore-pleasures' (VII, 310). Both feats are essentially related to *formal* considerations; thus Freud specifically admires the way Sophocles reveals Oedipus' guilt 'with cunning delays and ever-mounting excitement' (schrittweise gesteigerte und kunstvoll verzögerte Enthüllung) (IV, 262). The key quality is subtlety. Derivatives of repressed material arouse less resistance by slightly displacing the attention of the audience. Similarly, ambiguity is an important ingredient, decentring rather than crudely diverting attention. A blatantly neurotic protagonist is by no means impossible, but the dramatist must allow his audience to become gradually absorbed in the development of the illness (VII, 309). Clearly, Freud is not so much interested in content as he is in the economics of overcoming resistance, namely, the way in which content is subtly, gradually, and ambiguously communicated to the audience. This is another respect in which the psychoanalytical aesthetic concerns form and content in equal measure.

Freud's awareness of the absolute dependence of content on adequate form is not exhausted by his postulation of the need for subtlety. In order to demonstrate the full significance of form in Freud's conception of aesthetic pleasure, reference must be made to his 1905 book *Jokes and their Relation to the Unconscious*. The scope of this work is already highly literary in that the majority of the witticisms studied are taken from literary sources, such as Shakespeare, Schiller, and, above all, Heine. The complexity of, for example, Freud's conception of humour can best be appreciated in the highly sensitive passage concerning the subtleties of Falstaff and especially Don Quixote (VIII, 231n.). It is worth remembering that Freud's delight in the formal qualities of Cervantes's novel can be traced back even beyond his enthusiastic letters to Martha in the 1880s. At the age of sixteen he taught himself what was his seventh language with the express purpose of being able to read *Don Quixote* in the original Spanish.[7] As he had already enjoyed the work in German translation, this is striking evidence of the literary sensitivity to language and style which, in fact, permeates the book on wit. Even Francesco Orlando, who is critical of Freud's literary studies, admits that this work, at least, is highly sensitive to the 'text' of jokes.[8]

Nevertheless, the book is perhaps most appreciated by critics as a potential model for an aesthetic approach to literary texts in general. As it deals with the conscious communication of valuable ideas in complex verbal configurations specifically directed towards a listener 'of a more refined education' (VIII, 100), its paradigmatic relevance is clear. Critics such as Kris and Gombrich are usually credited with the elaboration of a psychoanalytical aesthetic on the model of Freud's book on wit, but such an analogy is already very much implicit in Freud's own texts concerning literature. His standard description of purely aesthetic pleasure as an 'incentive bonus' is a direct allusion to his theory of the pleasure mechanism of the joke. Indeed, in 'Psychopathic Characters on the Stage' he explicitly states that the aim of theatre is 'opening up sources of pleasure or enjoyment in our emotional life, just as . . . joking and fun open up similar sources' (VII, 305).

As the wit analogy is Freud's own, it is worth outlining its relevance to any account of his literary sophistication. Central to the analogy is the fore-pleasure principle, a mechanism which Freud himself in the book on wit says 'can be shown to hold good in many other aesthetic structures' (VIII, 135). This principle involves one kind of pleasure acting as an insidious vanguard, breaking ground for more powerful, primal satisfactions. In wit the pleasure generated by the form of the joke acts as an incentive bonus, reducing inhibitions and enabling a more significant discharge of instinctual tensions which would otherwise be impossible to achieve. Psychoanalytical aestheticians are attracted by the theory because of its emphasis on form. The central concept of *Jokes and their Relation to the Unconscious* is undoubtedly that of joke technique. This is originally completely distinct from any thought-content and pertains solely to verbal expression. Wit begins as pure word-play which generates pleasure in its own right simply from economies made in the activity of the psyche. It then develops by becoming meaningful and communicable, but the pleasure it generates is still self-contained and form-specific. Only in its ultimate form, tendentious wit, does it involve the satisfaction of repressed instinctual urges, and even then it remains utterly dependent on the vehicle of verbal form.

Peregrine Horden accuses Freud of having an 'impoverished' conception of aesthetics, one which reduces form to a superficial attempt to bribe an audience to pay attention.[9] Similarly, Rieff complains that the aesthetic uniqueness of a text thus becomes its inessential trappings.[10] The analogy with wit mechanisms, however, suggests that neither conclusion is quite accurate. The pleasurable relaxation of inhibitions caused by aesthetic pleasure is absolutely essential to the release of instinctual pleasure. It is no mere sugar-coating: Freud insists that for a genuinely successful joke the two elements must be fused to create a single 'overall impression'. Two distinct forms of pleasure are generated simultaneously, one from technique, the other from tendency, and the sum is *greater* than the parts (VIII, 136–7).[11]

No doubt, even despite its dynamic complexities, the fore-pleasure principle is still too crude a concept to account for the whole of aesthetic pleasure. Nevertheless, it is worth remembering that its extension into the literary sphere is really only implicit in Freud's works. The concept of joke technique, with its emphasis on condensation and displacement, is clearly a continuation of dream-work, but it is already significantly more elaborate. It may be reducible to a single principle, that of economy, but its subtle variations are endlessly complex, and Freud's elucidation of its relation to pleasure mechanisms and social dynamics places the wit book on an altogether higher plane of sophistication. Had Freud actually written a *Literature and its Relation to the Unconscious* based solely on his reading of literary texts, there can be little doubt that he would have made a similar qualitative leap forward in refinement.

Even critics who accept the relevance of Freudian theory to aesthetics continue to misrecognize Freud's own direct contributions. Norman N. Holland distinguishes three phases in the application of psychoanalysis to literature. Firstly, there were the crude origins consisting of a hunt for latent content, usually infantile sexuality. This was then followed by Anna Freud's psychology of the ego which caused psychoanalytical critics to read texts for defensive strategies, a much more creditable formalist approach. However, most sophisticated of all is the modern phenomenological approach which draws on the psychology of the self and constructs textual readings around the polarity of self and other.[12] With regard to Freud's *followers* this schematization is fairly accurate. Nevertheless, it fails to take account of the extent to which the 'later' sophistications are implicit in Freud's own texts. Qualities such as his formalist emphases on close reading and reception dynamics, his reliance on textual rather than biographical evidence, and his awareness of the overdetermined complexities of specifically literary contents all bespeak a degree of literary cultivation well in excess of that commonly attributed to him.

THE SUBLIME FATHER

Freud's literary studies occupy a much smaller fraction of his published works than might be expected. Considering his overwhelming bent for interpretation in general and his attraction to literature in particular, his restraint is remarkable. This apparent paradox can be resolved when viewed in the context of the extreme reverence which Freud felt towards great writers. Shoshana Felman attributes his vast superiority over his followers in the field of literary criticism precisely to his acute awareness of his own limitations.[13] Freud repeatedly refers to his own impotence before the sublime mystery of art. He never attempts to explain creative genius, which he describes as 'unanalysable' (XXI, 179), and he claims that psychoanalysis 'can do nothing towards elucidating the nature of the artistic gift, nor can it explain the means by which the artist works – artistic technique' (XX, 65). Such drastic agnosticism concerning a phenomenon belonging squarely in the realm of the human psyche is most uncharacteristic of Freud. In the opening paragraph of 'The "Uncanny"' he implies that it is the very complexity of aesthetics, with its 'subdued emotional impulses . . . dependent on a host of concurrent factors', that deters a psychoanalytical approach (XVII, 219). Elsewhere he attributes his reticence to his own personal shortcomings, as in the introductory paragraph of his Michelangelo study: 'I am unable rightly to appreciate many of the methods used and the effects obtained in art' (XIII, 211).

Consequently, Freud developed no theory of literature as such. He does, of course, approach literary texts from various angles, but these approaches seem always to be indirect, the central emphasis being on purely psychological themes. Thus he studies the dreams and delusions in *Gradiva*, the uncanny in 'The Sand-Man', and clinical characterology in Shakespeare and Ibsen. Alternatively, he restricts himself to marginal aspects of literary phenomena such as fantasies and jokes. The famous analyses of *Oedipus* and *Hamlet*, it will be remembered, are to be found under the heading 'Typical Dreams'. Freud's most overt piece of literary criticism is his essay 'The Theme of the Three Caskets', but in its introductory paragraph he deprecates the work as the solution of 'a small problem' (XII, 291), as if to confirm that he is not really tackling the sublime enigma of literature. Indeed, the motif he studies is, again, not specifically literary. He certainly acknowledges the potential literary applications of psychoanalytical techniques, but he is usually careful to shift responsibility for them onto other analysts whose interpretations he cites, such as Rank and Jones.

Freud's tentativeness seems to be confined to his published texts. In a letter to Jung, for example, he offhandedly describes Oedipus as a case of obsessional neurosis,[14] whereas in *The Interpretation of Dreams* he takes great pains to avoid the responsibility for diagnosing Hamlet: 'if anyone is inclined to call him a hysteric, I can only accept the fact as one that is implied by my interpretation' (IV, 265). This rhetorical ploy actually allows Freud both to resist and satisfy his urge to diagnose. There is evidence that he did indeed indulge in some less reverential pieces of literary criticism which were never published. He admits as much in 'Creative Writers and Day-Dreaming', where he claims that his biographical formula has, after 'some experiments', proved fruitful in application to literary texts (IX, 151). This does not, however, mean that Freud merely publicly conceals his own reductive tendencies. He is averse to essentializing or exclusive interpretations of any text, let alone literary ones. His readings tend to elucidate a single layer of an endlessly complex overdetermined network, and they are always left open to radical revision.

Richard Wollheim penetratingly argues that Freud's aesthetic is *systematically* fragmentary, its richness lying in the overlapping of various suggestions. Thus he warns against any attempt to synthesize the many marginal perspectives; Freud was himself aware that such a synthesis was impossible.[15] It could be argued that the thesis of 'Creative Writers and Day-Dreaming' attempts a totalizing perspective on literary production, but Freud is as cautious in this text as he is in any other. He tackles 'not the writers most highly esteemed by the critics, but the less pretentious authors [Erzähler] of novels, romances and short stories' (IX, 149). Of course, 'Delusions and Dreams in Jensen's *Gradiva*' is a far more exhaustive study than its title implies, and Freud's evaluative comments about the novella appear to be wholly positive. Nevertheless, he effectively ranks Jensen not far above the lowbrow authors referred to in 'Creative Writers and Day-Dreaming' [Der Dichter und das Phantasieren] when he speaks of this author as one of those who are 'in the habit of giving themselves over to their imagination [Phantasie] in a simple-minded joy in creating' (IX, 94). Correspondingly, his praise of Jensen in the essay is occasionally rather fulsome. When, for example, he strains to prove that Jensen's blatantly contrived coincidences are not arbitrary, Freud is clearly struggling to suppress his reservations about the writer. Finally in 1925, after Jensen's death, Freud explicitly refers to *Gradiva* as a short story 'which has no particular merit in itself' (XX, 65).

Freud's tentativeness about undertaking literary studies really pertains only to canonical works. Although Francesco Orlando is content to ascribe this 'excess of academic respect' simply to Freud's nineteenth-century humanistic *Bildung*,[16] it actually seems to be a specifically literary reticence. Freud's art criticism, after all, consists of an extensive account of Leonardo da Vinci's life and an exhaustive study of an acknowledged masterpiece, Michelangelo's *Moses*. Goethe meant far more to Freud than these Renaissance masters, yet Freud was singularly uncomfortable about publishing any analysis of him. In his dream of 'Goethe's Attack on Herr M.', Freud's apparently selfless wish-fulfilment is 'a contradiction of the idea that Goethe should be treated as though he were a lunatic' (IV, 327). Freud, it seems, would not even dream of attempting a psychoanalysis of the great poet. The exception, of course, is his 1917 essay 'A Childhood Recollection from *Dichtung und Wahrheit*'. This brief study addresses Goethe's life, not his works, and even then Freud only dares to voice his own conclusion through a proxy, Hitschmann: '"*Goethe, too, as a little boy saw a younger brother die without regret*"' (XVII, 151, Freud's emphasis). Furthermore, Freud makes it clear in the essay that he has held this interpretation back for years, hoping 'not to stretch the claims of psycho-analysis too far nor to apply it in unsuitable places' (XVII, 149). Despite this extreme restraint, his speech in acceptance of the Goethe Prize is primarily an apologia for the psychobiographical study of Goethe. Freud, who has so remarkably avoided analysing his favourite poet, still feels the need 'to justify oneself before him' (XXI, 208). It is very tempting to interpret this sense of guilt in the absence of any crime as an acknowledgement of a powerfully suppressed urge.

At the end of the same speech Freud attempts to reassure his audience by claiming that psychobiography has not led very far with Goethe:

This is because Goethe was not only, as a poet, a great self-revealer, but also, in spite of the abundance of autobiographical records, a careful concealer. (XXI, 212)

If Freud is so acutely aware that Goethe concealed much – his favourite quotation is Mephistopheles' 'the best of what you know may not be told to boys' – it is difficult to stifle the suspicion that he must have attempted a serious analysis. Almost twenty years earlier, significantly only in a letter, Freud had already referred to Goethe as a master of concealment, tantalizingly alluding to a study relating *Wilhelm Meister* to Goethe's infantile experiences.[17] In fact, Freud's initial impulse may have been to apply his new science to his favourite poet. An 1897 letter to Fliess even contains the sketch of a psychogenesis of *Werther*.[18] More significantly, it may be that his copious allusions to his favourite work, *Faust*, are traces of an unpublished interpretation of the play. His comments about Faust's detachment of libido (XII, 70–2) seem to be part of this fragmentary critique, as does his description of the premise of the tragedy as the 'transformation of the instinct to investigate back into an enjoyment of life' (XI, 75).

It is not merely fortuitous that the latter reference to *Faust* is made in Freud's study of Leonardo da Vinci. Both the legendary character and the Renaissance artist belong to a study of the complex process which is absolutely fundamental to his conception of all art, namely sublimation. Freud often mentions Goethe and Leonardo in the same breath, and usually in the context of sublimation. In the Goethe Prize speech he claims that Goethe approaches Leonardo for multifacetedness, and even surpasses him by virtue of his ability to reconcile the activities of artist and scientist, whereas Leonardo's scientific pursuits inhibited his artistry. Furthermore, Leonardo, unlike Goethe, sacrificed all sexual activity to these pursuits. It is not at all surprising, then, that Freud should interpret Faust's character in terms of sublimation. In *Civilization and its Discontents* he comments:

A satisfaction of this kind, such as an artist's joy in creating, in giving his phantasies body, or a scientist's in solving problems or discovering truths, has a special quality. . . . At present we can only say figuratively that such satisfactions seem 'finer and higher'. But their intensity . . . does not convulse our physical being. (XXI, 80–1)

Sublimation, then, is itself an inherently Faustian concept, a sublimated drive being incapable of final satisfaction. However, if Freud's analysis of *Faust* is fragmentary and implicit, his theory of sublimation is even more strikingly so. He often speaks of the artist's 'secret', and this is almost certainly a direct allusion to the capacity for sublimation. At the end of *Leonardo da Vinci*, for example, Freud writes that psychoanalysis cannot explain 'his extraordinary capacity for sublimating the primitive instincts', thus:

Since artistic talent and capacity are intimately connected with sublimation we must admit that the nature of the artistic function is also inaccessible to us along psycho-analytic lines. (XI, 136)

To some extent, the mystery of art *is* the mystery of sublimation.

Ironically, Freud's book on Leonardo is often cited as a source of reference for his theory of sublimation. It is, however, widely recognized that Freud only ever describes sublimation and positively avoids elucidating its dynamics. It may be that Freud, himself a scientist, found the subject too personal. However, his frankness in works such as *The Interpretation of Dreams* indicates that this explanation alone is inadequate.

Ricoeur's suggestion is more convincing; he implies that Freud has deliberately allowed sublimation to remain the 'empty concept' of psychoanalysis in deference to the artist's inexplicable mastery of repressed material.[19] Many critics, concerned about artistic integrity, are too eager to view sublimation as a mode of repression and thus to dismiss it as a slight on artists.[20] In the Leonardo study, however, Freud confirms that sublimation represents an *escape* of libido from the fate of repression, and he hardly needs to add that neurosis is thereby also avoided (XI, 80). It is a very common misconception that Freud equated artists with neurotics. On the contrary, Freud viewed neurosis as a universally human affliction surmounted only by those with a high capacity for sublimation, a quality he ascribes above all to great artists. W.H. Auden informs us that artists of his generation were most incensed by the passage in which Freud describes the artist as a man with 'excessively powerful instinctual needs' who is 'in rudiments an introvert, not far removed from neurosis'.[21] Nevertheless, Freud's repeated assertion that the greatest literature draws on material which is normally pathogenic implicitly ascribes enormous self-mastery to poets and uncanny therapeutic power to the techniques of literature. If artists are plagued with excessive drives, it is all the more remarkable that they should not only be largely healthy, but also socially valued.

Neurosis is, essentially, an 'uneconomic' way of dealing with reality. Freud, however, repeatedly emphasizes the true artist's supreme command of psychic economics. In *Beyond the Pleasure Principle* he stresses the fact that, via a 'system of aesthetics with an economic approach' (eine ökonomisch gerichtete Ästhetik), tragedy not only ensures mastery of 'the most painful experiences', it also transforms them into a source of great pleasure (XVIII, 17). His theoretical emphasis on art as self-treatment is reflected in his actual practice of literary criticism. It is actually most explicit in his study of Leonardo, where, for example, he remarks of the artist's predilection for androgynous figures: 'It is possible that in these figures Leonardo has denied the unhappiness of his erotic life and has triumphed over it in his art [künstlerisch überwunden]' (XI, 117–18). It is clear that Freud equally regards a literary creation as less a symptom than an attempted self-analysis and cure. In the letter to Fliess concerning *Werther* he claims that Goethe responded to his sexual trauma with Lotte Kestner and the news of Jerusalem's suicide with thoughts of his own suicide. He goes on to explain that the novel, far from representing a morbid fantasy, actually *protected* Goethe from suicide or mental illness.[22] Even the works of an author as lowbrow as

Jensen are viewed by Freud not as expressions of problems, but rather as outlines of a solution. Thus 'The Red Umbrella' and 'In the Gothic House' are, like *Gradiva*, 'attempts at a satisfactory poetical solution of the same problem in the psychology of love' (IX, 94).

Of course, in *Beyond the Pleasure Principle* even child's play is interpreted as an attempt to win pleasure from the mastery of painful experiences. Freud, however, draws an explicit distinction between the play and imitation of the infant and that of the adult artist: the latter directs his specifically at the audience (XVIII, 17). Similarly, when in *Totem and Taboo* Freud describes a case of hysteria as 'a caricature of a work of art', his vital distinction is that, whereas the former is asocial, art is a social and, therefore, healthy creation (XIII, 73). The poet does not only minister to himself, he plays a vital social role. Gay comments that one of Freud's slights on artists is his circumscription of their social function.[23] Admittedly, in *The Future of an Illusion* Freud gives a very limited view of the social value of art. It merely offers 'substitutive satisfactions' as compensation for socially-imposed renunciations, and it promotes feelings of identification by embodying the ideals and celebrating the achievements of a specific culture (XXI, 14). Worse still, art is ranked *below* religion for its cultural value in this respect. Such a conception of art smacks of utilitarian bourgeois idealism, but it is by no means the full extent of Freud's understanding. *Civilization and its Discontents*, in so many respects an essential complement to the naive – or, rather, polemical – optimism of the essay on religion, significantly modifies this conception of the social role of the artist. Here Freud speaks, somewhat cryptically, of certain great individuals who attain recognition for 'attributes and achievements which are completely foreign to the aims and ideals of the multitude', a recognition which is only possible due to 'discrepancies between people's thoughts and their actions' (XXI, 64). He is certainly referring to *Dichter* here, his only example of such an individual being his friend, Romain Rolland. Although the conception is no doubt still flawed, the suggestion that literature is an insidiously subversive and yet essential antidote to a culture's view of itself is considerably more complex and less condescending than the one which reduces its social function to that of a narcissistic and normalizing social narcotic.

In Freud's view, literature can offer a genuinely satisfactory and otherwise forbidden discharge of instinctual tensions to a social group whilst simultaneously promoting some kind of self-awareness. This is because the greatest *Dichter* are able to gain access to and master repressed material. A certain degree of preconscious control over the primary processes is essential if the artist is both to address an audience *and* circumvent socially-erected resistances. In Freud's scheme, aesthetic mastery consciously generates the fore-pleasure which lowers inhibitions, liberates repressed energies, and facilitates real end-pleasure. In *Jokes and their Relation to the Unconscious* even the sophisticated joke is seen to transcend various barriers of resistance – logic, criticism, inhibitions – and enable a healthily social and yet subversive release of instinctual tensions. The same techniques in the hands of a genuine *Dichter* can lead to even more remarkable feats. Auden does not point out that, in the same controversial passage in which Freud categorizes the artist as a near-neurotic, egotistical fantasist, he goes on to write, 'a man who is a true artist has more at his disposal':

[He knows] how to link so large a yield of pleasure to this representation of his unconscious phantasy that, for the time being at least, repressions are outweighed and lifted by it. (XVI, 376)

An artist, then, is capable of suspending repression. Freud acknowledges this as early as 1905 in 'Psychopathic Characters on the Stage'. Here he states that some of the pleasure generated by a 'psychopathological' drama is that of liberation. By effecting 'the revelation and the more or less conscious recognition of a repressed impulse' (VII, 309), the artist economizes with the spectator's expenditure of repressing energies and effects a satisfying discharge.

Such a socially invaluable and pleasurable suspension of repression, achieved aesthetically by a conscious mastery of the primary processes, is much closer to a therapeutic technique than it is to any neurotic mechanism. And this conception is not confined to Freud's abstract statements about the nature of art; it forms the basis, for example, of his analysis of Ibsen's *Rosmersholm*. Rebecca's incestuous past is never referred to explicitly in the play, but Ibsen has *not* simply repressed it. Freud acknowledges this by avoiding the term repressed, claiming instead the incest is 'so to speak, subterranean'. It has to be 'pieced together from hints . . . inserted with such art that it is impossible to misunderstand them' (XIV, 327). Freud, then, considers Ibsen to be in masterful control of this exquisitely aesthetic process of disguised revelation. Rebecca has been created by Ibsen with 'the most critical intelligence', and, through his 'conscious creative combination', the dramatist has *analysed* and deliberately manipulated the oedipal constellation. It is, for example, not Ibsen's own Oedipus complex, but rather 'laws of poetic economy' which have caused him to avoid any explicit reference to the underlying motif.

Resistance could easily have been aroused in his audience, the whole play being based on 'the most distressing emotions' (XIV, 329). The dramatist, however, via his supreme and subtle mastery of poetic economy, has not only managed to 'bind' painfully repressed emotions, he has liberated them from repression and transformed them into a source of pleasure and, to some extent, self-knowledge for an audience.

Critics who assume that Freud merely 'diagnoses' works of literature as morbid oedipal fantasies have failed to recognize the conscious analytical mastery which he imputes to authors such as Ibsen. A great work of literature is not a socialized neurotic fantasy; indeed, it is not even primarily in the thrall of the pleasure principle. Norman Brown believes that Freud vacillates in his attitude towards art as he vacillates between the pleasure principle and the reality principle, his fundamental dilemma.[24] Freud, however, does not simply equate artistic activity with the primary urge for gratification. He believes some artists achieve dominion over the complex economics of play and thereby gain access to unconscious realities. His abstract statements about art repeatedly refer to it as a *reconciliation* of the two principles, 'a region half-way between a reality which frustrates wishes and the wish-fulfilling world of the imagination' (XIII, 188). In 'Formulations on the Two Principles of Mental Functioning' of 1911 art is described as 'the way back to reality . . . from this world of phantasy'. Admittedly, the instance of reality here is essentially only the audience. They share the artist's dissatisfactions, and this shared discontent is the reality which the artist addresses (XII, 224). Nevertheless, Freud knows that a genuine artist's relationship with reality extends far beyond this awareness of shared discontents. Indeed, the most significant aspect of his genuine veneration of poets is his recognition of their secret knowledge of the human psyche.

At the very outset of his analysis of *Gradiva* Freud expresses his admiration with an allusion to *Hamlet*:

[Creative writers] are apt to know a whole host of things between heaven and earth of which our philosophy has not yet let us dream. In their knowledge of the mind they are far in advance of us everyday people . . . . (IX, 8)

This superior knowledge is not merely the result of intuition. On the contrary, apart from its aesthetic formulation, the poet's method follows the pattern of Freud's own self-analysis:

The author . . . directs his attention to the unconscious in his own mind, he listens to its possible developments and lends them artistic expression instead of suppressing them by conscious criticism. Thus he experiences from himself what we learn from others – the laws which the activities of this unconscious must obey . . .; as a result of the tolerance of his intelligence, they are incorporated within his creations. (IX, 92)

A *Dichter* is not restricted to self-analysis. As well as 'the courage to let his own unconscious speak', he possesses 'a sensitivity that enables him to perceive the hidden impulses in the minds of other people' (XI, 165). And, rather than considering his psychoanalytical insights to be mere endopsychic projections, Freud generally emphasizes the poet's conscious, or at least preconscious, understanding of them. In *The Psychopathology of Everyday Life*, for example, he demonstrates that Schiller has 'a clear understanding of the mechanism and the meaning of this kind of parapraxis' (VI, 97). Even more strikingly, Albrecht Schaeffer is described as having portrayed a figure in his novel *Josef Montfort* 'with intuitive poetic feeling and profound psycho-analytic understanding' (XVII, 243).

Such appreciation is a salient feature of Freud's literary criticism. Thus he speaks of his 'admiration' of Jensen's knowledge of the mechanism of the return of the repressed (IX, 49); an endopsychic perception of the process is ascribed only to the character Hanold, whereas another character, Zoë, understands it 'consciously' (IX, 51). In his study of *Rosmersholm* Freud imputes a much greater degree of scrupulous analytical tenacity to Ibsen, a 'great dramatist, who loves to pursue problems of psychological responsibility with unrelenting vigour' (XIV, 324). The very premise of 'Some Character-Types Met with in Psycho-Analytic Work' is the 'complete agreement' between traits in Freud's patients and 'figures which great writers have created from the wealth of their knowledge of the mind' (XIV, 318). Thus the works of Ibsen and especially Shakespeare are so analytically accurate that they are epistemologically interchangeable with clinical experience. Freud recognizes that such systematic insights are indeed proto-scientific: '[The poet] has from time immemorial been the precursor of science, and so too of scientific psychology' (IX, 44).

Freud's literary interpretations tend to assume that the author has already done extensive analytical work which merely needs explicating. While discussing the taboo of virginity, he claims of *Judith*:

Hebbel has intentionally [in klarer Absichtlichkeit] sexualized the patriotic narrative from the Apocrypha of the Old Testament . . .; with the fine perception of a poet, he sensed the ancient motive, which had been lost in the tendentious narrative, and has merely restored its earlier content to the material. (XI, 207)

Thus, the author's conscious, analytical penetration has stripped away any secondary tendencies to release the dynamic energies at the core of the subject matter. This process is precisely the opposite of the hypocritical secondary revision of dream-content undertaken merely to circumvent censorship. In *The Interpretation of Dreams* Freud quotes a passage from Keller's *Der grüne Heinrich*, which itself refers to a passage in *The Odyssey*, to illustrate the following claim:

It sometimes happens that the sharp eye of a creative writer has an analytic realization of the process of transformation of which he is habitually no more than the tool. If so, he may follow the process in a reverse direction and so trace back the imaginative writing to a dream. (IV, 246)

Freud is implying here that most authors merely extend or modify the unconscious secondary elaborations present in dreams, fantasies, and myths. An exceptional few, however, are able to use literary production as a means of actively analysing these scenarios of disguised wish-fulfilment. Freud's distinction between literary classics and lowbrow fiction, overlooked by almost all of his critics, could hardly be expressed more trenchantly.

Perhaps inevitably, the most extensive analytical powers are attributed to Shakespeare. This is most clearly demonstrated by Freud's analysis of the mythical motif of the choice between three women in *King Lear*.

We get an impression that a reduction of the theme to the original myth is being carried out in his work, so that we once more have a sense of the moving significance which had been weakened by the distortion. It is by means of this reduction of the distortion, this partial return to the original, that the dramatist achieves his more profound effect on us. (XII, 300)

Shakespeare achieves not disguised wish-fulfilment, but 'eternal wisdom', namely a full recognition of the necessity of death. This profound awareness of the ultimate aspect of Ananke has little to do with pleasure and everything to do with reality. And Freud need hardly have used psychoanalytical techniques to interpret the motif of the choice between three women. He merely had to read Shakespeare's treatment of this motif in *King Lear*. 'The regressive revision which he has thus applied to the myth, distorted as it was by wishful transformation, allows us . . . glimpses of its original meaning' (XII, 301). By regressive Freud means *interpretative*, the stripping away of wishful distortions to reveal the unconscious root. This process of making conscious the unconscious, tendentiously aimed at a more profound awareness and acceptance of reality, is most reminiscent of psychoanalysis itself.

Gay correctly discerns that Freud loves art less for art's than for truth's sake, a love Gay terms a 'higher philistinism'.[25] Although the description is, to some extent, fair, it must be recognized that Freud's emphasis is crucially different from the nineteenth-century bourgeois idealist belief that art embodies 'higher' truths. Far from being noble or spiritual, the universal truths which Freud imputes to the greatest poets are so subversive, indeed explosive, that he believes the *ars poetica* consists entirely in their controlled detonation. In one of his introductory lectures Freud points out that a cherished social ideal precludes any thorough evaluation of the aggressive impulses which exist within familial relations. He continues:

incidentally, this disavowal applies only to real life. Narrative and dramatic works of the imagination may freely make play with the themes that arise from a disturbance of this ideal. (XV, 206)

Thus, he goes on to claim that not psychoanalysis, but *literature* is the realm in which the ubiquity of the Oedipus complex is acknowledged (XV, 208). Freud does indeed imply that Sophocles' treatment of the Oedipus myth evinces the poet's understanding of its hidden meaning. As we have seen, he claims it is 'the dramatist's voice' (XVI, 331) which informs the audience that they, too, are guilty because of their own unconscious impulses. Similarly, according to Freud, Shakespeare has his Hamlet inform us that oedipal guilt is 'super-individual' (XXI, 189). Of course, in his *Autobiographical Study* Freud actually admits that he partly inferred the universality of the Oedipus complex directly from 'the overwhelming effect of its dramatic treatment' (XX, 63).

In his *Autobiographical Study* there is a striking contrast in Freud's discussion of priority. After fiercely asserting absolute independence from psychologists such as Pierre Janet, Freud is, if anything, conspicuously proud of the fact that 'poets and students of human nature' have always anticipated his findings (XX, 33). Goethe is honoured with the most categorical statement of this concession of priority:

He himself approached [psychoanalysis] at a number of points, recognized much through his own insight that we have since been able to confirm, and some views, which have brought criticism and mockery down upon us, were expounded by him as self-evident. (XXI, 208–9)

It is almost impossible to recognize Freud, the proud and doggedly independent innovator in some of his more humble statements of this kind – for example:

In the field of symptomatic acts, too, psycho-analytic observation must concede priority to imaginative writers. It can only repeat what they have said long ago. (VI, 213)

This uncharacteristic humility suggests that the great *Dichter* represent significant authority-figures to Freud. Not only does he enjoy invoking them as his protecting spirits, he all but admits that he has learnt directly from them. This relationship, however, is much more complex and emotionally involved than that between pupil and teacher. In his letter to Hugo Heller containing a list of ten 'good' books, he cites such authors as Zola and Keller, happily acknowledging that he owes some part of his 'knowledge of life and philosophy' to them. Nevertheless, he has restricted his list to these authors – omitting, as we have seen, Sophocles, Shakespeare, and Goethe – precisely because of the *absence* of 'the element of shy reverence, the conviction of one's own smallness versus their greatness'.[26] Good authors, then, have something to teach Freud, but the very greatest *Dichter* cause him to feel positively belittled. Even Jones, himself so reverential towards Freud, ventures to comment that Freud views artists as 'mysterious beings with a superhuman, almost divine, afflatus'.[27]

It does not seem unreasonable to turn to Freud's own works for an explanation of this unwonted piety. In *Moses and Monotheism* he writes:

If we unhesitatingly declare that, for instance, Goethe and Leonardo da Vinci and Beethoven were great men, we must be led to it by something other than admiration for their splendid creations. (XXIII, 108)

The dynamic element is that the great man must also represent a paternal authority. The first 'great man' is the *father*, and this infantile model remains in effect throughout adulthood. Admittedly, Freud is referring only to the attitudes of social groups towards great individuals. It would, indeed, be absurd to claim that the tone-deaf Freud had a relationship with Beethoven as intimate and dynamic as that with his own father. Nevertheless, with regard to Goethe – the first name that occurs to Freud – the claim is somewhat less outrageous. In *The Interpretation of Dreams* he includes great men amongst the universal dream-symbols of the father and continues: 'for that reason Goethe, for instance, appears as a father-symbol in some dreams' (V, 354). Freud attributes this example to Hitschmann, but even if he is not once again screening his own emotional involvement with the poet behind this analyst, it is at least worth questioning the extent to which his selection of this particular example of a father-symbol was purely random. Freud's Goethe Prize speech seems to justify such speculation. Here, on behalf of his fellow analysts, he defends his and their 'right to place ourselves under the patronage of Goethe' (XXI, 210). No one familiar with Freud's interpretative vigour could imagine he was ignorant of the etymological implications of the word *Patronanz*. Indeed, in this very speech he describes our powerful curiosity about the lives of great men as 'the need to acquire affective relations with such men, to add them to the fathers, teachers, exemplars whom we have known' (XXI, 211).

The strikingly filial nature of Freud's relationship to great poets sheds light on his hostility towards avant-garde artistic movements. Freud was not afraid of controversial innovation; indeed, he himself laid crucial foundations for the modernist revolution. His conservative tendencies in the arts cannot be explained away as a mere corollary of his bourgeois conventionalism. His attitude towards modern art is little short of reactionary: he describes surrealist and expressionist painters as lunatics and mockingly suggests that 'modern "art"' is the sorry product of men attempting to compensate for severe congenital defects of vision.[28] Predictably, his criticism of modern writers is more muted, but traces of it run throughout all his important texts concerning literature. In *The Interpretation of Dreams* 'modern dramatists' are deemed incapable of generating the effect that Sophocles achieves in *Oedipus* (IV, 262). Similarly, in 1905 he writes that a drama must deal with suffering, but in such a way as to generate pleasure in the audience and he adds: 'Modern writers have particularly often failed to obey this rule' (VII, 307). In a 1933 lecture he even makes an explicit criticism of writers. Regarding the inferiority complex he notes:

It especially haunts the pages of what are known as *belles lettres*. An author [Schriftsteller] who uses the term 'inferiority complex' thinks that by so doing he has fulfilled all the demands of psycho-analysis and has raised his composition to a higher psychological plane. (XXII, 65)

This expression of unalloyed contempt for authors – quite unique in Freud's works – focuses on a pseudo-psychoanalytical term and is, therefore, strictly limited to twentieth-century writers. Apart from this restriction to modern artists, there is another common theme in all of these criticisms: modern painters lack sufficient preconscious elaboration of unconscious material, their creations bear no recognizable relation to reality, modern writers cause their audiences to suffer because they lack awareness of dynamic resistance, they are derivative and arbitrary, believing they can substitute jargon for genuine painstaking analysis. In other words, they all lack the high degree of *mastery* – of self, of subject matter, of formal medium, of audience – which alone distinguishes the great artist.

It would be perfectly feasible to interpret Freud's attitudes in terms of an adherence to, say, the aesthetic of Weimar classicism. Nevertheless, his humility before great poets and his contempt for those who lack their powers of mastery both tend to suggest that there is a powerful emotional dimension in his conservatism. If great poets are fathers, then revolutionary modernists belong to the parricidal brother-clan who may, by joining forces, overthrow the primal father, but who will always fail to establish any authority in his place. It seems that Freud's contempt for modern writers is, to some extent, another expression of his filial piety towards classical *Dichter*. As representatives of the now sublime primal father, these great poets constitute something like a totem for Freud. He seeks knowledge and protection from them, and in return he offers his reverence whilst scrupulously avoiding any contact with them which may be interpreted as aggressive.

This element of taboo, of 'holy dread', sheds a fascinating light on Freud's reluctance to indulge in literary criticism. Sarah Kofman accurately discerns his dynamic resistance against making this Father-God a direct object of analysis.[29] Freud often appears not so much agnostic as positively awe-struck in his attitude towards works of art. Of Leonardo's most famous paintings he writes: 'These pictures breathe a mystical air into whose secret one dares not penetrate' (XI, 117). More commonly, Freud speaks of poets in such terms. The impression he gives of treating them as oracular deities is heightened by his preference for the generic term *Dichter* over the use of specific names. Freud even attempts to keep this significant word untainted by referring to lesser authors as *Erzähler* and to writers who use jargon in the place of psychological analysis as *Schriftsteller*.

Perhaps the most compelling evidence for the dynamically emotional, filial aspect of Freud's reverence for *Dichter* is his conversion to the eccentric theory of Shakespearean authorship forwarded by the unfortunately named Thomas Looney. In *Civilization and its Discontents* the 'cultural level of an English country town in Shakespeare's time' is one source of Freud's own discontent. He is clearly uncomfortable with the knowledge that Shakespeare's father was fined for keeping a large dung-heap outside his Stratford home (XXI, 93). Freud had long doubted that the man from Stratford was the author of the plays, suspecting Shakespeare was actually of French extraction, but Looney's thesis struck a deeper chord within him. In his Goethe Prize speech he admits he finds it 'painful' not to know the identity of the man who wrote the plays attributed to Shakespeare:

whether it was in fact the untutored son of the provincial citizen of Stratford, . . . or whether it was, rather, the nobly-born and highly cultivated, passionately wayward, to some extent *déclassé* aristocrat, Edward de Vere, Seventeenth Earl of Oxford, hereditary Lord Great Chamberlain of England. (XXI, 211)

On reading this passage it is difficult to disagree with Ernest Jones's suggestion that Freud's speculation represents 'some derivative of the Family Romance fantasy'.[30] Harry Trosman develops this suggestion and points out that, emotionally, such dubious theories about Shakespearean authorship usually correspond with almost a deification of the dramatist, a regression to the infant's idealization of the father.[31] It is certainly not social élitism which causes Freud to promote Shakespeare from the petty bourgeoisie to the aristocracy. Quality of education has little to do with the excessive instinctual drives and enigmatic powers of sublimation which he believes distinguish the literary genius. Nor is it merely a matter of playful curiosity for Freud. His Earl of Oxford theory rears its head in most of the major works of his last decade, including his 1930 revision of *The Interpretation of Dreams* and even, via a 1935 supplement, his autobiography. It is most revealing that his fullest reference to the theory should be made during the speech in which he openly speaks of his desire for Goethe's patronage and of his need to establish emotional ties to the poet in order to be able to relate to him as a father. This tends to confirm the suspicion that his conversion to Looney's thesis represents his need for Shakespeare to fulfil the role of an idealized parent. Although it has many genuine aspects, which are solidly grounded in his literary theory and fully sustained by his practice of literary criticism, Freud's reverence for the *Dichter* is, on one level, that of a son for a father.

PIOUS IMPIETY: BIOGRAPHY AND *DAS GEMEINE*

Freud's reverence for poets may be filial, but in the wake of the psychoanalytical revolution 'filial' has long ceased to be a synonym for 'reverential'. If Freud's tentativeness about undertaking literary studies is some form of 'holy dread', then it is difficult to avoid developing the 'taboo' metaphor to its logical conclusion. He himself describes taboo as a symptom of ambivalence (XIII, 66), and it is indeed the phenomenon of ambivalence which lies at the heart of his own relationships with poets. His subtly equivocal attitude must, of course, be appreciated precisely in the context of his high degree of literary cultivation and his profound veneration for *Dichter*. Many critics have correctly diagnosed Freud's ambivalence, but they have largely failed to evaluate its manifestations in his texts. Charles Rycroft provides a typical example. He speaks of Freud's 'ambivalence towards artists, whom he both admired . . . and disparaged, by trying to demonstrate that they were all neurotic'.[32] He has thus not only, like many others, misrepresented Freud's own literary studies, but perhaps also the concept of ambivalence itself.

Even the most careful readers of Freud's texts go astray. Trilling sees an emphatic shift in Freud's theories of art, beginning with the 'essential neuroticism of the artist' and gradually developing towards a recognition of poets as the true discoverers of the unconscious.[33] This is precisely the opposite of the trend detected by Kofman. She, too, speaks of Freud's relationship with poets as profoundly and dynamically ambivalent, but she attempts to read Freud's essay on *Gradiva* as 'pivotal', marking a shift from treating literature as an oracle, a model confirming psychoanalytical knowledge, towards 'treating' it as a patient.[34] The reason such astute critics are able to make plausible cases for diametrically opposed positions is that both fail to grasp the extent of the ambivalence which Freud felt towards poets. There simply was no epistemological break; the same equivocal attitude spans the whole of his adult life. In psychoanalytical theory, ambivalence is not merely an internal conflict liable to some form of dialectical resolution. It consists of a simultaneous coexistence of full-blooded affectionate and aggressive feelings, usually towards a paternal object, the affection often being conspicuous, the aggression latent. In his remarkably frank Goethe Prize speech, precisely in the context of his defence of psychoanalytical studies on Goethe, Freud avows:

Our attitude to fathers and teachers is, after all, an ambivalent one since our reverence for them regularly conceals a component of hostile rebellion. That is a psychological fatality . . . and is bound to extend to our relations with the great men whose life histories we wish to investigate. (XXI, 212)

The contradictory feelings, then, are both fully coexistent and radically ineluctable.

Not only the extent, but also the subtlety of Freud's ambivalence commonly escapes the attention of critics. Given Freud's high degree of literary sophistication and the extent of his genuine admiration for the poet's mastery, it must be appreciated that his aggressive tendencies are finely modulated and discernible only in subtle textual traces. The *Dichter* is a *sublime* father, an idealized, transcendental figure, and Freud's ambivalence towards him is correspondingly sublimated. Paradoxically, it is perhaps best to begin examining it by looking at Freud's explicit statements of piety and humility. Immediately, a striking pattern amongst these avowals comes into focus: they are almost exclusively to be found in his very opening paragraphs. Thus, on the second page of his *Gradiva* analysis he praises the poet's knowledge to the detriment of his own; in the opening paragraph of 'The Theme of the Three Caskets' he derogates the whole essay; and in the opening paragraph of 'The "Uncanny"' he declares aesthetics beyond the scope of psychoanalysis. The pattern is the same in his other works of art criticism. For example, in the opening paragraphs of his book on Leonardo he bows before the artist's 'perfection' (XI, 63), whilst the first line of his Michelangelo study is self-deprecating: 'I may say at once that I am no connoisseur in art, but simply a layman' (XIII, 211).

These acts of intellectual obeisance are suspect for a variety of reasons. Firstly, they are significantly absent in 'Psychopathic Characters on the Stage', the one text concerning literature which Freud never prepared for publication. It would seem, then, that they are secondary embellishments of his own texts, included primarily for rhetorical reasons. Kofman notes that Freud's reverence is strategic, a conspicuous lip-service paid to the conventional ideology of the 'divine' artist.[35] Whilst Freud's adherence to this ideology is more profound than mere lip-service, it is impossible to contest the opposition Kofman draws up between what Freud says – always modest and conservative – and what he *does*, this tending to be radical and deconstructive.[36] By the end of his study of Leonardo, for example, any idea that the artist is 'perfect' has been systematically undermined. Freud's most abject declaration of humility is contained in one of the opening paragraphs of his essay on Dostoevsky, written in 1927:

> The creative artist is the least doubtful: Dostoevsky's place is not far behind Shakespeare. *The Brothers Karamazov* is the most magnificent novel ever written; the episode of the Grand Inquisitor, one of the peaks in the literature of the world, can hardly be valued too highly. Before the problem of the creative artist analysis must, alas, lay down its arms. (XXI, 177)

Rycroft cites this latter sentence as evidence that Freud belatedly abandoned his 'homology' between poet and neurotic.[37] Freud's declaration is indeed extreme, culminating in a symbolic self-castration, no less. Even as it stands, however, its perfunctoriness is manifest. It clearly belongs with the other mechanical statements of humility inserted at the very beginning of his texts in an attempt to lower resistances in his reader. More strikingly, when contrasted with the rest of the essay, Freud's pretended humility seems to be *inversely* proportional to his actual deference. He lays down his weapons on the opening page of the text in which he most blatantly assassinates the author.

Freud's professed humility could, of course, be seen as purely expedient. It is not necessarily a screen for deeply rooted hostility. The poet is not a real father to Freud, he represents no prohibitive or punitive authority, no progenitor of unwanted siblings, no rival for a mother's affections. It would be too uncritical an application of Freudian theory to posit a whole Oedipus complex simply because of the quasi-filial nature of his respect. Trosman avoids this issue by reading the 'family romance' of Freud's Shakespeare hypothesis only in terms of the relationship with his actual father, Jakob – the poet representing the 'idealized parent of early childhood'.[38] Like Hamilcar Barca in the childhood fantasy described in *The Interpretation of Dreams*, then, the poet is merely a more suitable substitute for Jakob, whose imperfections were painfully perceived by the young Freud (IV, 197). The *Dichter* here would be the positive element of a 'splitting' of the real father and, as such, would be exempt from any hostile impulses. Unfortunately, this by itself is also an inadequate account of Freud's relationships with poets. Freud harbours specific animosities towards poets, not merely as revenants of Jakob Freud, but *as* poets. The oedipal constellation provides an excellent metaphor for the functioning of Freud's ambivalence, but its nonoedipal dynamics must be fully acknowledged.

Freud was fundamentally *envious* of poets. In a letter to Arthur Schnitzler he speaks openly of this envy and how it colours his admiration for *Dichter*. The reason he cites is the apparent ease with which they come by 'this or that piece of secret knowledge which I had acquired by a painstaking investigation of the subject'.[39] Thus Gay says of Freud's various slights on artists: 'The tortoise is maligning the hare'.[40] Freud usually expresses his somewhat flattering envy to contemporary authors of his own acquaintance such as Schnitzler, Lou Andreas-Salomé, and Thomas Mann. Nevertheless, even Goethe seems to inspire a certain competitive resentment. For example, shortly after referring to 'Goethe, who is immortal', Freud, in a separate but roughly contiguous dream analysis, writes: '"No, my own immortal works have not yet been written"' (V, 440 and 453). Whether or not these two passages are subliminally related, Freud certainly assumes he can never achieve the esteem enjoyed by poets. Although he believes they often deal with similar material, he critically lacks the *ars poetica* of circumventing the resistance aroused by this material. As Hélène Cixous puts it, Freud is jealous of the poet's capacity to *seduce*.[41]

Cixous may well be alluding here to the distinctly sexual dimension of Freud's resentment of artists. During his courtship with Martha, Freud's rivals included an artist and a musician. Jones recounts how Freud confessed to Martha the general enmity between scientists and artists, the latter possessing the key to female hearts, whilst men in Freud's profession had to puzzle hard over the lock.[42] This complaint is structurally identical to the one made to Schnitzler, suggesting the priority of the sexual over the intellectual jealousy. Correspondingly, many of his slights on artists betray a hidden agenda of sexual rivalry. Freud's infamous description of the artist as a near-neurotic fantasist ends with the assertion that, ultimately, he achieves '*through* his phantasy what originally he had achieved only *in* his phantasy – honour, power and the love of women' (XVI, 376–7). His rhetorical structuring of the whole passage surreptitiously suggests that the *telos* of artistic creation is the seduction of women. Such an aspersion may even be latent in his analogy between aesthetic pleasure and fore-pleasure, initially a purely sexual mechanism. Thus, his attribution of secret knowledge to the *Dichter* is occasionally somewhat two-edged. His 1933 lecture on femininity suggests: 'If you want to know more about femininity . . . turn to the poets' (XXII, 135). The suggestion that their specialist knowledge is conditioned by an ulterior sexual motive is by itself somewhat disparaging. Even more radically, in the same lecture Freud, for once, dares to doubt the poet's analytical powers precisely in regard to the subject of sexual attraction:

we scarcely know whether we are to believe seriously in the power of which poets talk so much and with such enthusiasm but which cannot be further dissected analytically. We have found an answer of quite another sort by means of laborious investigations. (XXII, 119)

Sexual jealousy is not the most important element of the grudge Freud harbours against poets. More than their power over women, he resents their power over *himself*, as a reader. Even in 'The Moses of Michelangelo', in which he professes his imperviousness to many artistic effects and techniques, he has to admit: 'Nevertheless, works of art do exercise a powerful effect on me, especially those of literature and sculpture' (XIII, 211). There is much evidence that Freud was powerfully gripped by literary narratives, and he sometimes betrays the naive enthusiasm of what was evidently a childhood passion. When, for instance, he points out that 'Gradiva' is not a ghost, but the character Zoë Bertgang, his overreaction suggests that, initially, he was himself 'inveigled' into a delusion: 'What a humiliation for us readers! So the author has been making fun of us' (IX, 18). Max Milner recognizes that Freud is uncomfortable with the passive role he must play as a reader. As an analyst he manipulates his patients' resistances and, from Olympian heights, exercises a powerful therapeutic effect on them. As a reader, however, it is *his* resistances which are aesthetically manipulated, and it is he who must suffer a powerful effect at the hands of the unchanging text.[43] In 'The "Uncanny"' Freud does indeed write of how a reader is constrained to follow the author into the world of his choosing. He regards this as just one of the many freedoms enjoyed by poets, and it is one he particularly resents. For example, he mentions authors who appear to locate their stories 'in the world of common reality' only then to achieve powerful uncanny effects by subverting this realism. Freud claims that such authors 'betray' and 'deceive' us and fail to achieve a pure effect. He continues:

We retain a feeling of dissatisfaction, a kind of grudge against the attempted deceit. I have noticed this particularly after reading Schnitzler's *Die Weissagung* [*The Prophecy*] and similar stories which flirt with the supernatural. (XVII, 249–51)

Freud even speaks of his revolt (Auflehnung) in this respect; and if the author circumvents this by avoiding specifying the nature of his narrative plane, Freud remains ambivalent, describing this technique as underhanded (arglistig). That the fundamental cause of his resentment is his *passivity* as a reader becomes clear later in the same passage:

But the story-teller has a peculiarly directive power over us; by means of the moods he can put us into, he is able to guide the current of our emotions, to dam it up in one direction and make it flow in another, and he often obtains a great variety of effects from the same material. (XVII, 251)

Milner is certainly correct to point out that Freud is unhappy about his own passivity and jealous of the author's active role. Nevertheless, he fails to notice how Freud seems to perceive the best *Dichter* to be positively *aggressive* towards the reader. To describe the effect of great works of literature Freud repeatedly draws on the same stock of verbs, ranging from 'seize' (packen) and 'grip' (ergreifen) to 'overwhelm' (überwältigen), 'paralyse' (lähmen), and – his favourite – 'shatter' (erschüttern). The aggressive undertone of these terms is quite evident. Freud even modifies his diagnosis of Dostoevsky as a masochist, citing as a sadistic trait 'the way in which, as an author, he treats his readers' (XXI, 178–9). It would certainly be possible to interpret this sense of submission to the violent authority of the *Dichter* in oedipal terms. Freud feels the poet achieves his effects by paralysing and dazzling the reader. For example, he speaks of Zweig's 'brilliantly told' (glänzend erzählte) story (XXI, 193), or of the 'splendour' (Glanz) of the language in Shakespeare (XIII, 213). This debilitatingly powerful 'blinding' effect could conceivably be read as a symbolic castration. In the light of his own interpretation of the monster (Ungeheuer) in *Oedipus* as a projection of the castrating father (XXI, 188), the same could even be said of his remarkable description of the 'overpowering effect [ungeheure Wirkung] of *King Lear*' (XII, 300). Nevertheless, Freud's grievances can also be adequately explained without recourse to psychoanalytical doctrine, namely in terms of his jealousy of the poet's many freedoms, privileges, and powers.

Freud does not simply acquiesce in his vulnerability at the hands of the *Dichter*. His interpretations contain an important element of resistance to his own particularly acute susceptibility to literary narratives. In his *Macbeth* study he writes:

The dramatist can indeed, during the representation, overwhelm [überwältigen] us by his art and paralyse [lähmen] our powers of reflection; but he cannot prevent us from attempting subsequently to grasp its effect by studying its psychological mechanism. (XIV, 323)

Psychoanalytical literary criticism, then, is both Freud's revolt against and his revenge for the poet's paralysing subjugation of the reader. In 'The Moses of Michelangelo' he claims that artistic studies which focus on minute details have 'something extraordinarily attractive' precisely because they accentuate isolated features which 'we usually fail to notice, being overcome [überwältigt] by the total impression . . . and as it were paralysed [gelähmt] by it' (XIII, 219). His use of verbs of aggression identical to those in the preceding quotation suggests that Freud's preference for studying detail is an act not of deference but of *defence*, a way of undermining the artist's overpowering effects.

Earlier in this text, Freud admits that if he is incapable of *understanding* the source of an artistic effect, as for example with music, he remains 'almost incapable of obtaining any pleasure'. He continues:

Some rationalistic, or perhaps analytic, turn of mind [Anlage] in me rebels against being moved [ergriffen] by a thing without knowing why I am thus affected and what it is that affects me. (XIII, 211)

His use of the word *Anlage* here is somewhat misleading. Rationalism is not a constitutional faculty, nor is analysis a primary activity. Wollheim astutely points out that Freud's comments here contradict assertions he makes elsewhere.[44] For example, when Freud quotes Leonardo's claims:

'One has no right to love or hate anything if one has not acquired a thorough knowledge of its nature', and 'great love springs from great knowledge of the beloved object', he dismisses these assertions, so similar to his own professed attitude towards the arts, as 'obviously false' (XI, 73–4). An even more fundamental contradiction lies in Freud's assessment of the 'apparently paradoxical fact that precisely some of the grandest and most overwhelming creations of art are still unsolved riddles to our understanding'. Here he claims:

I am not sufficiently well-read to know whether . . . some writer on aesthetics has discovered that this state of intellectual bewilderment is a necessary condition when a work of art is to achieve its greatest effects. It would be only with the greatest reluctance that I could bring myself to believe in any such necessity. (XIII, 211–12)

Now, at least one amateur aesthetician has made just such a finding, namely Freud himself! The circumvention of critical evaluation, and thus of emotional resistance, by means of various forms of displacement is the very essence of Freud's aesthetic.

This remarkable contradiction can best be explained with reference to Freud's urge to rationalize the powerful effect works of art have on him. His analytical understanding of a work of art, far from being the source of his enjoyment, is, in fact, his *reaction* to a primary response of abject pleasure. He resists this pleasure so forcefully it becomes a source of dissatisfaction to him until he can procure the more controlled pleasure of intellectual comprehension. For Freud, literary criticism is, to some extent, a means of self-defence, indeed of counter-attack. He particularly exalts in his interpretation of *Hamlet*. No doubt he was firmly gripped by the enigmatic power of this play, and his deepest satisfaction derives from his ability to *explain* the source of his own reaction. Thus he has not only defended himself honourably against Shakespeare's onslaught, he has even outwitted his other great mentor, Goethe. In *The Interpretation of Dreams* Freud cannot resist pointing out that his own oedipal interpretation surpasses 'the view which was originated by Goethe and is still the prevailing one to-day' (IV, 265). The reading he rejects is one in which Hamlet is 'paralysed by an excessive development of his intellect'. This cannot have been a comfortable idea for Freud; indeed, he deploys his intellect precisely in order to prevent his own paralysis at the hands of the great *Dichter*. I earlier claimed that in one essay Freud even 'assassinates' Dostoevsky. Naturally he does not openly attack a *Dichter*. Nevertheless, by naively – or, rather, disingenuously – splitting Dostoevsky into creative artist, neurotic, moralist, and sinner, he paves the way for what he, perhaps unconsciously, acknowledges is an attack: 'The moralist in Dostoevsky is the most readily assailable [angreifbar]' (XXI, 177).

Freud's need to rationalize his own submissive response to literary texts sheds some light on an aspect of his literary-critical practice which often provokes charges of reductionism. This is his tendency to view a work of art as a riddle or a problem that is susceptible to solution. For example, his attempt to 'crack' *Macbeth* remains inconclusive, which clearly rankles with him: 'One is so unwilling to dismiss a problem like that of *Macbeth* as insoluble' (XIV, 323). His response is to refer to Jekels's theory that Shakespeare often split individual creations into two characters. Freud claims: 'I shall not follow this clue any further', only then to produce a flood of textual evidence to demonstrate that Macbeth and his wife are indeed 'two disunited parts of a single psychical individuality' (XIV, 323–4). Problem-solving clearly satisfies an emotional need in Freud. When he has explained the riddle of his own response, his complacent pride does indeed resemble crass reductionism. In his *Outline of Psychoanalysis* of 1938, for example, he comments 'how easily the riddle of another dramatic hero, Shakespeare's procrastinator, Hamlet, can be solved by reference to the Oedipus complex' (XXIII, 192).

Freud's rationalistic attitude is better explained by the emotional dynamics of his profound susceptibility to literary texts than by any charge of philistinism. There is a wealth of evidence demonstrating his sophisticated appreciation of multiple layers of textual meaning sustained by ambiguities. His problem-solving approach is not a deficiency of his literary culture, but an active *misrecognition* motivated by ambivalence. This rationalizing approach does, however, have significant repercussions for his literary criticism, above all in his tendency towards homogenization. In 'The Theme of the Three Caskets', for example, not only two vastly different scenes from Shakespeare, but also various myths and fairy-tales are treated as a single problem with a single solution. More dubiously, Freud attempts to homogenize literary response. He regards his interpretation of *Hamlet*, for example, as a solution to the *problem* of the 'mass of differing and contradictory interpretative attempts' (XIII, 212). He hopes to disambiguate the text and resolve the multivalency of critical response it has provoked. Of the connoisseurs of artistic masterpieces he writes:

But usually in the presence of a great work of art each says something different from the other; and none of them says anything that solves the problem for the unpretending admirer. (XIII, 212)

Correspondingly, he goes on in this text to 'solve' Michelangelo's *Moses* with very little regard for its aesthetic specificities. He is not even primarily attracted by the statue's ambiguity. He asks rhetorically: 'Has then the master-hand indeed traced such a vague or ambiguous script in the stone, that so many different readings of it are possible?' (XIII, 215), and his essay answers firmly in the negative. This is, however, only to be expected in the light of Freud's admission: 'no piece of statuary has ever made a stronger impression on me' (XIII, 213). For such an overpowering effect to be worked through, he must needs solve a riddle.

It is a work not of sculpture, but of literature which critics most commonly accuse Freud of misrepresenting, namely Hoffmann's 'The Sand-Man'. Hélène Cixous and Neil Hertz, amongst others, have given detailed accounts of the shortcomings of Freud's interpretation of this novella, published in the 1919 essay 'The "Uncanny"'. Essentially, Freud focuses his plot synopsis exclusively around Nathaniel's 'castration complex', thus universalizing Hoffmann's multiple perspectives. The shifting viewpoints of the opening letters are disregarded, as, in fact, is Hoffmann's narrator; the only text Freud quotes is dialogue. He unravels the complex narrative to produce a linear account which rationalizes all the fantastic elements, the uncertainties, and the shifts of perspective used by Hoffmann to sustain essential ambiguities.[45] As Freud unwittingly admits: 'This short summary leaves no doubt' (XVII, 230). Later in 'The "Uncanny"' he does demonstrate a theoretical awareness of how a writer can create effects by keeping us in the dark about the nature of his narrative plane (XVII, 251). In his literary analysis, however, he does not consider the possibility that Hoffmann has systematically and ironically sustained the ambiguities in his novella.

The most problematic element of Freud's interpretation of 'The Sand-Man' is a footnote, over forty lines in length, which seems to have bypassed his usual pre-publication vetting of his own literary criticism (XVII, 232–3n.). His tactics of arrogant misrecognition are evident from the very opening sentence: 'In fact, Hoffmann's imaginative treatment of his material has not made such wild confusion of its elements that we cannot reconstruct their original arrangement.' In this 'original' arrangement all four adult males in the story are Nathaniel's 'father', and Olympia 'can be nothing else than a materialization of Nathaniel's feminine attitude towards his father in infancy'. However brilliant and original his analysis is, such a psychologizing approach strips away the delicate structure and ambiguities of a text which clearly had an uncomfortably powerful effect on Freud as a reader. There is little doubt that such disregard for what Rieff calls 'the autonomy of the aesthetic imagination'[46] constitutes a significant element of his counter-attack on *Dichter*.

The same footnote reveals much about an equally important element of Freud's literary-critical armoury. When he reads characters as psychic projections of Nathaniel, himself only another character existing on the same narrative plane, Freud overprivileges him as a character. This is particularly blatant when he describes Olympia as 'a dissociated complex of Nathaniel's'. In fact, Freud is implicitly assuming that all these characters are projections of *Hoffmann's* own psyche. It is no surprise that his only biographical reference to Hoffmann is contained in this very footnote. Here Freud mentions the author's life-long sensitivity about his father's abandonment of the family when Hoffmann was only three years old. Clearly, this single scrap of information is not in any way a premise of Freud's interpretation. Indeed, he has not made any study of Hoffmann's life; he has casually picked up this information from the biographical introduction to his copy of Hoffmann's works. His literary interpretations are never biographical in the sense that they use an author's life to 'explain' his works. On the contrary, Freud considers the ultimate goal of a literary interpretation to be access to otherwise unavailable information about the author's emotional life.

In his study of Michelangelo's *Moses* Freud claims that in order to be able to discover the 'intentions and emotional activities of the artist . . ., I must first find out the meaning and content of what is represented in his work' (XIII, 198). This implies that the interpretation of a work of art is a means to an end, the end being an analysis of the *artist*. A year earlier, in the 1913 paper 'The Claims of Psycho-Analysis to Scientific Interest', he writes:

The connection between the impressions of the artist's childhood and his life-history on the one hand and his works, as reactions to those impressions, on the other is one of the most attractive subjects of analytic examination. (XIII, 187)

For Freud, the hidden life of the artist is not just the most interesting element of a piece of art criticism, it is actually the most tempting object of psychoanalysis as a whole. In his 1914 history of the psychoanalytical movement he explains that his science has moved on from studying literature to studying writers themselves, and he openly admits that these latter studies are 'the most fascinating among the applications of psychoanalysis' (XIV, 37). Freud's claim here that literary psychobiography is a recent development is, moreover, blatantly inaccurate. His analysis of

C.F. Meyer's novella *Die Richterin* in an 1898 letter to Fliess is his first literary-critical essay, and its central subject is clearly Meyer himself.[47]
Even a year earlier, *Werther* is viewed in relation to its author's experiences, and, more significantly, Freud's interpretation of *Hamlet* is, ultimately, biographical. In *The Interpretation of Dreams* he writes: 'For it can
of course only be the poet's own mind which confronts us in Hamlet'
(IV, 265). Freud does not allow his drastic change of heart about
Shakespeare's identity to affect his interpretation of the *text* of the play
in the slightest, but in 1900 he reflects that the man from Stratford wrote
Hamlet just after his father's death, 'under the immediate impact of his
bereavement', whilst in 1938 his new 'Shakespeare' also fits the Hamlet
bill, and he points out that Edward de Vere 'lost a beloved and admired
father while he was still a boy and completely repudiated his mother,
who contracted a new marriage very soon after her husband's death'
(XXIII, 192n.). His bizarre combination of flexibility and inflexibility
here reveals much about his biographizing tendencies.

Adorno recognizes that psychoanalytical art criticism places the
emphasis on the individual producer of art. Although he fails to appreciate the epistemological subtlety of Freud's biographical concerns, he
does usefully remark that this emphasis at least frees art from its 'enthral-
ment to absolute spirit'.[48] Rieff makes a similar point when he describes
Freud's uncovering of not the higher, but the lower stratum of a text as
an 'inverse' hermeneutics.[49] It is this aspect of Freud's ultimately biographical approach which sheds most light on the dynamic tendency of
his literary criticism. His emphasis on the poet's person is a vital element
of his attempt to 'work through' the disturbingly powerful effect literary
texts have on him. It is Freud's revolt against his passive position in the
hands of this apparently self-creating Father-God. Richard Ellmann,
referring to the genre as a whole, but with specific reference to Freudian
techniques, accurately sums up this dynamic when he describes biography as a pious impiety.[50] Freud certainly has only scorn for those biographers whose infantile idealization of their subject admits of 'no vestige
of human weakness or imperfection' (XI, 130). He regards biography,
rather, as a means of escaping his own filial submission to artists. In his
agonistic 'riddle-solving' guise he views a literary text as a revealing
attempt to *conceal* weaknesses and imperfections. He may consider
Heine's Hirsch-Hyacinth to be Heine himself 'under a thin disguise'
(VIII, 141), but generally he believes a poet's mask is not so easily pene-
trable. For example, standing in front of his massive Weimar edition of
Goethe's works, he told Hanns Sachs: 'All this was used by him as a

means of self-concealment.'[51] Freud assumes that *Dichter* are compelled to write about themselves, but with the privilege of rearranging the material to suit their own needs and, ultimately, to recreate themselves. In his defiant attempt to eradicate this privilege, Freud trusts the tale – thus his biographical approach remains text-immanent – but never the teller. For example, he disregards Dostoevsky's account of his own illness, suggesting that the author may be attempting 'to interrupt disagreeable causal connections' (XXI, 182n.). Freud impiously restores such connections, if not demeaning the author, then at least democratizing relations with him.

Freud claims psychoanalysis illuminates art by examining what the artist shares in common with all men (das allgemein Menschliche) (XX, 65), and whilst this does not degrade artists as human beings, it does undermine all pretence to superhuman status. In *The Interpretation of Dreams* Freud refers to the physical humiliations his own father suffered on his death-bed, and he quotes two lines from Goethe's epilogue to Schiller's 'Das Lied von der Glocke', in which the poet refers to his dead friend:

> Und hinter ihm in wesenlosem Scheine
> lag, was uns alle bändigt, das Gemeine.
>
> (behind him, a shadowy illusion,
> lay what holds us all in bondage – the things that are common.)
> V, 428

This particular reference to *das allgemein Menschliche* points to a profound element of latent filial aggression. It involves not only his father's final humiliating physical collapse, but also, by extension, that of one of Freud's most highly revered poets, Schiller. A humiliation suffered by Goethe himself is re-enacted when, earlier in the same book, Freud quotes Herder's pun on the poet's name: 'Thou who art the offspring of gods or of Goths or of dung [Kote]', to which Freud responds immediately with a quotation from *Iphigenie*: 'So you too, divine figures [Götterbilder], have turned to dust' (IV, 207). This free association appears to confess the sacrilegious element of his own emphasis on the common mortality of his 'fathers', the dirt of their bodily existence and their inevitable return to dust. Of course, in his Leonardo book Freud quotes from Schiller precisely in order to *deny* that psychoanalysis seeks to 'blacken the radiant and drag the sublime into the dust'. He claims: 'there is no satisfaction for it in narrowing the gulf which separates the perfection of the great from the inadequacy of the objects that are its usual concern' (XI, 63). Nevertheless, this disclaimer is not unequivocally sincere. It is made in the opening paragraph of a text which, in fact, goes on to reveal Leonardo to be a narcissistic, infantile, obsessional, and frigid latent homosexual – traits evinced, moreover, by the very masterpieces on which his fame rests. Clearly, Freud's emphasis on *das Gemeine* constitutes an important vent for his ambivalence towards artists. The biographical element of his reading of *King Lear* actually highlights Shakespeare/de Vere's *paternal* inadequacies. In a 1934 letter Freud claims that the play concerns the Earl of Oxford's sense of guilt at having been a wretched father to his three daughters,[52] useful evidence, incidentally, that his Shakespearean 'family romance' does not serve only to ennoble the poet.

Freud is most honest about the ambivalent tendencies of analytic biography in his Goethe Prize speech. When he first answers the reproach that psychoanalysts have insulted Goethe by having 'degraded the great man to the position of an object of analytic investigation', he flatly denies that this constitutes a humiliation, and he makes his usual reverential declaration that no biography could ever explain either artistic talent or artistic effects: 'Even the best and fullest of them could not answer the two questions which alone would seem worth knowing about' (XXI, 211). The very subtle echo here of Freud's favourite *Faust* quotation may be designed to reinforce his expression of reverence, but it is an allusion to Mephistopheles' 'Das Beste, was du wissen kannst', the line which introduces the scene with the student in which the devil cynically and irreverently debunks any pretence to intellectual dignity. Eventually, Freud does indeed admit that there is something like a Mephistophelean dimension to all biographical curiosity:

All the same, we may admit that there is still another motive-force at work. . . . It is true that the biographer does not want to depose his hero, but he does want to bring him nearer to us. That means, however, reducing the distance that separates him from us: it still tends in effect towards degradation. And it is unavoidable that if we learn more about a great man's life we shall also hear of occasions on which he has in fact done no better than we, has in fact come near to us as a human being. (XXI, 211–12)

Crucially, this is the very paragraph in which Freud speaks of the inevitable ambivalence in all relationships to great men. Freud was initially requested to write an acceptance speech concerning his own personal relationship with Goethe.[53] His actual speech, however, both decisively shifts the emphasis onto Goethe as an object of psychobiographical analysis *and* all but admits that precisely this is a salient manifestation of the negative aspect of his ambivalence towards the great poet.

Freud's normally rather restrained biographical revelations are never intended simply to debunk the artist by revealing his human failings. The fundamental tendency of his approach is altogether more subtle and yet at least as aggressive. Freud has a powerful fascination with the source of the poet's material, his *Stoffwahl*. He believes that this 'choice' of material is, in fact, *determined* by the author's life history, and that it, in turn, determines the shape of the literary product. This emphasis on psychological determinism aims a severe blow at the heart of literary creativity. In the opening sentence of 'Creative Writers and Day-Dreaming' Freud avows his fascination and even seems to hint at its motive:

We laymen have always been intensely curious to know . . . from what sources that strange being, the creative writer, draws his material, and how he manages to make such an impression on us with it [uns mit ihnen so zu ergreifen]. (IX, 143)

He is, of course, extremely tentative about ascribing literary production to forces beyond the author's control, and he immediately acknowledges that no amount of insight into 'the determinants of his choice of material' could ever account for the poet's creativity. In his book on *Gradiva*, though, he cautiously admits

Since our hero, Norbert Hanold, is a fictitious person, we may perhaps put a timid question to his author, and ask whether his imagination was determined by forces other than its own arbitrary choice. (IX, 14–15)

In fact, faced with an author as unprepossessing as Jensen, Freud is far from timid. In the 1912 postscript he speaks of having plucked up sufficient courage to demand to know 'the material of impressions and memories from which the author has built the work' (IX, 94), and to Jung he admits 'I became indiscreet and asked for information about the subjective share of the work, where the material came from, where his own person is hidden etc.'[54]

When he has asked Jensen about the biographical element in his novella, he is disappointed that the author seems 'altogether incapable of entering into any other but his own poetic intentions'.[55] Freud actually wanted information about those determining biographical factors which were *beyond* Jensen's control. Evidently, he considers *Stoffwahl* to be no more a real 'choice' than *Neurosenwahl*. Indeed, with regard to a neurotic author such as Dostoevsky, Freud is far less tentative about elucidating biographical determinants. He writes at length about how Dostoevsky, in the thrall of his sense of guilt, has boundless sympathy for criminals, and he boldly asserts: 'There is no doubt that this sympathy by identification was a decisive factor in determining Dostoevsky's choice of material' (XXI, 190). However, it is not only lowbrow or neurotic authors who are subjected to banal, biographical determinants. In a 1917 introductory lecture Freud's confidence in its universal validity gives him the courage to make the general statement that the Oedipus complex is a major determinant (höchst bestimmend) of literary production as a whole (XVI, 337). In 1928 he writes: 'It can scarcely be owing to chance that three of the masterpieces of the literature of all time . . . should all deal with the same subject, parricide' (XXI, 188); and in *The Interpretation of Dreams* he almost presumes to give advice to writers: 'an author who, like Ibsen, brings the immemorial struggle between fathers and sons into prominence in his writings may be certain of producing his effect' (IV, 257). This latter claim implies that literary effects are grounded primarily in *Stoffwahl*, this being the dynamite for which the *ars poetica* is merely the technique of controlled detonation. If the raw material both determines literary effects and is itself determined by biographical factors beyond the author's volitional control, then Freud can convince himself that he is seized, overwhelmed, and so on not by the will of the poet, but by universal psychological truths to which the poet, too, is subject. Naturally, he denies that this deterministic emphasis is degrading to artists. In his Leonardo biography he writes: 'there is no one so great as to be disgraced by being subject to the laws which govern both normal and pathological activity with equal cogency' (XI, 63). Nevertheless, as this contention is made in the opening paragraph of the essay, it is reasonable to speculate that it belongs to that group of statements which screen a hostile intent. The 'screen', in fact, is somewhat transparent. Freud seems to be echoing Goethe's Prometheus, who defiantly goads Zeus by referring to universal powers which are 'my masters and yours'.

The truly Promethean aspect of Freud's 'biographical determinism' is the question mark it places over the cherished notion of artistic creativity. If an author's *Stoffwahl* is indeed determined by his life history, then creativity ceases to denote the invention of something wholly new and becomes inextricably bound up with the author's *past*. Freud delivers his most iconoclastic blow when he claims: 'The "creative" imagination, indeed, is quite incapable of *inventing* anything; it can only combine components that are strange to one another' (XV, 172; original emphasis). The central process of creativity, then, is 'condensation', the superimposition of banal 'day residues' over each other. When he fails to convince the novelist Arnold Zweig of his dubious Shakespeare theory, Freud becomes almost irritated: 'That all Shakespeare's material is second-hand . . . is, for me, inconceivable.'[56] He is implying that the petty bourgeois, provincial actor simply did not have a rich enough *life* to give rise to Shakespeare's oeuvre. This conception, according to which the poet cannot recreate himself, nor even transcend the conditioning cause-and-effect of his own life history, aims a powerful blow at the ideology of the poet as sovereign Father-God. The determinism underlying Freud's interest in *Stoffwahl* robs the poet both of the freedom *from* his own biography and of the freedom *to* create.

THE UNCONSCIOUS ANALYST: A BLOOMIAN PERSPECTIVE

Freud's impious emphasis on biographical determinism exists directly alongside his genuine reverence for poets, giving rise to unresolved contradictions in his practice of literary criticism. For example, on the very same page on which he vaunts Hebbel's analytical powers with regard to the biblical story of Judith, he also refers to an analysis by his pupil Sadger which demonstrates 'how Hebbel was determined in his choice of material by his own parental complex'. This biographical element is even used to explain Hebbel's profound empathy for women; thus the author not only has his creativity, but also his very masculinity questioned by this 'penetrating analysis'. Screened by his pupil, Freud even dares to doubt Hebbel's analytical powers. Sadger claims the author's pretended motive for altering the biblical narrative is 'artificial and as though intended to justify *outwardly* something the poet himself is unconscious of, while at bottom concealing it' (XI, 207–8). Admittedly, Freud takes Sadger's theory of an infantile fantasy of the virgin mother no further, returning to his elucidation of the author's 'sensitive imagination'. His ambivalence is, as always, finely balanced. Nevertheless, his suggestion that Hebbel is unconscious even of his own poetic analysis belongs to a particularly virulent line of attack.

When his subject is a painter, Freud himself makes the point quite explicitly. Of Leonardo he writes: 'Kindly nature has given the artist the ability to express his most secret impulses, which are hidden even from himself, by means of the works that he creates' (XI, 107). With regard to writers, this emphasis tends to be more muted. Having just read Arnold Zweig's novel *Erziehung vor Verdun*, Freud can scarcely conceal his envy, and he showers the author with questions about his creative powers such as: 'By what means does one conjure a Sister Klara into existence?' The backlash is delivered, however, when he continues: 'It would be interesting to question you sometime about the "day residues" which have gone into this literary creation.'[57] Thus Freud admires creativity only to undermine it, both by anchoring it to the author's own past history and by paralleling it with the unconscious processes of dream-work.

Freud's book on wit asserts that not only content, but also form itself is attributable to the unconscious. He describes the process of joke creation thus: '*a preconscious thought is given over for a moment to unconscious revision*' (VIII, 166). Admittedly, the 'primary' formal modification must be carefully controlled and easily traced back, but only because wit is 'the most social of all the mental functions that aim at a yield of pleasure' (VIII, 179). The implication is that literature is less social than wit, therefore closer – in terms of conscious comprehensibility, if not of sophistication – to the dream. Thus, there is some ambiguity in, say, Freud's implication that *Hamlet* is more subtle than *Oedipus*, the oedipal wish-fantasy being fully realized in the Greek drama, whereas in Shakespeare's play it is present only in its inhibiting consequences. This does not necessarily denote Shakespeare's aesthetic or analytical superiority over Sophocles, it simply represents 'the secular advance of repression in the emotional life of mankind' (IV, 264) – in other words, the Elizabethans were more repressed than the Greeks. Freud's famous letter to Fliess about Shakespeare does indeed indicate only that 'his unconscious understood the unconscious of his hero'.[58]

According to Rieff, Freud's literary-critical approach elevates interpretation into a necessity by positing a generic source of meaning that is unconscious.[59] Freud admits as much in his analysis of Stefan Zweig's novella:

It is characteristic of the nature of artistic creation that the author, who is a personal friend of mine, was able to assure me, when I asked him, that the interpretation which I put to him had been completely strange to his knowledge and intention. (XXI, 192)

Having Zweig's own testimony that the essential element of literary meaning is unconscious to the author and yet conscious to the psychoanalyst, Freud can simultaneously respect and humble the author here. In fact, Freud positively prefers to believe that an author would, like a patient, *resist* the analyst's interpretation. Of the meanings he imputes to Jensen, he writes:

Our opinion is that the author need have known nothing of these rules and purposes, so that he could disavow them in good faith, but that nevertheless we have not discovered anything in his work that is not already in it. (IX, 91–2)

Accordingly, Freud claims that Jensen responded 'in the negative, and, indeed, somewhat brusquely' to the analysis of his novella (IX, 91), but, in a letter to Freud, Jensen denies this, adding:

here and there you do in fact read things into the novella which the author did not have in mind, at least, not consciously. But on the whole, in all the most important respects, I can confirm without reservation that your essay thoroughly gets to the bottom of and does justice to the intentions of my little book.[60]

It seems Freud has deliberately msinterpreted Jensen's response as gruffly dismissive in order to imply he is an unconscious fantasist who, like any analysand, 'denies' the hidden intentions he cannot help but reveal. He can only be embarrassed by the suggestion that his analysis merely elucidates the author's conscious poetic intentions.

A fascinating example of the pitfalls generated by Freud's assumption that authors are largely unconscious of the meanings they create is provided by his analysis of Goethe's childhood memory from *Dichtung und Wahrheit*, in which the infant Goethe smashes the household crockery by throwing it into the street. Freud's eagerness to find the meaning of this earliest memory, and thus 'the key to the secret pages of his mind' (XVII, 149), seems to have led him astray. He insists that before the advent of psychoanalysis such a memory would never have been interpreted. It is not only indifferent, it is actually alien to Goethe's later life:

the episode does not seem in itself to admit of any traceable connection with important impressions at a later date. A mischievous trick with damaging effects on the household economy, carried out under the spur of outside encouragement, is certainly no fitting head-piece for all that Goethe has to tell us of his richly filled life. (XVII, 149)

Furthermore, Freud reads Goethe's stilted description of a motive for the act of destruction as 'a confession that at the time of writing it down . . . he was not aware of any adequate motive for his behaviour' (XVII, 150). Having established that Goethe is unconscious of the meaning of a passage in his own autobiography, Freud goes on to translate the memory into rational dialogue, ultimately: '"My strength has its roots in my relation to my mother"' (XVII, 156). Nevertheless, the childhood memory is, in fact, a singularly pertinent vignette for another reason, and Goethe's own wording suggests that he is fully conscious of this deeper meaning. Firstly, he acknowledges that childhood memories are often embellished, and he emphasizes that this one was 'narrated' to him by his family. His description of the event then centres on the vicarious pleasure enjoyed by his eager audience, whose 'applause' and whose calls for encores inspire him to provide 'an even finer show [Schauspiel]'. Finally, in return for the devastation caused by this public exposure of something fragile, something usually kept inside, Goethe concludes that he has at least provided entertainment: 'there was at least an amusing story, which the rascals who had been its instigators enjoyed to the end of their lives' (XVII, 148). Freud's dubious presumption that he can provide the conscious meaning of Goethe's 'unconscious' utterances has caused him to overlook the fact that the poet considers this memory – an apocryphal account of his first piece of theatre – to be an ideal prologue to his life story.

Freud's 1898 analysis of Meyer's *Die Richterin* reveals perhaps the most reprehensible aspect of his need to consider himself conscious of what remains unconscious to *Dichter*, in other words his urge to *diagnose*. He describes the novella as a 'poetic defence' which 'proceeds *exactly* as it does in neurosis'.[61] In 1898, of course, defence was still merely a synonym for pathological repression. This diagnostic tendency is *not* essential to Freud's literary criticism. In fact, it long preceded his creation of psychoanalysis. Tellingly, it can be traced back as far as his engagement to Martha, to whom Freud wrote a letter which relates *La Tentation de Saint Antoine* to Flaubert's hallucinatory epilepsy.[62] Freud is actually well aware that diagnosis can serve aggressive tendencies, and he keeps a correspondingly tight rein on it. Only in his study of the manifestly neurotic Dostoevsky does he give full vent to his diagnostic urge, going as far as to read *The Brothers Karamazov* as an unconscious confession 'that the epileptic, the neurotic, in himself was a parricide' (XXI, 189). Even in the case of Dostoevsky Freud feels the need to erect, with the last sentence of his essay, a screen for his own aggression. He claims, with excessive modesty, that most of his conclusions have been prefigured by Jolan Neufeld's work in a 1923 issue of *Imago*. The 'cover' provided by this attempt to displace priority onto a pupil is, in fact, easily stripped away. A letter to Stefan Zweig written in 1920 demonstrates that Freud had already ascertained what, in 1928, he arrogantly calls 'the formula for Dostoevsky' (XXI, 185), namely his crippling guilt from oedipal ambivalence, his masochism, his hysterical epilepsy, and so on. To Zweig, of course, he makes the usual disclaimer:

With you I do not have to fear the misunderstanding that this emphasis on the so-called pathological is intended to belittle or explain away the splendour of D.'s creative power.[63]

Nevertheless, he reveals the essence of the master/slave dialectic he subtly tries to impose on his relationships with authors when, in the very same letter, he speaks of 'the psychopathologist, whose property Dostoievski must inevitably remain'.

Freud's emphasis on the neuroticism of the artist is very much a marginal aspect of his ambivalent counter-attack on them. More significant are his repeated allusions to the, albeit healthy, *infantilism* of artistic activity. Although this emphasis is inherent in psychoanalysis as a whole, Freud's biographical interest in authors is almost exclusively confined to their earliest childhood. His reference to Hoffmann's life begins: 'Hoffmann was the child of an unhappy marriage' (XVII, 232n.). In fact, his only other mention of Hoffmann reduces him to 'an infant at his mother's breast', receiving a wealth of impressions which would subsequently determine the extent of his creativity (XXIII, 126). Hoffmann may himself authorize this account, but Freud is particularly gratified by the juxtaposition of infancy and creativity. His insistence on the importance of the Oedipus complex in literature, for example, is much more concerned with infancy than it is with pathology; *Oedipus, Hamlet*, and *The Brothers Karamazov* are all traced back to what Freud calls the 'primaeval wishes of our childhood' (IV, 262). In his *Hamlet* analysis he does briefly refer to the death of Shakespeare's own son, Hamnet, but his conception of 'the deepest layer of impulses in the mind of the creative writer' pertains solely to the dramatist's own infancy. The play was written in response to the death of his father, therefore 'while his childhood feelings about his father had been freshly revived' (IV, 265).

Similarly, Freud's biographical essay on Goethe centres on a childhood memory; thus he deals not with the great poet, but with Goethe as a little boy (der kleine Goethe). By itself, this is not necessarily demeaning. Nevertheless, in his essay on Leonardo, which is again structured around a childhood memory, Freud writes:

Indeed, the great Leonardo remained like a child for the whole of his life in more than one way; it is said that all great men are bound to retain some infantile part. (XI, 127)

If there is an aggressive tendency underlying this pathography, its salient aspect concerns Leonardo's infantilism, which, unlike his mild obsessional neurosis, say, or his latent homosexuality, provokes something like a reproach from Freud. In this text even the revered capacity for sublimation is traced back to infantile sexual curiosity. This general tendency does not pertain only to Leonardo. Indeed, Freud confides to Stefan Zweig that the entire range of literary themes can be traced back to a small number of primal motifs, above all, childhood fantasies.[64]

It is no indignity for a poet to concentrate on infantile material; indeed, he has this in common with the psychoanalyst, who, presumably, is also driven by a sublimation of infantile sexual curiosity. Nevertheless, the poet differs from the analyst in his *aesthetic* treatment of this material, and Freud gives many indications that aesthetic activities are themselves fundamentally infantile. In *Jokes and their Relation to the Unconscious*, play is regarded as the infantile predecessor of mature wit. This play is quintessential to all aesthetic activity – for example, the treatment of words as objects derives from infancy, as does the predilection for repetition which is fundamental to rhyme, refrain, and alliteration (VIII, 121–2). The more obsessed the artist is with aesthetic concerns, the more infantile is his activity. In a letter to Jones Freud complains about a group of artists with whom he has spent an evening: 'Meaning is but little with these men, all they care about is line, shape, agreement of contours. They are given up to the *Lustprinzip*.'[65] Ultimately, the fore-pleasure principle, essential to Freud's conception of aesthetics, relates to foreplay, and thus to polymorphously perverse *infantile* sexuality.

'Creative Writers and Day-Dreaming' systematizes these various suggestions. Here Freud claims: 'The creative writer does the same as the child at play' (IX, 144). He is acutely aware that his readers will find this emphasis disparaging, hence the restriction of his thesis to lowbrow authors. Nevertheless, this act of deference paves the way for an entirely irreverent account of the similarity between literary creativity and child's play, or rather its adult counterpart, fantasy. Artistic activity is repeatedly viewed by Freud as a kind of daydreaming. It is only undertaken by 'a man who is consumed by [erotic and ambitious] desires' (XIII, 90) who is unable to adjust to unsatisfying reality. Although it engenders real satisfaction, this is achieved 'without following the long roundabout path of making real alterations in the external world'. Thus, only indirectly does the artist actually become 'the hero, the king, the creator, the favourite he desired to be' (XII, 224). At the centre of all these fantasies Freud discerns 'His Majesty the Ego, the hero alike of every day-dream and of every story' (IX, 150). In this scheme, then, art is ineluctably hedonistic and egotistical.

Freud is fully aware that sophisticated works of literature have evolved far beyond these blind, narcissistic fantasies, but he can scarcely conceal his gratification when pointing out the family resemblance:

We are perfectly aware that very many imaginative writings are far removed from the model of the naive day-dream; and yet I cannot suppress the suspicion that even the most extreme deviations from that model could be linked with it through an uninterrupted series of transitional cases. (IX, 150)

This is no mere abstract hypothesis; it is an emphasis present at the heart of his literary criticism. His analysis of Stefan Zweig's novella, for example, reveals 'that its invention is based fundamentally upon a wishful phantasy belonging to the period of puberty' (XXI, 193). And, whilst Ibsen's masterfully analytical *Rosmersholm* may represent the greatest work of art of its class, it, too, is descended from a 'common phantasy' (XIV, 331). Despite the fact that Ibsen has portrayed an essentially female fantasy, Freud apparently assumes that a poet is incapable of genuine objectivity. Of the central character of 'what are known as "psychological" novels', he writes: 'The author sits inside his mind, as it were'; and where the narrative consciousness appears to be a detached observer, as in Zola's later novels, Freud feels he 'must' mention certain 'individuals who are not creative writers, and who diverge in some respects from the so-called norm' – in other words, patients – who have fantasies in which their ego plays the role of an observer (IX, 150–1). Clearly, the *Dichter*, however distantly related to the blinkered fantasist, is congenitally incapable of observing reality with any kind of objectivity. He will always be impeded by the desire which motivates his productions.

In a letter to Jung Freud gives full vent to this vaguely contemptuous condescension. He cites Jensen's comment that he wrote *Gradiva* without having to think as *proof* that it was driven by repressed infantile sexual impulses, and concludes: 'So the whole thing is once again an egocentric phantasy'.[66] Kofman argues that Freud elevates poets into fathers only then to reveal them, by means of analysis, to be children.[67] This tendency, again reminiscent of Goethe's Prometheus who scorns Zeus for his childishness, is certainly an important element of Freud's ambivalent attitude. Nevertheless, Kofman's portrayal is often too one-sided. For Freud, the infant's psyche is by no means merely an inferior version of the adult's. In *The Future of an Illusion*, for example, he writes: 'Think of the depressing contrast between the radiant intelligence of a healthy child and the feeble intellectual powers of the average adult' (XXI, 47). Nor is Freud's filial reverence for the poet merely a polemical strategy. Again Kofman fails to recognize the subtlety of the ambivalence which she correctly identifies.

Nevertheless, the most exquisitely ambivalent aspect of Freud's attitude towards *Dichter*, his conception of their status as proto-psychoanalysts, is incisively appraised by Kofman. She does not simply claim that Freud looks at the 'childhood of art', she also elucidates how Freud reads literature *as* 'l'enfance de l'art', namely as a primitive mode of psychoanalysis. Freud thereby both pays homage to literature *and* imperiously reduces it to the status of an early, imperfect attempt at science. Kofman claims, for example, that Freud's analysis of 'The Sand-Man' arrogantly inscribes an ambiguous text into an exterior and anterior 'analytic truth'.[68] The insights which Freud imputes to poets are indeed almost always articles of psychoanalytical faith, a strategy which Trilling also condemns for its 'covert denial of the autonomy of literature'.[69] Such a utilitarian emphasis causes art as a whole to lose its dignified independent status. Freud all but suggests that Leonardo's artistic activity is mere child's play when measured against his scientific researches 'which represented the latest and highest expansion of his personality' (XI, 128–9). It is, therefore, actually Freud's own love of literature which appears to fulfil the stipulation he ascribes to Leonardo:

one *should* love in such a way as to hold back the affect, subject it to the process of reflection and only let it take its course when it has stood up to the test of thought. (XI, 74)

This is certainly the case for the pleasure he derives from Jensen's *Gradiva*. The novella has only limited aesthetic merit, its real value lies in its corroboration of psychoanalytical law, hence Freud's appreciation of it as a 'perfectly correct psychiatric study' (IX, 43). In a transparently polemical passage Freud claims that the novella not only passes muster 'before the judgement of science', but that science 'cannot hold its own before the achievement of the author' (IX, 53). Of course, the only science to which *Gradiva* is superior is the non-psychoanalytical variety. That it is inferior to psychoanalysis is subtly indicated by Freud's insinuation that Jensen's insight is somehow only 'preconscious': 'How was it that the author arrived at the same knowledge as the doctor – or at least behaved as though he possessed the same knowledge?' (IX, 54).

Freud most appreciates *Dichter* when they behave like scientists. For instance, his praise of Zola as 'a keen observer of human nature' (VII, 239n.) and 'a fanatic for the truth' (XVI, 260) is not specific to any literary qualities he may possess. Diderot seems to be appraised in similar terms. In Freud's later works a passage from *Le Neveu de Rameau* is allowed to join the ranks of *Hamlet* and *Oedipus* in expositions of Oedipus complex theory; in fact, it is especially privileged by being quoted in full.

Nevertheless, Freud is primarily attracted by the *discursive* nature of the passage. It offers little indication of its literary origins; indeed, it is strikingly devoid of any 'aesthetic' strategies of displacement. It could almost be a statement of fact made in a scientific – that is, a psychoanalytical – discourse:

If the little savage were left to himself, preserving all his foolishness and adding to the small sense of a child in the cradle the violent passions of a man of thirty, he would strangle his father and lie with his mother. (XVI, 338)

The privilege enjoyed by this passage, 'which was rendered into German by no less a person than Goethe', owes just as much to the vicarious sanction Freud thus receives from his favourite poet. Before conjecturing about how Goethe himself would have viewed psychoanalysis, Freud surreptitiously loads the dice by referring to the poet as 'attentive to every innovation in science' (XXI, 208). Thus, despite Goethe's many poetic anticipations of psychoanalytical insights, Freud believes it is the scientist in Goethe who will endorse psychoanalysis. His emphasis on the poet as analyst does not, therefore, admit of any direct literary influence. When he points out that a passage in Goethe's poem 'An den Mond' anticipates his own theory of the unconscious meaning of dreams, he is careful to add that 'the riddle of dream-distortion finds no solution here' (XXI, 209). This piece of one-upmanship asserts both Freud's independence from and superiority over the poetic insight.

Adorno claims that, by its exclusive privileging of the reality principle, psychoanalysis is an 'anti-aestheticism'.[70] Aesthetic qualities are, indeed, cast in a somewhat unflattering light by Freud's praise for the poet as psychoanalyst. In a letter to Arthur Schnitzler, he implies a more or less complete divorce between the novelist's artistic talents and the insights *beneath* his poetic surface 'which I know to be my own'.[71] Aesthetic technique, then, is neither an end in itself nor is it a means to any kind of autonomous signification. The fore-pleasure it generates is not even required by the hardened analyst; it becomes a mere façade to be stripped away. Freud is therefore surprised that Jensen appears to have produced a straightforward and correct case history, 'as though the author's mind were an absolutely transparent medium and not a refractive or obscuring one' (IX, 41). A literary text is fundamentally an egotistical fantasy, and it would, by itself, merely provoke shame in the poet and revulsion in the audience. The poet's 'innermost secret', then, and 'the essential *ars poetica*' consist in the overcoming of this revulsion (IX,

153). By apparently mystifying the *Dichter* here, Freud manages simultaneously to portray him as a mere disguiser of something shameful.

Of course, the greatest poets courageously reveal uncomfortable truths. Sophocles, who has Oedipus acknowledge and punish his crime, is the 'most honest'. To this high praise of the dramatist Freud adds: 'But poetic treatment is impossible without softening and disguise.' In this case, the 'indispensable toning-down' consists of the projection of desires onto an external fate (XXI, 188). In *The Interpretation of Dreams* Freud dismisses the play's 'theological purposes', writing: 'Its further modification originates once again in a misconceived secondary revision of the material' (IV, 264). In fact, a poetic treatment is not just misleading, but can be positively mendacious. With regard to Zweig's 'Four-and-Twenty Hours in a Woman's Life', Freud points out 'how the *façade* given to the story by its author seeks to disguise its analytic meaning' (XXI, 193). This mendacity is sometimes portrayed as a self-seeking and fraudulent act of bribery:

The writer softens the character of his egoistic day-dreams by altering and disguising it, and he bribes us by the purely formal – that is, aesthetic – yield of pleasure which he offers us in the presentation of his phantasies. (IX, 153)

This aesthetic bribery paves the way for the 'actual enjoyment', namely forbidden releases of instinctual tension. Even in his mythopoeic speculation, Freud's emphasis on literature as transgressive and, above all, deceitful is sustained. In a highly speculative supplement to his *Group Psychology and the Analysis of the Ego* he suggests that the first epic poet was a prehistoric son who, wishing to supplant the primal father, invented the heroic myth in order to give vent to his parricidal desires: 'This poet disguised the truth with lies in accordance with his longing' (XVIII, 136).

Freud was by no means insensitive to aesthetic effects, rather he found them uncomfortably hypnotic. He is certainly speaking for himself when he writes: 'People who are receptive to the influence of art cannot set too high a value on it as a source of pleasure and consolation in life.' He retaliates, however, by going on to set up an opposition between aesthetic pleasure and Ananke: 'Nevertheless the mild narcosis induced in us by art can do no more than bring about a transient withdrawal from the pressure of vital needs' (XXI, 81). Art's very pleasurableness, then, distances it from reality. This is quite distinct from the alienation from reality which characterizes neurosis, but both fall short of the realism of science. Jensen's Norbert Hanold is a scientist, but he lets his profession down when he becomes fixated on his fantasies: 'This division between imagination and intellect destined him to become an artist or a neurotic; he was one of those whose kingdom is not of this world' (IX, 14). In fact, Freud cannot even cede sovereignty to the poet in his own realm. In a letter to Arnold Zweig referring to the problematic relationship between poetic licence and historical reality, Freud claims that the author should be allowed complete freedom where the historical facts are not known or are obscure: 'On the other hand he should respect reality when the facts are established.'[72] Correspondingly, he calls G.B. Shaw a fool for his inaccurate portrayal of Caesar, and even Goethe and Schiller are implicitly reproached for failing to comply with these 'rules'.

By subordinating aesthetic pleasure to the reality principle, Freud undermines even the proto-scientific insights he freely attributes to poets. What he values most in art are qualities specific not to art, but to his own scientific profession. As for specifically aesthetic concerns, the artist can only be hampered by them. In the introductory paragraph of his 1910 paper 'A Special Type of Choice of Object made by Men', immediately after speaking of the sensitivity, insight, and courage evinced by poets in their portrayal of human love, Freud continues:

> But there is one circumstance which lessens the evidential value of what he has to say. Writers are under the necessity to produce intellectual and aesthetic pleasure, as well as certain emotional effects. For this reason they cannot reproduce the stuff of reality unchanged, but must also isolate portions of it, remove disturbing associations, tone down the whole and fill in what is missing. These are the privileges of what is known as 'poetic licence'. . . . In consequence it becomes inevitable that science should concern herself with the same materials whose treatment by artists has given enjoyment to mankind for thousands of years, though her touch must be clumsier and the yield of pleasure less. (XI, 165)

Freud's abasement of his own métier here cannot disguise the fact that he is actually enjoying the ultimate revenge on *Dichter*. Not only are even the best poetic insights unreliable, it is the very pleasure generated by their aesthetic formulation which compromises them. Furthermore, the poet is constrained to make this compromise – it is a 'condition' to which he must passively submit. Freud has good reason, then, for placing poetic licence in quotation marks, a typographical device he reserves for his most aggressive ironic sideswipes. Finally, that Freud should portray the poet's privileges as obstacles to his insight into – of all things – human love constitutes the *ne plus ultra* of this counter-attack. Freud not only takes revenge on poets for their pleasurable and effortless insights, their universal popularity, and their freedom to create, he also evens the score against them as envied sexual rivals, a grudge dating back to his long and arduous engagement with Martha.

With the final sentence of this apparently gratuitous opening paragraph Freud delivers the fatal blow: 'Science is, after all, the most complete renunciation of the pleasure principle of which our mental activity is capable' (XI, 165). In the essay on *Gradiva* Freud explains that poets have superior knowledge 'for they draw upon sources which we have *not yet* opened up for science' (IX, 8, my emphasis). But because art only finds a compromise between pleasure and reality, whereas science represents a complete victory over the pleasure principle, the implication is that psychoanalysis will not only catch up with *Dichter*, but ultimately supersede them. Freud did not generally recommend therapy to artists lest it sap their creativity. As Rieff comments, therapy renders art much less necessary.[73] If the psychoanalytical ideals of Logos and Ananke were ever realized, it can only be assumed that art would be rendered all but obsolete. What Freud values most in poets, their psychological knowledge, is undermined precisely by the literary treatment and presentation of this knowledge to which the poet is bound. Consequently, only psychoanalysis can complete the work which great poets have begun.

The way Freud vaunts literature for its corroboration of psychoanalysis only then to point out how this corroboration is inherently inadequate appears to be related to the rhetorical strategy which Harold Bloom calls 'tessera', a strong misprision whereby a poet antithetically 'completes' a precursor. The 'revisionary ratios' which he propounds in *The Anxiety of Influence* are, in fact, singularly pertinent to Freud's misrecognition of his literary precursors. For example, he defines 'kenosis' as an apparent humbling of the self which actually screens an aggressive humbling of the precursor. Equally relevant is 'apophrades', a strategy whereby the latecomer holds his own work open to that of the precursor in such a way as to make it seem as though, uncannily, he has written the precursor's work.[74] Bloom actually points to the Freudian theory of the family romance as a model for the relations between 'strong' poets and their literary predecessors.[75] Interestingly, Freud elucidates a particular aspect of the family romance in 'A Special Type of Choice of Object made by Men', the very text onto which he appears to have grafted that most Bloomian opening passage about writers. *Dichter* reappear in the reference to the element of the family romance which Freud goes on to discuss, namely the 'rescue-motif'. Here the son fantasizes about rescuing his father in order to settle the account for owing him his life, a motif which, when slightly displaced, Freud claims 'may even be made use of by creative writers' (XI, 172–3). In fact, it seems to be particularly germane to Freud's own treatment of his literary 'fathers'. He presumes to redeem the poet's illusory and escapist fantasies by demonstrating their corroboration of psychoanalytical truth. Thus, Freud reappropriates his predecessors on his own terms by causing them to owe *him* for the psychoanalytical doctrine which retroactively confers value on their work. Needless to say, this act of 'rescue' screens Freud's fundamentally aggressive desire to rid himself of his own indebtedness, hence his insinuations that the poet's highly valuable corroboration of psychoanalysis is, nonetheless, inherently inferior, being biographically determined, infantile, mendacious, hedonistic, and, most damningly, not even altogether conscious.

The veiled hostility of Freud's various strategies for humbling the *Dichter* must, however, always be viewed in the context of his genuine respect for literature. Despite its fragmentary nature, Freud's literary criticism evinces a profound understanding of the nature of literary meaning. In his approaches to literary *texts*, he is both sensitive and innovative. Indeed, Rieff partly attributes the twentieth century's 'efflorescence of academic literary criticism' directly to Freud.[76] The *Dichter* themselves, however, represent significant father-figures to him and are, perhaps inevitably, subjected to a wide variety of postures, ranging from devout prostration to jealous and contemptuous iconoclasm. This latter is more covert than is generally recognized; Freud most decidedly does not simply equate poet and neurotic. He *sublimates*, so to speak, the aggressive component of his ambivalence, and therefore his counter-attack on the privileges and powers of the *Dichter* is manifested only through subtle and ambiguous traces within his own literary-critical texts. His extensive literary cultivation cannot help but engender in him a sophisticated literary awareness and a profound, authentic reverence for *Dichter*, which nevertheless coexists with a latent, but virulent Promethean revolt. Freud's relationship to his literary idols can only be understood in terms of this sublime, yet ultimately intractable ambivalence.

CHAPTER THREE

The literary-critical paradigm: sources of Freud's hermeneutic

GRADIVA AND THE RETURN OF THE REPRESSED

Two paradoxes regarding the relevance of Freud's theories to the practice of literary criticism are often noted by critics. The first is that, although he considered himself to be a natural scientist, indulging only occasionally in literary criticism as an amateur, his pretension to scientific status has been widely discredited, whilst his influence has saturated most spheres of literary criticism. The second is that literary critics are almost invariably more interested in texts in which Freud does *not* directly address literature. *The Interpretation of Dreams* and *Jokes and their Relation to the Unconscious* are most popular with literary critics, but Bloom, for example, is equally interested in *Inhibitions, Symptoms and Anxiety*, whilst Peter Brooks looks to *Beyond the Pleasure Principle* for specifically literary insights.[1] This could be explained most easily by pointing to the correspondences between the 'primary processes' of unconscious thought and the stylistic features of literary writing. However, I wish to shed light on these paradoxes from a rather different angle. It seems to me that the effects of psychoanalysis were felt most forcefully in the literary sphere because the roots of Freud's 'scientific' practice were themselves literary in a very specific way.

As we have seen, Freud rarely allows himself to indulge in literary criticism for its own sake. He always justifies himself by framing his analyses, however flimsily, in specifically psychological studies. Nevertheless, he cannot disguise just how attractive he finds the idea of analysing literary texts. In a 1907 letter to Jung he describes literary criticism as a 'territory that we have barely touched upon so far, but where I might easily settle down'.[2] Despite this claim, evidence suggests that the practice of literary criticism is, in fact, *essential* to psychoanalysis, not just as a diversion in its creator's twilight years, but from its very inception. Indeed, it is tempting to say that literary criticism is, to some extent, the mother of psychoanalysis, vitally procreative and yet taboo. Clearly, even when intended only metaphorically, such a claim smacks of 'wild' analysis, but to justify it I shall look in detail at Freud's creation of a hermeneutic.

Freud would not have denied that his practice of interpretation had libidinal origins. The imagery he uses to describe it, such as uncovering and exposing, tends to indicate voyeuristic motives. A disguise must be undone, a fabric unravelled, or a screen removed in order to reveal the naked truth.[3] This is particularly true of literary studies which, it will be remembered, Freud calls 'the most fascinating [die reizvollsten] among the applications of psycho-analysis' and 'one of the most attractive subjects [anziehendste Objekte] of analytic examination'. In 'Creative Writers and Day-Dreaming' he admits he is 'intensely curious' (mächtig gereizt) to understand more about creative writing, and immediately after this he lets slip something even more interesting: 'If we could at least discover in ourselves or in people like ourselves an activity which was in some way akin to creative writing!' (IX, 143). Of course, Freud only means that he can use the fantasy as a parallel model with which to understand literature, but the statement opens up the possibility that literature itself has actually supplied Freud with a paradigm for understanding other phenomena. Literature was, after all, the earliest and the most pleasurable object of interpretation for Freud, the self-confessed bookworm. To suggest that this first and most attractive object was the 'mother' which gave birth to his interpretative method may lead to nothing more than a hopelessly mixed metaphor. Nevertheless, Freud clearly both desired and in his own written works largely avoided (or at least disguised his indulgence in) this primal source of pleasure.

If literary interpretation is a form of quasi-sexual gratification which Freud repressed, it is worth remembering his own theory that no one can renounce a source of pleasure without adopting some form of substitute. Furthermore, this very substitute will tend to be the site of the return of the repressed. After the strictly medical application of his newly invented science of psychoanalysis, his major works seem to offer evidence of just such a return. The sequence *Studies on Hysteria* (1895), *The Interpretation of Dreams* (1900), *The Psychopathology of Everyday Life* (1901), *Jokes and their Relation to the Unconscious* (1905), and 'Delusions and Dreams in Jensen's *Gradiva*' (1907) seems to bespeak a graduation from the pathological to the more sophisticated – ultimately, literary – dialects of the unconscious. Freud was himself aware that this was a 'regressive development'. In 1935 he writes of it:

My interest, after making a lifelong *détour* through the natural sciences, medicine and psychotherapy, returned to the cultural problems which had fascinated me long before, when I was a youth scarcely old enough for thinking. (XX, 72)

Yet his own theory of the return of the repressed suggests a rather more radical dynamic: his suppressed literary urges would not just eventually reassert themselves, they would, from the very outset, be unconsciously present *within* his clinical work, the rigorous 'science' with which he tried to subdue them.

Freud offers an excellent example of the return of the repressed in his *Gradiva* analysis. He tells of a patient who attempted to renounce women by immersing himself in mathematics. The attempt failed when mathematical formulae themselves started making sexual allusions (IX, 36). Freud's paper on Jensen's novella is itself a fascinating example of how the 'repressed' – the practice of literary criticism – overwhelms this ostensibly purely psychological study of 'correctly' formulated delusions and dreams. Freud's initial intention is to look only at these respectable objects of clinical analysis, but he ends up analysing the entire novella, with the central emphasis on specifically literary criticism. He explains this away by claiming that he also needs to know a patient's life story before he can interpret a single dream. However, the entanglement goes much deeper than this. It is as if Freud's method has returned to its literary-critical origins, invigorated Antaeus-like by this contact with the mother country.

In the analysis Freud uses associations in narrative detail instead of his usual interpretative tool of the analysand's free associations. This is no mere makeshift; it is actually *more* appropriate than the method he uses in dream analysis, freed as it is from any nagging doubts about arbitrariness. Using this technique he discovers the double determination of the elements in Hanold's dreams and delusions, in the name Gradiva, for example. In each case there is a plausible surface meaning and an alternative, 'unconscious' meaning pertaining to Hanold's repressed infantile memories. The same is true of the sustained ambiguities in Zoë's speech; in fact, there is hardly a single element in the story which is not both determined and overdetermined by this schema of meaning.

Although Freud is very impressed by this correspondence with the results of his technique of reading symptoms and dreams, it seems he is actually overestimating the 'clinical' significance of a whole series of *literary* conventions. Linguistic ambiguities, doubly determined story elements, a symbolic key pointing to a subtext, and symbolically prophetic dreams are perfectly common literary devices, especially in novellas. The relentlessly meaningful repetition and the contrived structuration around a central symbolic nexus are all too blatant in *Gradiva*. The Vesuvius dream, for example, is patently artificial and so coherently 'meaningful' as to convince this reader only of Jensen's desire for absolute symbolic closure. Freud himself comments that Jensen presses the 'key to the symbolism' into the reader's hand (IX, 40). And yet he is so enthralled by his interpretation that he does not notice how tautological his argument becomes. He is effectively claiming that symbolism, metaphor, and ambiguous word-play are present not only in dreams and symptoms, but even in literature.

The logical flaw in this argument is no mere *non sequitur*, it is, rather, a circularity. From his earliest years Freud was both familiar with and delighted by such literary conventions, especially the structuring of over-determined meaning around symbolic nodal points in a complex 'fabric of thought'. Intellectually, this was his first love, established long before and, it seems, profoundly influencing his development of the psychoanalytical mode of interpretation. It is as if to extricate himself from this implication that he claims *Gradiva* is not so much a novella as a 'perfectly correct psychiatric study' (IX, 43). However, Freud is rather more impressive when interpreting the subtle unconscious ambiguities of a neurotic patient's speech in real psychiatric studies than he is in this elucidation of Jensen's overt symbolism.

Freud's approach to interpretation is by no means invalidated by its possibly literary derivation. He and Jensen may indeed both simply have hit upon the same laws of the unconscious. Nevertheless, the following boast at least becomes suspect: 'the conclusion seems inescapable that either both of us, the writer and the doctor, have misunderstood the unconscious in the same way, or we have both understood it correctly' (IX, 92). There is a third alternative, namely that amongst their common creative sources were the conventions of the novella. Freud actually checks his own rage for interpretation by reminding himself that Norbert and Zoë are not real persons, but poetic creations. This distinction, however, is not of the essence. When he hesitated about collaborating on a psychological study of Woodrow Wilson, the consideration that held him back was precisely the reverse, namely that Wilson was *not* a product of literary imagination as Gradiva was.[4] The distinction between reality and fiction does not seem to have any bearing on Freud's technique. Many critics complain that Freud analyses literary characters not only as if they were real people, but also as if they were his patients. Such critics may well be missing the subtler point that Freud analyses the real individuals who lay on his couch as if they were themselves the products of a literary imagination.

The literary origins of Freud's approach to interpretation may have been 'repressed' very early on by the strictly scientific rigour of his neurological studies, but the repressed appears to return – and moreover to return *within* the instance of repression. At the heart of Freud's clinical practice itself, above all in the assumptions underlying his interpretation of dreams and symptoms, there is evidence of a paradigm shift from the objectivity of the natural sciences towards the heterogeneous discipline of literary criticism. Occasionally Freud even seems to be trying to pre-empt just such a claim. In his Dora analysis he offers a lengthy denial that is worth quoting in full. Before claiming that Dora was unconsciously in love with Frau K., he makes the following rather curious apology:

I must now turn to consider a further complication to which I should certainly give no space if I were a man of letters engaged upon the creation of a mental state like this for a short story, instead of being a medical man engaged upon its dissection. The element to which I must now allude can only serve to obscure and efface the outlines of the fine poetic conflict which we have been able to ascribe to Dora. This element would rightly fall a sacrifice to the censorship of a writer, for he, after all, simplifies and abstracts when he appears in the character of a psychologist. But in the world of reality, which I am trying to depict here, a complication of motives, an accumulation and conjunction of mental activities – in a word, overdetermination – is the rule. (VII, 59–60)

In order to distance himself here from the status of literary critic to Dora's poetic conflict, Freud has to claim that poets expressly avoid complications, contradictions, and overdeterminations. This claim is all too easily refuted. Edward Timms, for example, notes that Musil's novel *Die Verwirrungen des Zöglings Törless* matches the complexity of Dora's circumstances,[5] whilst Neil Hertz points out strong parallels between her case history and Henry James's *What Maisie Knew*.[6] Freud's claim falls so far short of his usual insight into his literary precursors that it begs to be read as a symptomatic 'negation' of the literary dimension in his clinical practice. The repressed is allowed full access to consciousness but only in the context of being, unconvincingly, denied. The claim that psychoanalysis is partly derived from a paradigm of literary criticism is indeed a disturbingly radical evaluation of the degree to which it is penetrated by its creator's literary culture. To substantiate it I shall now look in detail at Freud's hermeneutic theory and practice.

THE ART OF READING DREAMS

Critics who insist that Freud degrades literature by treating it as if it were neurotic discourse forget the simple fact that his first detailed hermeneutic grew out of the study of a non-pathological object, the dream. More importantly, however, they fail to recognize that, to a significant extent, Freud reads dreams as if they were poetic. It was Freud's *a priori* assumption not only that dreams are meaningful and interpretable, but also that they are inexhaustibly so. Admittedly, Ricoeur claims that in this respect Freud actually distinguishes between works of art and dreams. In *The Interpretation of Dreams* Freud remarks that his interpretation of *Hamlet* uncovers only one layer of meaning and that the play, like all genuine works of art, is capable of 'over-interpretation' (Überdeutung). Ricoeur believes this implies genuine multivalency of meaning, unlike the over-determination (Überdeterminierung) found in dreams which is due to condensation and displacement and is, therefore, ultimately univalent.[7] He is, however, misrepresenting Freud who, in this respect at least, confers the same status on dreams as he does on literature. He states that however complete an interpretation seems, the ability of the dream-work to 'hit seven flies at a blow' must never be underestimated: there may always be a further – and he uses the same word – *Überdeutung* (V, 523). Earlier in the same work he claims: 'There is at least one spot in every dream at which it is unplumbable – a navel, as it were, that is its point of contact with the unknown' (IV, 111n.). Such a claim is distinctly at odds with Freud's positivist training and provides further evidence of a conflict of intellectual influences which in fact runs through the whole of the dream book. When, for example, Freud claims that dreams give us a glimpse into 'the composition of that most marvellous and most mysterious of all instruments' (dieses allerwunderbarsten und allerge-heimnisvollsten Instruments) (V, 608), the noun may belong to the mechanistic Helmholtzian tradition, but the quasi-Romantic adjectives point to a powerfully conflicting influence.

Freud's overt emphasis was, of course, always on the dream as an object of scientific study. The literary influence is usually most in evidence in a kind of subtext, for example in Freud's use of analogies. It was Freud himself, in *The Psychopathology of Everyday Life*, who remarked on the significance of the imagery we use to express our thoughts:

The images and turns of phrase to which a person is particularly given . . . often turn out to be allusions to a theme which is being kept in the background at the time, but which has powerfully affected the speaker. (VI, 216)

His own imagery regarding dreams often reveals a latent equation with works of literature, for example his parallel between the dream-work's considerations of representability and the rhyming of two lines of poetry, or the simile he uses of dreams which have undergone extensive secondary revision and are 'smoothly constructed like a literary composition' (XXII, 10). Indeed, Ricoeur should have noted that in an introductory lecture Freud even draws a parallel with a Shakespeare play in order to warn against oversimplifying a dream's meaning. He points out that we may know the stimulus of a dream, but this does not mean it is solved. *Macbeth* was an occasional play written for the accession to the throne of James I: 'But does this immediate historical occasion cover the content of the tragedy? Does it explain its greatnesses and its enigmas?' (XV, 96). Dreams, he implies, must be given the same respect as literature if their enigmatic grandeur is to be appreciated.

Freud's breakthrough in dream interpretation is in no small part attributable to his painstaking attention to detail, and his respect for the dream as an organic work of art clearly played a groundbreaking role here. In *The Interpretation of Dreams* he makes a declaration of faith in the significance of even 'the smallest, least conspicuous and most uncertain constituents of the content of dreams' (V, 513). Ironically, his example here of how a tenuous detail can become significant depends entirely on the intermediacy of four lines from a Heine poem. However, more important here than the literary element is the fact that Freud trusts not details as such, but the *associations* they evoke. It was indeed his use of the method of free association which he believed distinguished his 'scientific' interpretations from the intuitive feats of less methodical colleagues, such as Stekel. Nevertheless, this cornerstone of Freud's hermeneutic is itself permeated with literary influences.

Freud applied the method of analysing patterns that emerge from absolutely uncensored free associations in almost all his interpretative practices. As I have said, the substitute he uses in analysing literary texts is, if anything, superior to the original. It is perfectly suited to a text-immanent study of a piece of literature, establishing, as it does, the meaning of any element only in relation to the author's subjective constellation of signification. When used with a patient, it retains this key quality of structuralist literary criticism. The meanings it yields are not absolute, but relational and contextual, the context being the patient's own semiotic idiosyncrasies. Freud's insistence that his therapy has no pre-established line of procedure already distinguishes his approach from any controlled scientific technique. Each patient is treated as a unique object, and the method of free association encourages patients to concentrate on their spontaneous subjectivity freed from the restraints of propriety, logic, and critical judgement. In a letter which Freud quotes at length in his own *Interpretation of Dreams*, Schiller names precisely this, the 'ground rule' of psychoanalysis, as the precondition of literary crea-tivity. The patient, then, is asked to improvise and produce something closely related to poetry. The results of this suspension of inhibitions do indeed display certain poetic qualities. The associations are subtle, evoc-ative, and unpredictable, relying on connotation rather than denotation. It would even be accurate to say that they fulfil a more 'modern' criter-ion of literary language – the priority of the signifier over the signified.

In response to the patient's streams of associations Freud recom-mends what he calls 'evenly suspended attention' (gleichschwebende Aufmerksamkeit). The analyst immerses himself without prejudice in the patient's utterances, respecting every detail, hovering over ambigu-ities, constantly modifying interpretations, and avoiding premature con-clusions. It is perhaps because this is an approach so closely related to literary response that it is one quality the master usually failed to pass on to his pupils. The preservation of ambiguities does not correspond to any postmodernist notion of literary *jouissance*. Freud's objective is much more traditional and yet is still very much in keeping with a literary-crit-ical paradigm. From the mass of multivalent associations to the radically fragmented dream Freud ultimately detects recurring motifs and synthe-sizes them into broad themes which form the basis of his interpretation.

The clearest evidence that free-association technique has literary origins can be found in the brief paper 'A Note on the Prehistory of the Technique of Analysis' written in 1920 (XVIII, 263–5). In response to Havelock Ellis's claim that analysis by free association is more an artis-tic than a scientific achievement, Freud counters that it is a purely scientific faith in absolute determinism which led him to this technique. Nevertheless, he ends the article with a most uncharacteristic admission. He mentions his youthful admiration of the German poet Ludwig Börne, whose collected works are the only book he has retained from his childhood. He then points out that an essay in this very book, 'The Art of Becoming an Original Writer in Three Days', prefigures free-associ-ation technique – Börne recommends the would-be poet to write down streams of totally uncensored associations for three days. Freud finally admits the likelihood that this was a source of cryptomnesic influence on his own technique, and it is extraordinarily telling that this, his most explicit acknowledgement of indebtedness to a literary source, is made *anonymously*. Freud refers to himself in the article in the third person and signs it simply 'F'. Furthermore, the implications of the admission are even greater than Freud realizes. It is not merely that he has borrowed an idea from a literary precursor. He often claims the poets as his forerunners, but he always means the poet-as-analyst. Börne, however, has nothing to say about the scientific doctrine of determinism; for him free association is simply the key to poetic creativity. Freud's status in analysing his patients' dreams, then, is that of literary critic to their proto-poetic utterances, their streams-of-consciousness *avant la lettre*. This is no mere static borrowing of a piece of analytic truth. If free association is an idea from a literary source, then this source is one which continues to flow through the centre of his interpretative practice.

Reluctantly, Freud came to accept that apparently gifted analysts such as Stekel could interpret dreams without the dreamer's associations, by reading them for their use of symbols. Freud conceded that many of these were universal, and this recognition led to the greatest revision of his own interpretative technique. Nevertheless, the Freud who has entered popular consciousness, the monotonous reader of sexual symbols, is not to be found in any of his own works. At the outset of *The Interpretation of Dreams* Freud rejects both 'symbolic' interpretation and the 'decoding' method. He thought the symbolic method treated the dream as a complete whole, a technique which suited only the artificial dreams found in literature (IV, 97). Conversely, he rejected the decoding method for its crass simplicity and its purely mechanical transcription of dream elements. This clearly offended his literary-critical paradigm of interpretation, and nothing more was to be heard of it. The symbolic method, however, was to return. Admittedly, it remained subordinate to free-association technique, which Freud continued to trust far more than symbolism. He viewed the interpretation of symbols as at best intuitive and at worst witty and artificial. Indeed, it is the 'artistic' taint that he found most disturbing. He claims of symbolic interpretation: 'It is not our business to perform acts of virtuosity [Kunststücke]' (XV, 151). Free-association technique, on the other hand, is, like any good scientific method, painstakingly detailed and free of arbitrariness.

Nevertheless, much of Freud's aversion to symbolic equivalences simultaneously bespeaks a certain literary sensitivity. He seems to have seen the arbitrariness in the symbolic method as evidence of disrespect towards the unique and subjectively constituted fabric of a dream. Fixed symbols have too many qualities in common with clichés, and Freud considers them to be useful in a dream interpretation only if their elucidation yields new associations, that is, they belong to the intricate network of signs unique to the dreamer. With this proviso, though, the symbolic method of interpretation certainly became increasingly important to Freud's hermeneutic. His initial resistance to it seems to have stemmed from his 'repression' of literary influences – it was simply too literary. Ultimately, his central objections to it, that it is intuitive and 'artistic', could not endure because such qualities conformed perfectly well with his literary-critical paradigm.

When Freud does analyse visual symbols, he tends to use verbal associations to reconnect them to the linguistic fabric of the dream. Indeed, the lack of inhibitions which many of his pupils display in translating symbols, Freud himself shows only in his indulgence in this kind of word-play. Almost any of his published dream analyses demonstrates his preference for verbal structures over symbolic equivalences. For example, in the dream of the Wagner opera where the dreamer sees a man on a high tower in the stalls, Freud opts to take the tower at its word (wörtlich), rather than fall back on sexual symbolism. Via word-play such as 'towered high above', 'Fool's Tower', and 'highly-placed' he establishes the identity of the man and ultimately the dreamer's secret love for him (V, 342–3). Freud's preferred route to the latent content is always via 'word bridges' like these, with the result that his hermeneutic is almost entirely language-specific. Indeed, he interprets not dreams as such, but the verbal mechanisms and word-play of their narrative formulation. He has absolutely no difficulty dismissing objections that a dream-narrative misrepresents the dream itself, tending to make it more coherent. His answer is simple: 'The wording chosen is itself part of what is represented by the dream' (V, 455n.). This is not a sophisticated evasion; he is proud to acknowledge that he treats the dream 'as Holy Writ' in which 'every shade of the form of words' is respected (V, 514), a claim that is absolutely borne out by his analyses. It is precisely the fact that Freud elevates the dream to the status of *text*, as Geoffrey Hartman puts it,[8] that made his breakthrough possible.

Freud pays most attention to the precise letter of the dream-text, believing that in the primary processes words are treated like objects and to understand this mode of signification he must do the same. He sometimes disingenuously claims that he expects readers to find this approach absurd, unaccustomed as we are to concentrating on associations based on verbal similarities (Gleichklangs- und Wortlautassoziationen) (V, 596). Freud is 'forgetting' here that most readers are perfectly used to *poets* attaching the greatest significance to the play of syllables. He actually calls the dream's word-play a 'syllabic chemistry' (IV, 297n.), but the strictly scientific analogue fails to draw attention away from the literariness of his concentration on verbal textures; often the streams of associations are based purely on alliteration and assonance. Freud is interested in the 'nodal points' where signifiers overlap and generate ambiguities. Dreams – or at least Freud's dream interpretations – thrive on these polysemic junctions. He positively welcomes hesitations, distortions, gaps, and minute revisions in dream narratives, and his attentiveness to language is often so painstakingly *literal* that it bespeaks a literary reverence for the word. His decision to impute such central importance to language must indeed have derived, at least in part, from his profound literary culture.

*

Freud is often pleased by the beauty of a dream interpretation. He is aware, however, that the satisfying element is neither the dream content itself nor the underlying dream-thoughts, but the intricate dream-work that has transformed the latent into the manifest content. In fact, throughout the whole of *The Interpretation of Dreams* he is less interested in repressed infantile wishes, the 'true' dream content, than he is in the *form* of the dream and the meaning that can be inscribed in form. Orlando overstates the significance of this when he claims that, for Freud, form is the essence of a dream, whereas in literature form is merely a disguise.[9] This distinction between literature and dream is invalid because, ultimately, however 'poetic' the effect, the *raison d'être* of form in the Freudian dream *is* disguise. That dream-work is the essence of the dream is, however, an acute insight with far-reaching implications. Freud makes the point very clearly himself:

At bottom, dreams are nothing other than a particular *form* of thinking . . . . It is the *dream-work* which creates that form, and it alone is the essence of dreaming – the explanation of its peculiar nature. (V, 506n.)

Freud claims this other way of thinking is not inferior to, but merely qualitatively different from what we are familiar with in conscious thought. Thus, for example, he affects surprise that the formal elements of a dream so regularly carry meaning: '*The form of a dream . . . is used with quite surprising frequency for representing its concealed subject-matter*' (IV, 332). Of course, the notion that form can be purposively and richly meaningful is perfectly familiar – it is eminently literary. Perhaps this is why the ingenuity with which Freud synthesizes meanings gleaned from the form and content of every single dream element into a coherent construction often makes him so uncomfortable. He insists that it is not the dream-interpreter, but the dream-work which is witty; and yet anyone familiar with his works cannot accept the excessive modesty with which he disavows any claim to wit (IV, 298n.). It is not the dream-work which cleverly inscribes meaning into the dream's every element, but Freud's reading of the dream through a grid of literary-critical expectations that forces him to use his own immense ingenuity to ascribe meanings which sometimes seem not to be there.

It is in his 1901 précis 'On Dreams' that Freud admits just how literary his conception of the dream's 'unusual form' is. The dream-thoughts are 'represented symbolically by means of similes and metaphors, in images resembling those of poetic speech [wie in bilderreicher Dichtersprache]' (V, 659). Freud's familiarity with literature engendered in him a sensitivity towards imagery which he brought to his reading of dreams and used in his formulation of the basic processes of dream-work. Condensation (Verdichtung) is the term he assigns to the process whereby one element of a dream is superimposed over another. Via an intermediate common entity a new unity is created, richer in meaning and perceptually more intense. Freud claims that it is this condensation which makes dreams so alien to us, 'for nothing at all analogous to it is known to us in mental life that is normal and accessible to consciousness' (V, 595). Yet this process is at the root of overdetermination and, as such, is remarkably closely related to a device of *poetic* economy, namely meta-phorization. Lacan even implies that Freud has incorporated the word *Dichtung* into the term *Verdichtung* in order to denote that it is a poetic process.[10] He was certainly subjecting dreams to a metaphoric reading well before he conceived of condensation. Witness the nonchalance of this juxtaposition of a dream fragment and its interpretation as a meta-phor in his very first dream analysis: 'She would then have *opened her mouth properly*, and have told me more than Irma' (IV, 111). Freud's *a priori* assumptions were literary long before they found a rationalized justification in terms of a scientifically established 'economic' process.

Alongside condensation, Freud names displacement as the other key factor governing dream-work. This is the process whereby the dream shifts its focus onto trivial, decentred elements of the dream material. Freud always reads these as *allusions* to material that is absent from the dream content but at the centre of the true nexus of meaning. Again Lacan parallels this with a poetic device, metonymy, and Kenneth Burke expresses this insight more simply when he claims that to read a dream in terms of condensation and displacement is to read with an essentially literary awareness that an element may be both more than and less than its literal self.[11] During his summary of dream theory in *Jokes and their Relation to the Unconscious* Freud himself admits how familiar this process is when he describes the most common form of displacement, 'representation by the opposite', as the technique of irony (VIII, 174).

Dream-work employs many other techniques with which it transforms the latent into the manifest content. The procedure which Freud calls 'considerations of representability' (Rücksicht auf Darstellbarkeit) seems to correspond most closely to what he terms the *bilderreiche Dichtersprache* of the dream. Here a 'colourless and abstract expression' is replaced by 'a pictorial and concrete one' (V, 339), often resulting in an idiosyncratic kind of symbolism which, however, is usually based on linguistic usage. For example, Freud claims that dreams often dramatize the metaphors which are embedded in linguistic usage. Not only is this a highly literary way of reading a dream, but Freud's only truly convincing example (the others are as ingenious as they are dubious) is taken from a 'dream' in a novel by Gottfried Keller (V, 407). When, however, he admits that this aspect of dream-work is similar to the work of a poet (ähnlich wie bei der Arbeit des Dichters) (V, 340), his analogy could hardly be more shallow. He only wishes to illustrate a limitation, namely that what dreams choose to portray is conditioned by what can be represented in concrete form, just as the content of a line of poetry is conditioned by its need to rhyme with the previous line. Surely, though, this is another of those analogies that reveals far more than was intended.

It may be argued that Freud was less a literary critic than he was a linguist in his approach to the dream-work. His account of the dream's 'means of representation' constitutes the beginnings of a syntax of the primary processes: how they represent relationship, opposition, causality, and so on. Condensation stems from the logical relation of similarity which is particularly favoured by the dream but which is only one aspect of a whole grammar of unconscious processes. It is, however, precisely this grammar, or 'rhetoric', which Bloom sees as the essential feature of poetic language. He reproaches Lacan for his equation of condensation and displacement with metaphor and metonymy, considering it to be a drastic oversimplification of the potential parallel between defence mechanisms and literary tropes.[12] It is for this reason that Bloom sees Freud's *Inhibitions, Symptoms and Anxiety*, which deals with defence mechanisms, as such a suggestive text for literary critics. Whether Bloom is simply adopting Freud's psychoanalytical insights as a model for his own poetics, presupposing that the mind's basic manoeuvres are innately poetic, or whether he is implying that Freud himself has actually conceived of the various defences in terms of the traditional discipline of rhetoric, there can be little doubt that a correspondence between the two does exist. One critic produces an impressive list of the rhetorical devices which Freud detects in dream-work including, amongst others, allusion, euphemism, antiphrasis, synecdoche, and ellipsis.[13]

My own position, of course, is that Freud's conception of dream-work was indeed radically influenced by the literary culture he brought to it. The aims Freud attributes to the dream-work are: to make the abstract concrete, to superimpose elements in order to heighten intensities, to replace logic in content with logic in form, and to shape the elements into a coherent whole (V, 507). All of these could conceivably be named as basic principles of poetic economy. Freud does list another aim of the dream-work which few writers would recognize as an essentially 'poetic' aspiration, namely the avoidance of censorship. Nevertheless, it is true that, to some extent, literary expression avoids explicit statement, preferring to evoke, ironize, ambiguate, and so on. Literature, then, is a suitable model, if not of disguised meaning, at least of *latent* meaning. Furthermore, the paradigm of literary response which Freud employs in his interpretation of dreams includes, it must be remembered, his own culture-bound prejudices and even misconceptions. On the whole, however, it is quite sophisticated and serves him well, teaching him to seek meaning in such poetic devices as metaphor, allusion, symbolism, irony, and, above all, ambiguity.

*

If Freud's conception of dream form is demonstrably literary, does he show any prejudice towards conceiving of the dream's latent content as 'poetic'? This is a more difficult question. If there is little consensus about what constitutes poetic form, then there is none about poetic content. Of course, drives and their vicissitudes (Triebe und Triebschicksale) are the content which Freud believes to be the result of any interpretation, be it of dream or literary text. Perhaps his own remarkable use of the word *Schicksal* (fate) in this respect provides a clue. In his works Freud tends to associate fate either with the Fates of Greek mythology or with the *Schicksalstragödie* of Greek drama. This is by no means the only hint of how literary his conception of the latent themes of the unconscious is. For example, he describes the dreams of the Rat Man, which centre on incest, murder, and punishment, as 'an imaginative production [Dichtung] of a positively epic character' (X, 206n.). For Freud, the latent content of a dream has to fulfil two essential conditions. It must consist of only the most powerful impulses, and these must be in dynamic conflict with equally powerful repressive instances. There is little evidence of this conflict in the manifest content of dreams, which is often strangely neutral. With a vivid metaphor Freud insists this is merely 'the peace that has descended upon a battlefield strewn with corpses; no trace is left of the struggle which raged over it' (V, 467). It is, however, only his own *a priori* assumptions which cause him to read dramatic emotional battles into dreams where there is no manifest sign of them. That these assumptions are literary in origin is at least suggested when, for example, in 'Psychopathic Characters on the Stage' Freud describes such dynamic conflicts as the quintessential subject matter of dramatic literature. He certainly uses corresponding terminology to describe dreams, for instance, 'they "dramatize" an idea' (IV, 50) or the dream wishes are 'represented as a scene' (V, 534). He may describe this latter quality in grammatical terms, as a shift from the optative to the present tense, but as the single most characteristic aspect of the dream he names 'dramatization' (V, 653).

Strictly speaking, these points overlook a confusion between latent and manifest content. The 'dramatized' scenes are manifest, whereas the 'dramatic' conflicts are latent, and the distinction is crucial. Freud notes, for example, that some dreams have something like a plot: 'they start from a possible situation, carry it on through a chain of consistent modifications and . . . bring it to a conclusion'. It is, however, precisely such dreams that Freud trusts least: 'they appear to have a meaning, but that meaning is as far removed as possible from their true significance' (V, 490). He is eager to undo such suspiciously coherent structures, seeking meaning not in the manifest content, but through the holes he can unravel in this 'cover'. His literary analyses also follow this pattern, and many critics surmise from this that Freud is the first deconstructive critic, having first learnt deconstruction on the model of the dream. Nevertheless, this conclusion erases from the picture Freud the *traditional* reader of literature, and it is this Freud who belongs in the foreground of any discussion about psychoanalytical hermeneutics. In any dream analysis Freud picks out motifs and recurrent themes, establishing more 'rational' connections in the dream-text which he confidently fuses into a coherent pattern of meaning. This logocentric hermeneutic, through which the 'poetic' text is transcribed into rational discourse, is often overlooked by those who claim Freud for the camp of deconstruction, and yet it is fully consonant with my hypothesis of a culture-bound literary-critical paradigm at the heart of Freud's hermeneutic.

To illustrate this point I should like briefly to juxtapose one of Freud's literary-critical essays with one of his dream analyses. In 'The Theme of the Three Caskets' Freud interprets what he considers are two related scenes from Shakespeare. His method is essentially that of traditional and often very subtle literary criticism. He finds correspondences between scenes from *The Merchant of Venice* and *King Lear* and seeks their meaning in a common source which he traces back through Greek mythology. He explains the development of the myth of the three Fates at great length and comes to his conclusions by reading the Shakespeare scenes in the light of the genesis of this myth. In the course of his interpretation Freud relies on various theories culled from his study of dreams, such as sexual symbolism and 'representation by the opposite'. This, however, is not the central emphasis of his study. Nor are his interpretations of the kind that is generally expected from Freud. His nineteenth-century humanism leads him to seek the 'human content' hidden by the poetic veil, leading in this case to the 'primaeval identity' of love and death, the pain of man's acceptance of the necessity of death as part of Nature, and the three forms in which a man relates to his mother: as his bearer, as the model of his beloved, 'and lastly the Mother Earth who receives him once more' (XII, 301).

It is interesting to compare this excellent literary-critical essay with the analysis of his own dream of the three women in the kitchen, carried out about fifteen years previously and published in part in *The Interpretation of Dreams* (IV, 204). Here Freud uncovers its 'human content' by looking at it in the light of his own free associations. This method throws up a wealth of literary 'sources' including the first novel Freud ever read, Shakespeare's *Henry IV*, Goethe's *Faust* and *Iphigenie auf Tauris*, and the Greek myth of the three Fates. Amongst the meanings towards which this leads him are the primal co-existence of love and hunger in the child's relationship to the mother, and the painfully realized inevitability of death expressed in the Shakespeare quotation: 'Thou owest God a death.' In fact, Freud misquotes Shakespeare here – for God, he substitutes a more suitably 'maternal' instance of Fate, and he writes: 'Thou owest Nature a death.'

I do not wish to claim any mysterious connection between the literary analysis and the dream analysis. Many of the common elements – the Fates, Shakespeare, the multiple guises in which a mother appears to her child, the theme of the inevitability of death – are simply coincidental. What, however, is not coincidental is the similarity in Freud's approach to two very different phenomena. He seeks the hidden meaning by studying both the sources of and the interaction between each element, and he reads these as meaningful by imputing latent connections and synthe-sizing them into an account of the most basic human concerns. A scep-tical reader may admit this but point out that the reading of the dream came first, thus the reading of Shakespeare is simply a later extension of the interpretation of dreams. This would be a very familiar argument: Freud 'reduces' the literary text to the level of a dream, then applies his technique to produce a 'typically Freudian' interpretation. As I demon-strated in the previous chapter, however, far from reducing Shakespeare to a mere disguiser of his own indulgent day-dreams, Freud has Shakespeare himself effecting a 'reduction of the distortion' present in the mythological material, thereby accessing a more powerful core of wisdom and pathos. In fact, it is the sceptical reader's argument which must be turned on its head. Freud was reading Shakespeare, and much else besides, long before he 'read' his first dream, and this experience clearly served him as a paradigm for his later encounters with other 'texts'. Rather than reducing literature to the status of a dream, Freud seems, rightly or wrongly, to *elevate* the dream to the status of literary text.

THE ART OF READING NEUROSIS

It was, of course, the neuroses which Freud described as the 'mother country' of psychoanalysis, and he would sometimes show anxiety when protégés such as Jung strayed too far from it. Symptoms were indeed the first phenomena to which Freud ascribed purposive, communicative *meanings*, and in his Dora analysis he even claims that without its thera-peutic dimension the interpretation of dreams is 'an art, which would otherwise be useless' (VII, 114). There is an element of unconvincing denial in this statement. Freud was already highly sensitive about his practical method being seen as artistic, so any suggestion of *l'art pour l'art* was sheer anathema. Nevertheless, he did indeed conceive of the inter-pretation of dreams as a mere auxiliary to his all-important clinical tech-nique. As I have suggested that his medical studies were the vehicle of 'repression' of his literary inclinations, my hypothesis of a repressed par-adigm of literary interpretation at the heart of the psychoanalytical her-meneutic is worth nothing unless there are substantial traces of it in his approach to neurotic illness.

One such trace which Freud does nothing to disguise is the utter dependence of his method on *language*. Already in the *Studies on Hysteria* he can be seen learning to let patients speak, and to respect the exact wording of what they say. This becomes essential to his diagnostic approach. For example, Freud tells us that the Rat Man's attempt to recount the history of his illness suffered (litt) from inner contradictions and sounded incurably (heillos) confused (X, 169). The correspondence here between the language of illness – suffered, incurably – and that of linguistic incapacity – contradictions, confused – is not fortuitous. The sickness manifests itself in language, or perhaps even *as* a language. Freud refers to symptoms as 'the language of hysteria' (VII, 278) and to neuroses themselves as languages, for example: 'The language of obsessional neurosis . . . is, as it were, only a dialect of the language of hysteria' (X, 156–7).

Neurotics have a 'primitive' attitude towards language, responding to repetitions rather than logic, treating words like objects (dinglich), and ascribing magical powers to them. Not only did Freud develop a great sensitivity towards language in order to respond adequately to this, but for his own curative method he claims: 'And incidentally do not let us despise the *word*. After all it is a powerful instrument' (XX, 187). Language retains some of the magical powers ascribed to it by primitives, and it is the vehicle of the psychoanalytic cure. Freud made these claims in 1926 when his method of treatment had changed immensely since the days of his work with Breuer. The emphasis on language was, however, the unchanging bedrock of his technique. In the 1890s he saw hysterical symptoms dissipate when the sufferer '*put the affect into words*' (II, 6), and he defined the cathartic method as 'a discharge of the excitation by talking' (III, 50). Not only are symptoms themselves a language, they can also be cured by language.

Perhaps the most telling evidence of the language-specific nature of Freud's approach is that some of his most famous cases are based on an encounter not with a person but with a *text*. His analysis of the 'demonological' neurosis centres on his study of a fragment of the sufferer's diary and receives its main impetus from some meticulous detective work applied to a minute textual discrepancy. More strikingly, when Freud read Daniel Paul Schreber's *Memoirs of a Nerve Patient* in 1910 he was prompted to produce a full case history, even though he did not know if Schreber was dead or alive as he was psychoanalysing him. Far from being daunted by the prospect of working only with a text, Freud not only gains important insights by taking Schreber's account of himself at its very word, he positively delights in Schreber's suggestive neologisms such as 'soul-murder'. Freud does make use of his knowledge of Schreber's age, but he is otherwise very proud of the text-immanence of his analysis: 'Apart from this one fact, however, I have made use of no material in this paper that is not derived from the actual text of the *Denkwürdigkeiten*' (XII, 46n.). He even suggests that paranoia is particularly well suited to being analysed in the form of a written report (XII, 9).

The most revealing instance of such a purely textual 'case history' is his pathography of Leonardo da Vinci. Here Freud believes he is relying on authentic biographical information, but he scarcely disguises the fact that his main source is Merezhkovsky's *novel* about Leonardo. In fact, he clearly prefers this fictional source of information, believing that it is a *Dichter* rather than any biographer who has been able to portray the 'key' to Leonardo's character, 'not indeed in plain language, but (after the way of writers of imagination) in plastic terms' (XI, 73). Even when his real patients present him with accounts of themselves, Freud's primary concern is not with whether their stories are true or not. He positively rules out the idea of establishing the 'real' story, for example, by contacting a patient's family (XVII, 14n.). Indeed, it is tempting to say that his breakthrough was made when he stopped taking his patients literally – the mistake of his seduction theory – and he began to take them *literarily*, that is, suspending disbelief in 'truth' content and concentrating instead on the wording of their utterances. Some of the most vital elements of his theory of neurosis resulted from this shift in emphasis, for example the Oedipus complex, the primal fantasies, and the family romance, in which the neurotic is described as 'the hero and author' (der dichtende Held) (IX, 240). His sophisticated biographical approach enables him to treat all his patient's utterances, fictional or truthful, as legitimate objects of interpretation.

From the Freudian perspective, neurotics live by fiction even more than artists. Both have 'fled' reality, but artists reconcile their fantastic creations with a certain kind of reality, namely an audience. As far as Freud is concerned, then, it is essential only that patients verbally formulate their emotions and experiences, however distorted. As he puts it in his Dora analysis, the patient presents the analyst with a *text* (VII, 116). He insists the analyst plays no creative role in the production of this text; he must merely show due respect, with minimal intrusions and evenly suspended attention, to this already existing object. Although Freud's metaphor for this total assimilation into the realm of the patient's utterances is economic – the analyst adopts the 'neurotic currency' – his assumption of the immanent meaningfulness of a fictional construction in its own semiological terms appears, rather, to be derived from the model of the sensitive reading of literature. To emphasize the necessity for such subtlety and delicacy during analysis, Freud refers us to 'the words of a world-famous neurotic', namely Hamlet. He quotes a full eight lines in which the hero berates Rosencrantz and Guildenstern for believing they can play him more easily than a pipe (VII, 262). The musical reference within a literary allusion subliminally reinforces Freud's plea for an *aesthetic* sensitivity towards the object of analysis.

It is not necessary to go into great detail about the literary elements of his hermeneutic approach towards neurotic symptoms – the parallels between this and his interpretation of dreams are well known. His reading of symptoms as dramatizations of inner conflicts, distorted but readable in a metaphoric or metonymic mode, is in evidence throughout his published works. One interesting discrepancy is how receptive Freud was to symbolism in symptoms long before he fully accepted its significance in dreams. As early as 1893 he was describing the symptom as a symbol, there being only a symbolic relationship between the trauma and its pathogenic effects. Again Freud directly links such symbolism to the neurotic's sensitivity to language. Cäcilie M. is a striking example. Freud describes her as 'a woman who possessed quite unusual gifts, particularly artistic ones, and whose highly developed sense of form was revealed in some poems of great perfection'. Perhaps he hopes this ostensibly extraneous information justifies his own highly literary reading of her symptoms. Freud traces most of these to 'symbolization by means of a verbal expression', for example facial neuralgia resulting from a figurative 'slap in the face', and throat seizures attributed by Freud to other insults that she has been forced to 'swallow' (II, 179–81).

Although Freud is often criticized for treating artists as if they were neurotics save for their knack of manipulating an audience, in the field of the neuroses this perspective is reversed: Freud respects patients as if they were artists without an audience. As we have seen, in his 1914 paper on narcissism, whilst pointing out that we must love in order to be healthy, he quotes the following lines from Heine:

> Illness was no doubt the final cause
> of the whole urge to create.
> By creating, I could recover;
> by creating, I became healthy. XIV, 85

The quotation is strangely at odds with his assertion, and yet there is a good reason why he is so attracted to these lines. As he sees it, neurotics do not love, but rather, in their attempt at a self-cure, they *create*. Freud's unique therapeutic approach is indeed to read symptoms with an implicit faith in the patient's complex and meaningful creativity.

When his interpretation of Dora's unconscious ruses becomes extremely intricate, Freud denies this is a '*jeu d'esprit*' on his part. He admits that the network of connections is 'a clever *tour de force*', but one created by the *patient* (VII, 40–1). Although he would no doubt have insisted that this creativity was entirely 'primary', that is, independent of a patient's *Bildung*, it is remarkable that in 1896 he claimed his technique was useless with children, the feeble-minded, and the uneducated (III, 282). In other words, the patient has to meet him half-way in intelligence and culture. In his dream book Freud points out the important role played by 'jokes, quotations, songs and proverbs in the mental life of educated people' (V, 345). He is trying to explain why dreams use this material so extensively, but a sceptical reader is more likely to be struck by how often *Freud* relies on his patients' more cultivated associations in order to be able to construct a meaning for the dream. When he finally does analyse a child, Little Hans, some of his less convincing interpretations result from his crediting the five-year-old boy with an almost literary sophistication. For example, Freud interprets Hans's ridiculous story of his baby sister riding a horse in terms of the child's revenge on his father for being expected to believe the stork story: 'Oh no, it was no nonsense: it was parody' (X, 70).

Once again, Freud's analogies offer an insight into his approach to the patient's creativity. Elements in Dora's account of herself are variously called a story (Erzählung), a fairy-tale (Märchen), and a farce (Komödie), and almost a decade earlier Freud was describing all hysterical reminiscences as 'romances [Romane] which they themselves invent', especially his patients' 'stories of being assaulted' (Attentatsdichtungen) (III, 164). The most striking analogy is his description in *Totem and Taboo* of hysteria as 'a caricature of a work of art' (XIII, 73). He is probably referring here to the way such patients create unconsciously overdetermined, fantastic constructions which they tend to dramatize in symbolic form. There is something aesthetically sophisticated about this form; it offers a multi-layered wealth of meanings but always only *indirectly*. Freud greatly admired precisely this quality in Shakespeare, writing with regard to *Richard III*: 'A bungler in his place would give conscious expression to all that he wishes to reveal to us' (XIV, 315).

Of course the implication here, that neurotic discourse is inherently subtle, is extremely faint. Jung, however, was less inhibited than his teacher about the affinities between clinical cases and literature. In one letter to Freud he writes, 'every properly analysable case has something aesthetically beautiful about it', and he calls one case 'an exact copy of Ibsen's *The Lady from the Sea*'.[14] In letters Freud is himself a little freer in his aesthetic appreciation of his patients' illnesses. The Rat Man is a case in point, and at times Freud seems as proud of the case history's intricate complexity as he is of the cure. Gay writes of it: 'Freud, the most literary of psychoanalysts, could not rest satisfied with serving up a dry case report . . . he wanted to reconstruct a human drama.'[15] Whilst Gay's assessment of Freud's inclinations is insightful, it is worth pointing out that Freud himself makes a very different emphasis. He does not believe he has transformed the case into an aesthetic object; on the contrary, he writes to Jung: 'How bungled our reproductions are, how wretchedly we dissect the great art works of psychic nature!'[16] The Rat Man's illness, then, is *already* an organic work of art to which Freud believes his interpretative critique has failed to do justice.

Although Freud's various analogues for neurotic discourse cover nearly every literary genre, his emphasis on densely symbolic, word-playing narratives which present meaning only in a latent form appears to be most closely related to his familiarity with the nineteenth-century novella. One correlation, at least, seems to be that Freud consistently locates the poetic tension of these tales in their submerged erotic themes, a notable feature of the Biedermeier novella. It is, of course, in his *Studies on Hysteria* that Freud makes this much-quoted apology:

> it still strikes me myself as strange that the case histories I write should read like short stories [Novellen] and that, as one might say, they lack the serious stamp of science. I must console myself with the reflection that the nature of the subject is evidently responsible for this, rather than any preference of my own. (II, 160)

As with the statement about Dora's 'poetic conflict', there is something unconvincing about the way Freud raises the subject of an affinity with the novella form only to dismiss its significance. It is far from 'evident' that neurotic case histories are in themselves novella-like; neuroses were, after all, dismissed by generations of investigators before Freud as meaningless degenerative conditions. It is Freud's *interpretation* of the illnesses that first creates the impression of an affinity. Moreover, although this disclaimer was made many years before the denial in the Dora case history, it is in this earlier work that Freud admits a greater kinship with the poets. He goes on to claim that those neuropathologists who dismiss neurotic symptoms as nonsensical can make no headway with hysteria:

whereas a detailed description of mental processes such as we are accustomed to find in the works of imaginative writers enables me . . . to obtain at least some kind of insight into the course of that affection. (II, 160–1)

The relevance of a literary tradition to his therapeutic practice is, of course, admitted only in the context of a *denial* of any literary inclinations of his own having an influence on this practice.

*

Although Freud is uncomfortable about there being any subjective dimensions in his clinical work, his therapeutic success clearly depends on his sensitivity towards the meaningful creativity of his patients. A vital ingredient of any analysis is, therefore, what he terms empathy (Einfühlung). From his earliest published works onwards he makes claims such as the following:

I cannot imagine bringing myself to delve into the psychical mechanism of a hysteria in anyone who struck me as low-minded and repellent, and who, on closer acquaintance, would not be capable of arousing human sympathy. (II, 265)

He never manages to reconcile this dependence on empathy with his assertions of the scientific status of psychoanalysis – for example, his analogy between psychoanalysis and infinitesimal calculus (XXI, 36). He must have been aware that no mathematician considers it essential to enter into a personal relationship with a difficult equation. His sensitivity towards the problem can be seen in his insistence on a 'training analysis', believing that this would promote insight and objectivity in the analyst. However, an exhaustive training analysis really only fosters sensitivity towards a patient based on the model of an extremely intimate personal experience. In other words, it promotes not objectivity, but empathy, and the circle of inherent subjectivity remains unbroken. In less polemical texts Freud admits that the analyst's main therapeutic instrument is emotional influence, and that his is a cure through love.

It was Freud's less scientifically-minded pupils who saw a positive advantage in this feature of psychoanalytical therapy. His most literary follower was Lou Andreas-Salomé, and Freud complained to her: 'I silently accept the limits imposed by our subjectivity, whereas you draw express attention to them.'[17] If psychoanalysis is judged in terms of a paradigm of the natural sciences, it can indeed only be harmed by the taint of subjectivity. However, a literary-critical paradigm can, to some extent, rehabilitate its relevance as a hermeneutic technique. A patient, like any literary text, is unique, thus an analysis is already excluded from scientific status – though not from relevance – by its intrinsic unrepeatability. However, if the patient is interpreted as a unique 'text', then the *ad hoc* nature of Freud's approach can be seen as less a logical flaw than a positive asset. I do not simply mean that by relegating psychoanalysis to the status of a transposed literary criticism it can be allowed to indulge in rampant subjectivism. In fact, Freud's emphasis on empathy and the training analysis seems to transcend the crude distinction between objectivity and subjectivity. In this respect, his hermeneutic shows more than a passing similarity to the highly sophisticated area of literary criticism known as reception theory. For the meaning of a text to be generated it must not only be 'expressed', but also 'received' by another, who plays an active, creative role in the establishment of meaning.

Freud's recognition of the importance of the other in psychoanalysis is most evident in his theories about the transference. The 'text' studied in a psychoanalysis is not the patient's monologue, and the cure does not consist in patients merely 'expressing' themselves. The text is actually the transference, a result of the 'productive powers of the neurosis', which Freud specifically refers to as if it were indeed a written work. Sometimes they are 'merely new impressions or reprints. Others are more ingeniously constructed. . . . These, then, will no longer be new impressions, but revised editions' (VII, 116). It is the literary genre of drama which seems to have most deeply penetrated transference theory; indeed one psychoanalyst even went on to develop a form of transferential therapy called 'psychodrama'.[18] The emphasis in Freud's own descriptions of the transference is equally on a histrionic reconstruction of the patient's past, for example: 'the patient produces before us with plastic clarity an important part of his life-story. . . . He acts it before us, as it were, instead of reporting it to us' (XXIII, 176). In 1920 Freud states that with the discovery of the transference psychoanalysis ceased to be merely 'an art of interpreting'. Patients must not only understand the symbolic meaning of symptoms and remember suppressed traumas, they must *repeat* the pathogenic experiences of their past history as if they were present. In the analytical session the neurosis is replaced by a transference neurosis, and it is this 'illness' which is interpreted and treated (XVIII, 18). Although the transference is a real experience, it is also essentially fictional, as Freud realized when he found himself cast in roles in the drama which were originally played by others, mainly parents.

It is not surprising to find traces of a literary paradigm in his conception of this process. After all, Freud believed that the greatest drama was itself a form of therapeutic analysis by way of which a *Dichter* could work through unresolved conflict. He is certainly aware that such conflict is the essence of all drama. In 'Psychopathic Characters on the Stage' he writes: 'It must be an event involving conflict and it must include an effort of will together with resistance' (VII, 307). Even apart from the term resistance (Widerstand), the name Freud gave to the key concept in his theory of the transference, the parallel with the tenets of his theory of neurosis is evident. In 1938 he admits that he has never really been interested in the normal, stable mind, only in 'states of conflict and uproar' (XXIII, 165). In the terms of the neurotic currency the criteria of reality have no value, the only legal tender is 'what is thought with intensity and pictured with emotion' (XIII, 86). In such circumstances psychotherapy is, by necessity, the language-specific interpretation of a dialogue which is itself an emotionally charged but fictional drama.

Even before the discovery of transference Freud's conception of therapy was markedly dramatic. For instance, in 1893 he wrote:

Recollection without affect almost invariably produces no result. The psychical process which originally took place must be repeated as vividly as possible; it must be brought back to its *status nascendi* and then given verbal utterance. (II, 6)

This climactic reconstruction of the past in the medium of language was termed catharsis, a concept derived from Aristotle's *Poetics*. Admittedly, it was Breuer who coined the term in its therapeutic application, but it was not this literary aspect which caused Freud to leave the concept behind. It is more likely that in the 1880s precisely this element initially attracted him away from his dry medical studies. In the long term, however, Freud preferred analysis to catharsis. One might say his vocation was not theatre director, but theatrical critic.

Occasionally, the covert literary dimension rises to the surface of Freud's therapeutic interpretations. It is not merely for polemical reasons or to rationalize an indulgence in literary criticism that Freud uses characters from plays by Sophocles, Shakespeare, and Ibsen to exemplify clinical character types, nor even simply to make certain neurotic complexes comprehensible to his readers. Rather, he draws on his extensive knowledge of drama to make neurosis comprehensible to himself. In 'Some Character-Types Met with in Psycho-Analytic Work' Freud's only scruple about moving from actual case histories to *Richard III* is that he is 'indulging' himself. His pleasure clearly derives from his returning to home territory. As I have already pointed out, Freud quickly forgets the

second part of his title and gets carried away analysing the literary substitutes. Despite the charge of philistinism commonly levelled at Freud,
it seems that the emphasis throughout this paper is not excessively on
psychopathology, but rather excessively on traditional literary criticism.
For example, Freud has Lady Macbeth represent the type of patient who
falls ill on achieving success. Nevertheless, in the scheme which Freud
constructs at length from details in the play, it is only because of Lady
Macbeth's *failure* to produce children and secure a dynasty that she eventually breaks down. The essence of his interpretation is not the psychopathology of 'those wrecked by success', but a literary convention,
namely that Macbeth's crimes against parents and children are punished
by childlessness, 'a perfect example of poetic justice' (XIV, 321).

After six pages of such specifically literary analysis Freud finally
admits that he has not been able to explain why Lady Macbeth cannot
accept success. His response to his own failure is not to question the procedure of using a literary character to elucidate a neurotic character
trait. On the contrary, he simply moves on to Rebecca from Ibsen's
Rosmersholm. When he finally returns from literature to clinical experience at the very end of the essay it is 'only to establish in a few words the
complete agreement [volle Übereinstimmung] between them' (XIV,
331). This paper is, admittedly, rather exceptional amongst Freud's
works, but it is by no means anomalous. Indeed, Freud uses precisely the
same words, *volle Übereinstimmung*, to describe the correspondence
between the process of psychoanalytical therapy and the plot of another
work of literature, Jensen's *Gradiva* (IX, 89).

Of course, due to his belief that poets gropingly find access to psychoanalytical truths, Freud feels no need to address the possibility that they
have actually influenced his own conception of the neuroses. One critic
who does consider this issue is Gunnar Brandell. He makes much of the
fact that Freud developed the basic tenets of psychoanalysis whilst Ibsen
and Strindberg were at the height of their influence, and that their plays
called for a fusion of literary criticism and psychological analysis. Ibsen,
in particular, specialized in plays in which the past – the locus of the
play's tension and meaning – is gradually revealed, a genre which
Schiller termed the 'analytical drama'.[19] In the famous passage in *The
Interpretation of Dreams* I have already quoted from (see p. 71 above), in
which Freud points out that the nuclear complex of the neuroses corresponds in content with Sophocles' *Oedipus*, he makes an almost equally
fascinating parallel between the *form* of the play and the process of a
psychoanalysis:

The action of the play consists in nothing other than the process of revealing, with cunning delays and ever-mounting excitement – a process that can be likened to the work of a psychoanalysis – that Oedipus himself is the murderer. (IV, 261–2)

Sophocles merely inherited the themes of parricide and incest from the Oedipus myth, but Freud is equally interested in his specific treatment of these themes, the way the unconscious is made conscious by the gradual overcoming of resistances.

Although Brandell does not refer to this passage, it clearly corroborates his argument. He is perhaps too anxious to associate Freud with contemporary literary movements such as psychological naturalism and symbolism. He points to Freud's attaching such significance to symbolic interpretation 'at precisely the time when the current literary watchword was "symbolism"'.[20] However, despite Freud's admiration for writers such as Ibsen, Zola, and Schnitzler, contemporary literature did not have such a great influence on him. Even if symbolism were central to his hermeneutic, he would not have needed modern artistic trends to inspire him. When 'dream' symbolism became popular in surrealist art and literature, Freud was singularly unimpressed. Brandell himself finally concedes not only that Freud was not enthusiastic about contemporary literature, but also that his interest in symbolism could just as easily have been inspired by Goethe and the Romantics.

*

There is, however, at least one important respect in which the late nineteenth-century literary *Zeitgeist* may have influenced Freud's clinical practice. Despite my emphasis so far on dramatic literature, ultimately it is *narrative* which provides Freud with a paradigm of health. Furthermore, this narrative paradigm can – tentatively – be placed in a specific literary-historical context. Freud's emphasis on therapy as drama does endure in his concept of the transference, but he never ceased to grow away from Breuer's naive therapy of catharsis. The discontent he felt with the transference was not due to the fact that it made of therapy a literary-critical interpretation of a symbolic, fictional dialogue. It was simply that he, too, was an unwilling player in this drama. Although he recognized that unconscious repetition during therapy was inevitable, he much preferred traumas to be *remembered*, and he developed a new emphasis on the process of 'working through'. This involves recalling, verbalizing, and coherently ordering the raw material delivered up by the transferential drama. It represents a decisive shift in favour of the essential qualities of narration.

Catharsis tended to rely on a venting of emotion occasioned by the repetition of a single traumatic scene. Freud, however, came greatly to expand his diagnostic scope to include a patient's whole life history. He sought an extension of self-consciousness in his patients which would elucidate not just a single pathogenic event, but ideally their entire past. In his *Autobiographical Study* he claims that *Breuer* was the first doctor to take an interest in a patient's life history as told by the patient. This claim comes shortly after his own admission that medicine never interested him: 'I was moved, rather, by a sort of curiosity, which was, however, directed more towards human concerns than towards natural objects' (XX, 8). It seems this frankness has made him uncomfortable, hence his unconvincing attempt to deflect some of the 'blame' for his own unscientific interests onto his earliest collaborator. As Freud explains in 'Dora', he always begins by asking the patient to tell 'the whole story of his life and illness', including 'the purely human and social circumstances' (VII, 16–8). He compares Dora's and other patients' accounts to a river made unnavigable by rocks and sandbanks. These decentred and fragmented self-accounts may be 'poetic' in their rhetoric, but they are the very locus of neurotic illness. This narrative incoherence is what Freud diagnoses, what he interprets, and what he attempts to cure.

Patients are incapable of telling their own story, they leave gaps, riddles, and confusions in logic and sequence. Indeed, when one patient told her life story 'clearly and connectedly', Freud was able, from this evidence alone, to diagnose her illness as organic (VII, 16n.). It is in the gaps in a text that he seeks meaning, namely desire and its repression; and he positively trusts distortions, preferring an incoherent earlier version to a more slick correction. Although he is sensitive to the quasi-poetic manoeuvres of such disjointed texts, his priority is to reconstruct them and make them intelligible. Whilst techniques such as the deciphering of symbols and the synthesis of elements into coherent patterns may indeed be derived from a literary-critical paradigm, Freud's approach to narrative actually goes far beyond mere interpretation (I shall deal with it more fully in chapter 4). With the help of the transference, itself only a means to an end, he ultimately seeks to *construct* a coherent narrative of the pathogenic events in a patient's life history. This narratological approach is essential both to the psychoanalytical cure and to Freud's hermeneutic, a coherent story being, for him, the very essence of explanation. By way of various analogies, one could say that Freud uses a literary-critical approach in order to help patients transform their native poetry and unconscious drama into a coherent autobiographical novel narrated from an omniscient perspective.

From the beginning Freud saw discharge (Abfuhr) as the vehicle of cure. Catharsis is based on a very simple notion of discharge, whereas the later narratological emphasis is based on a much more sophisticated and controlled form of release. Merely experiencing repressed emotions is no longer sufficient, the patient must literally come fully to terms with them. Of course, remembering the past also means repeating it, but with the essential difference that it is recognized *as* the past. Freud greatly prefers this detached narrative perspective, formulated in the past tense. The emphasis is on *binding* the poetic energy and dramatic tension by stably investing them in a coherent story of the patient's most formative or traumatic years. A patient ultimately achieves intellectual and emotional insight by becoming his or her own self-conscious – ideally, omniscient – narrator. The analyst directs the procedure, but, Freud believes, only as the instance of objective detachment:

[The analyst] must get [the patient] to re-experience some portion of his forgotten life, but must see to it, on the other hand, that the patient retains some degree of aloofness, which will enable him, in spite of everything, to recognize that what appears to be reality is in fact only a reflection of a forgotten past. (XVIII, 19)

If, for Freud, narrative incoherence is the signal, indeed the very essence of illness, then narrative authority is the mark of psychic health, and it is this assumption which can be placed in a literary-historical context. Susan Suleiman implies the same when she writes that Dora was alienated by Freud's drive for absolute narrative coherence 'based on the only model Freud appreciated, that of the nineteenth-century realist novel'.[21] This literary ethos, often loosely termed 'bourgeois realism' by the postmodern age, does seem to share many ideals with Freud's narratological therapy. The urge for objective detachment, preferably narrative omniscience, the equation of coherence with health and rationality, the rejection of the notion of Fate in favour of the determining influence of a precisely detailed environment (in 'Wolf Man' the survey of the patient's milieu is accorded the same status as the history of his illness), and, above all, the faith in a linear narrative – all of these are in evidence in Freud's therapy. Treatment leads to 'an intelligible, consistent, and unbroken case history', a story which can be narrated now it is cured of its memory gaps (VII, 18). The dénouement of the Wolf Man case history is a fourteen-page summary of the patient's infancy. It comprises the oral phase, the anal-sadistic phase, actually masochistic due to the perverting influence of his early seduction, the genital phase, which due to his unsuccessful attempt at seduction and the trauma of his wolf dream regressed to anal sadism, followed by a castration trauma, then latency with the patient's sublimation of libido into compulsive religious practices (XVII, 106–19).

This ingenious fusion of Freud's own master narrative with the constructions evolved during therapy takes the form of a seamless chronological sequence, confidently narrated in the past tense. Freud reads the fragmented 'text' a patient offers him often with a very modern poetic sensitivity, but, ultimately, he reconstructs this text along the lines of the nineteenth-century novel. Despite this evidence, I do not wish here to categorize Freud's literary assumptions. I have formulated these so vaguely that they seem to correspond with traditions other than just 'bourgeois realism'. The emphasis on awareness, order, and self-mastery could easily be pigeonholed into, say, the tradition of Weimar classicism (indeed, Goethe's towering presence is at least as tangible here as the influence of bourgeois realism, which Suleiman is certainly wrong to name as Freud's only literary model). What I wish to emphasize is the broad literariness of his therapeutic practice.

One element in particular of Freud's hermeneutic seems to be dependent on a literary-critical model. Psychoanalytical interpretations arise from a dialogue between analyst and patient. In order to be effective they must not merely be internally consistent, they must make *sense* to both patient and analyst. The gaps in the initial text generate the possibility of the two participants mutually *constructing* a plausible new text. The emphasis is on not a single objective truth, but rather a workable, dialogic 'reasonability' capable of generating one of, presumably, an unlimited number of meanings. This kind of 'truth' is closest to that of literary criticism, especially as this is conceived in reception theory. Psychoanalytical therapy consists in the analyst and patient collaborating to construct and ascribe a meaning to a patient's life history. As in literary criticism, the essential criterion is not objective truth, but the wealth of plausible meaning that can be generated by one of many readings, hence Freud's claim that the only 'proof' he needs for a new construction is that it generate new associations.

Freud was aware that this procedure could lead to the production of *fictional* constructions. He demands only that these be consonant with other elements elucidated in the treatment such as the transference, symptoms, fantasies, screen memories, and dreams. In other words, the fiction only has to be consistent with a series of other fictions. Freud, especially in his theories of primal fantasies and screen memories, explicitly recognizes that humans constitute their identity in part through their own fictions. His 'Constructions in Analysis' of 1937 particularly emphasizes this feature of his hermeneutic. A construction is a *hypothetical* narrative which is already inescapably 'literary', taking as it does the form of a coherent, linear, and omniscient narrative. Freud helps his patients narrate not so much their own autobiography as their own autobiographical fictions. The objective facts of their life history are not of primary importance, what matters is *how* these constructions are conveyed to the patient, namely gradually and with sensitivity to their resistances – in short, 'aesthetically'. A fiction that is plausible to both participants in the analytical session is as therapeutic in effect as if it were objectively true. It is this feature perhaps more than any other which makes Freudian therapy most consonant with a model of literary criticism. It consists in the establishment of a 'text' which is then read with literary sensitivity and rewritten, under Freud's editorial aegis, in a more suitable genre. The emphasis is always on *meaning* rather than truth, even if this meaning is itself wholly dependent upon nothing more than a series of fictions.

THE RELUCTANT POSTMODERNIST?

The 'fictionality' at the heart of Freud's therapeutic practice raises certain pressing questions. Does it make of Freud a literary critic, or rather a narrator of his own fictions? And does it correspond with my description of him as a traditionalist, or does it indeed bear out those critics who see in him a pioneer of postmodernist interpretation? In chapter 4 I shall deal with some of Freud's literary aspirations which go beyond literary criticism. For the moment it suffices to say that I agree with Steven Marcus's assessment that in 'Dora' Freud is novelist, narrator, character, and a 'representative Victorian critic'.[22] I should particularly like to emphasize the traditional, 'humanist' dimension of Freud's literary-critical paradigm. For example, his insistence on the normalizing effect of coherent narrative, so essential to his therapy, is firmly rooted in nineteenth-century culture. His hermeneutic is best suited to 'texts' embodying a traditional conflict between desire and its repression which must be capable of a narrative articulation. Its most appropriate object is probably the novella, a highly traditional narrative genre, and the result of a successful analysis is the rational, non-symbolic narrative of a life history which has most in common with the omnisciently narrated nineteenth-century realist novel.

The modernist and postmodernist trends which have undermined beliefs in such things as the notion of language as a tool of expression and the validity of linear narrative would be as alien to Freud as the pathological texts presented to him by patients. Indeed, Trilling ascribes the loss of prestige suffered by psychoanalysis to the 'contemporary disenchantment with narration' as a mode of explanation,[23] whilst Marcus claims that psychoanalysis and narrative literature are both as old-fashioned as the bourgeois-liberal culture from which they arose: 'Both retain a primitive and charming belief in the sufficient authority of narrative as a means of constructing and legitimating human reality.'[24] This may seem surprising coming from a critic who has just read the Rat Man case history as a modernist novel. Marcus, however, seems to figure the Rat Man himself as the modernist 'text'. He claims that Freud's failure to reconstruct a coherent narrative is due to the fact that this text simply cannot be therapeutically edited in this way; the Kafka-like narrative cannot be straightened out.[25] The implication is that Freud's *traditional* hermeneutic is inadequately equipped to deal with such an object.

Brooks tries to rescue Freud for the modernist camp by concentrating on the 'structure of indeterminacy' at the heart of Freud's very solution to the Wolf Man case, the neurosis being the result of a dream which was itself the result of a 'fictional' primal scene.[26] However, it is in precisely this case history that Freud, rather than anticipating Proust, Kafka, or Faulkner, appears, as we shall see, to be drawing on his reading of detective novels. Brooks misses the point when he remarks that the break came between 1914 and 1918, as Freud switched his emphasis from a real trauma, the primal scene, to a fictional scenario, the primal fantasy. Firstly, Freud was fully aware of the role fictions played in the aetiology of neuroses from as early as 1897, when he abandoned the seduction theory. Secondly, his belief that the 'fictional' primal fantasies are phylogenetically inherited from human prehistory reveals the extremes to which he will go in order to achieve narratological determinacy.

Freud seeks a narrative understanding of almost all the phenomena he investigates. Even a slip of the tongue or a statue by Michelangelo possesses its meaning in the form of a story. To unravel the phenomenon of the joke, Freud tries to establish a linear narrative of its dynamic development. Initially, play conflicts with reason and this leads to the jest, which in turn conflicts with criticism leading to the joke. Joking then takes on a new opponent, inhibition, resulting in the tendentious joke. Such agonistic, developmental narratives are always the ultimate objective of Freud's interpretations. In his book on wit he claims that other authors have provided 'a series of anecdotes' to explain the phenomenon whereas he demands 'a biography' (VIII, 14). The image could hardly be more telling. However, it is important to remember that his emphasis is not on factual but on *narrative* truth. If a narrative – internally coherent and comprehensible as a development due to dynamic conflicts – possesses genuine explanatory power, then the facts are of only incidental importance. This explains how Freud managed to construct a detailed narrative of infantile sexual development in 1905, several years before he had ever analysed an infant.

One critic determined to cleanse Freud of the taint of nineteenth-century narratology is Leo Bersani. Given his political perspective, this is hardly surprising:

The mythologizing of the human as a readable organization is a fundamental political strategy, and the eagerness with which both literature and psychoanalysis have contributed to that mythology may be the surest sign of their willingness to serve various types of orders interested in the shaping of the human as a precondition for . . . controlling it.[27]

One way in which Bersani attempts to rescue Freud is to show how his narratives deconstruct themselves. For example, in 'repressively' narratological terms, any adult who has not achieved the *telos* of genital heterosexuality is abnormal, having failed to complete the narrative. For Freud, however, this ultimate finding of an object is a 'refinding', hence we are returned to the start of the story and the narrative line becomes a circle. Bersani claims this non-narrative repetition deconstructs the whole narrativization of sexuality, just as sexuality itself deconstructs the ego's attempts to control it.[28] But the phase in which the mother is the sole love-object is not simply 'repeated' in the mature phase, in which a love-object is sought on her model. Between the two there is an entire *Bildungsroman* of development and maturation. There are elements of repetition and circularity in the dénouement of this narrative, and these certainly disrupt any moralizing concept of normality, but they do not disrupt Freud's narrative. Far from being intrinsically deconstructive, narrative repetition and circularity conform, rather, to the oldest narrative traditions. Bersani's initial move of allying Freud with the urge to make human behaviour intelligible by making it narratable is much more convincing than his subsequent attempt to extricate him from this alliance. His hermeneutic is firmly and traditionally narratological.

The arrogance of nineteenth-century rationalism is often evident in

Freud's works. He may, for example, treat the dream as if it were a holy text, but for him the only gospel truth resides in his *interpretation* of the dream. Bloom rightly points out that Freud sees the interpretation as a 'truer text', whilst the dream is merely 'an inadequate commentary upon a missing poem'.[29] Freud casts himself as a rational authority, constantly aspiring to (if not actually arrogant enough to claim) the 'last word'. If he does deconstruct texts, it is only a means to the end of restructuring them to his own liking. In the Wolf Man case he claims the constructions arose 'independently' during the sessions, but this is a most disingenuous claim from the pioneering explorer of unconscious motivation. In fact, far from being unconscious, Freud's desperate drive to make the details of the Wolf Man case conform to his own master narrative is, at times, embarrassingly blatant. When he is in the grip of an interpretative train of thought, he will go so far as to use his own associations to the material produced by his patients, and even when he scrupulously avoids this temptation, the restructured texts he produces are still clearly of his own creation.

Such hermeneutic imperialism does not gainsay my hypothesis of a literary-critical paradigm. Long before developing psychoanalysis, Freud responded to works of art from the perspective of a sometimes naively rationalist aesthetic, gaining much of his pleasure from the valuable moral and scientific insights which he believed were dressed up in beautiful form. This assumption was certainly not the full extent of his understanding of aesthetics, but it was one aspect of his bourgeois-liberal mode of artistic response. This rationalism, however, is not that of the natural sciences. On the contrary, Freud initially imputes extremely complex meanings to psychic phenomena by reading them quasi-Romantically, as creative expressions of the Unconscious. His rationalism is more that of traditional literary criticism, whose only object of study is the meaning of creative expressions, but which assumes that this meaning can be made intelligible in rational language. In fact, it is partly because Freud's hermeneutic was derived from a literary-critical paradigm that it was able to suspend the opposition between scientific positivism and irrationalism. Nevertheless, critics who mistake the Romantic retentions of psychoanalysis for early deconstruction are turning a blind eye to the rational positivism which also pervades Freud's hermeneutic. If, like the deconstructionists, he perceives a radical disjuncture between language and 'reality', he diagnoses this as illness and attempts to cure it with rational narrative. He may read the texts of psychic phenomena as if they were literary discourse, then, but he ultimately seeks to transpose this discourse into an authoritative meta-language.

In the name of Reason, which he refers to, albeit ironically, as 'our god Λόγος', Freud does not necessarily reduce symbolic texts, but in appreciating their symbolism he attempts to demystify them. As Kofman puts it, psychoanalysis is governed by 'the traditional logic of the sign'.[30] It seeks the content hidden by form, the cause behind effects, the truth veiled by illusion. Freud's hermeneutic does respect that the latter terms in these binary oppositions – the signifiers – are the *means* to the signified, but it is the signified which is given ultimate priority. The content which Freud privileges is always biographical truth, and his literary-critical paradigm could be categorized as that which French postmodernists scornfully term 'l'homme explique l'oeuvre'. In 'Wolf Man' he even states, as a 'strict law', that every single detail of a dream must be interpreted in terms of the patient's life (XVII, 42) and when he manages this remarkable feat, he speaks of a 'solution' as if the whole has been a mathematical problem.

Again, however, I do not believe that such logocentrism contradicts my hypothesis that Freud's approach is literary-critical. In his 'The Theme of the Three Caskets' he even uses the word 'solution' to describe his interpretation of two texts by the master of 'over-interpretation', Shakespeare. Furthermore, Freud hardly rode roughshod over the Wolf Man's dream – he spent several *years* interpreting it. Given his respect for the inexhaustible complexity of meaning in a psychic text and the sophistication of his notion of biographical truth, it may be fairer to categorize his approach as 'l'oeuvre explique l'homme'. This is why he can allow the primal scene, the 'real' event behind the Wolf Man's dream, to be a fiction of his patient's invention. This does not, however, imply that Freud was somehow happier with a Kafkaesque indeterminacy at the heart of his narratives. Such fantasies as the primal scene, infantile seduction, and castration threats can be allowed to be fictional because Freud fixes them, if not in life history, then in prehistory. In 'Wolf Man' he claims that phylogenetic inheritance 'fills in the gaps in individual truth with prehistoric truth' (XVII, 97). His emphasis, then, is on establishing a logocentric truth. Furthermore, the phallocentric image which he uses to describe this process, the filling of gaps, indicates again the quasi-sexual pleasure which Freud derives from interpretation. It seems the ponderous term 'phallogocentric' could have been coined for his hermeneutic.

In Freud's defence, I could point to a genre of literature that does indeed structure itself around meaningful gaps which, when filled, lead to a 'solution', namely the detective novel. In *Moses and Monotheism* Freud draws the following analogy: 'In its implications the distortion of a text resembles a murder: the difficulty is not in perpetrating the deed, but in getting rid of its traces' (XXIII, 43). It does indeed often seem that Freud reads every text as if it has been written by Conan Doyle. Eysenck scornfully describes psychoanalytical logic as *post hoc ergo propter hoc*,[31] a kind of logic which, in fact, is rather appropriate in the reading of detective fiction. It is a genre whose conventions require that every ambiguous element, every gap presented to the reader be an indication of the absent presence of a crime. This crime is the absolute signified hidden in a mass of equivocal signifiers. In his reading of psychic texts Freud similarly assumes that there is an intricate design whose every detail is a fragment of a fixed and reconstitutable truth which is both brilliantly hidden and crying out to be read. His insistence on interpreting every phenomenon he encounters, from historical developments to physical symptoms to the accidental breaking of ornaments, does indeed seem to correspond with a literary-critical paradigm in which detective fiction has played a formative role.

This has been noted by certain critics, for example Stanley Fish, who uses Freud's assertion that every single detail of the Wolf Man's dream must be interpreted in order to contradict Brooks's claim that the case history is a postmodernist narrative. He argues that it is, in fact, rhetorically structured like a detective novel so as to induce a false credulity in his readers.[32] The Wolf Man himself spotted the resemblance between his analyst and Sherlock Holmes, and was surprised to hear that Freud had read and enjoyed several Conan Doyle novels. It is also known that in later life Freud's favoured light reading was the fiction of Agatha Christie and Dorothy L. Sayers. However, it is not necessarily detective novels themselves which influenced Freud. They are merely an extreme epitome of bourgeois-liberal literary tastes. The communication of omniscience from narrator to reader, the strictly causal sequence of events, and the ultimate satisfaction of an objective solution were sought by Freud in every text he encountered. The rationalist and utilitarian assumptions which he brought to his reading of all literature, from Homer to Ibsen, were related to the Victorian tastes which inspired the very creation of the detective novel.[33]

Much of what is considered 'deconstructive' in Freud's hermeneutic simply stems from the fact that his literary assumptions are largely unconscious. For example, his hermeneutic may render the distinction

between fiction and reality irrelevant, but this is largely due to the precedent of literary interpretation. In 'The "Uncanny"' Freud claims it is
one of. the many freedoms of the *Dichter* that he may choose his own
'world of representation', and the reader must follow him into this
'poetic reality' (XVII, 249–50). Freud abides by this not only when
reading literature, but when reading *all* texts, and it is this literary-critical assumption which causes him to suspend the distinction between
reality and fiction, rather than any postmodernist problematizing of the
notion of 'reality'. Similarly, he recognizes, in a precocious anticipation
of reception theory, that the 'truths' he ascertains are always only partial,
constructed, and open to constant modification. In these constructions
he seeks the very 'unity, connection and intelligibility' which elsewhere
he claims is the mark of secondary revision and must, therefore, be dis-
mantled (XIII, 95). This does not, however, imply that the meanings he
establishes are infinitely deferred and deconstructed. Like a respectful, if
traditional, literary critic, he believes he can establish only a workable
'truth', itself grounded in fiction and only one of an infinite number of
constructible meanings, but still one aspiring to a genuine core of
meaning. He believed in the reality of the unconscious but he held this
to be radically inaccessible, hence his concentration on language.
Despite this, he felt nothing but contempt for critics who attempted to
reduce the unconscious itself to a mere trick of language, a *façon de parler*.

Geoffrey Hartman convincingly describes how, in *practice*, Freud's
method of interpretation is deconstructive.[34] The more he interprets,
the more structures he undoes, and the more 'polysemic' the text
becomes. Free association discards the arbitrary link between signifier
and signified, throwing up chains of signifiers which are potentially
endless. Meaning, therefore, is radically decentred and infinitely
deferred. Ricoeur is referring to the same tendency when he claims that
in addition to the first 'reductive' reading there is a second psychoanalytic reading which aims to 'set free the interplay of references between
signs'.[35] I cannot, however, agree that there are *two* distinct psychoanalytical hermeneutics. The contradiction Ricoeur detects actually exists
within Freud's literary-critical paradigm itself, which is both rationalist
and extremely sensitive to literary discourse. Freud does indeed read like
a forerunner of deconstructive criticism. In his 'lacunary mode',[36] he
focuses on gaps, allusions, substitutions, and marginalizations, using
them to unravel deceptively univocal structures. It is, however, Freud's
rationalist belief in the mechanics of *censorship* which causes him to
adopt this mode of reading. Only his highly literary awareness of the

elaborateness of the unconscious response to this censorship rescues him from crass reductionism. He relentlessly seeks out gaps in a text because, in his eagerness to establish interpretative closure, he is intent on filling them all in. His literary-critical paradigm does teach him that the meaning of a text is inexhaustible, and this prevents him from trying to make the interpretative closure absolute. Nevertheless, critics wishing to turn a blind eye to Freud's positivistic leanings are misguided when they use this assumption of Freud's – actually quasi-Romantic and literary-critical in origin – to rewrite him as a pioneer deconstructionist. Freud's hermeneutic *practice* is more radical than his theory, and his highly sensitive and language-specific deconstruction of texts is more convincing than his sometimes arrogant reconstruction of them. Nevertheless, everything 'postmodern' in his interpretative technique can be traced back to a paradigm of traditionally humanist, sometimes naively rationalist, yet always highly sensitive literary response.

PSYCHOANALYSIS AS SCIENCE: FACT AND MEANING

The very idea of a hermeneutic is now somewhat old-fashioned due to its logocentric emphasis on deriving a rational 'message' from an ambiguous, arcane, or poetic text. Nevertheless, my emphasis on the traditional elements in psychoanalytical interpretation should not obscure the fact that Freud's paradigm of literary criticism helps him transcend the crude positivism which pervades much of his own theory. His concentration on studying *meaning* represents an important shift away from nineteenth-century mechanics towards twentieth-century semantics. Of course, Freud believed his assumption of psychic determinism was strictly in line with the anti-vitalist Helmholtzian school of thought. This school, however, had never attempted to extend its doctrines to the realms of 'pure' psychology. Even if it had, it is unlikely it would have reached Freud's conclusion that every psychic phenomenon is meaningful in its own terms. In *The Interpretation of Dreams* the mechanistic theorizing of the final chapter is noticeably detached from the bulk of the book in which Freud freely indulges his search for meaning in dream texts. As Ricoeur explains, Freud was primarily concerned to establish a natural science of 'energetics', but, due to the fact that this energy manifests itself only in the processes of symbolization, psychoanalysis remains a *hermeneutic* discipline from beginning to end.[37] Far from being merely one psychoanalytical tool amongst others, interpretation is the very essence of both therapeutic and applied psychoanalysis.

Gerald Izenberg attributes most of the existentialists' dissatisfaction with psychoanalysis to its underlying scientific positivism, its faith in absolute truth and its reduction of human behaviour to pseudo-materialist mechanisms.[38] Of course, Freudian theory is tarred with the biophysicalist brush. Freud places a strong theoretical emphasis on such ideals as absolute objectivity, 'quantities' of energies, and causalistic accounts of phenomena leading to the elucidation of predictable 'mechanisms'. Izenberg is quite correct to describe Freud as suffering from reminiscences of his Helmholtzian training.[39] Nevertheless, he fails to recognize how much Freud *gains* from even older reminiscences which free his hermeneutic practice from the confines of scientism. Rycroft points out that Freud only adopted the model of natural science, and with it the emphasis on the mind as a machine conforming to Helmholtzian principles, because he was educated in the late nineteenth century. He claims that in the twentieth century his model would have been linguistics and he would have produced a 'pure' theory of meaning.[40] Nevertheless, those twentieth-century cultural critics who do use a linguistic model are at least as profoundly influenced by Freud as they are by Ferdinand de Saussure. Freud unconsciously employed a paradigm quite distinct from that of nineteenth-century mechanics, and this led him to produce, almost inadvertently, a modern theory of meaning.

In Freudian theory, even the process of symbolization is 'mechanical', consisting of the displacement of a quantity of energy in the psychic apparatus towards more primitive mechanisms of representation. Freud even showed some interest (though not much) in establishing a symbolic 'key' with universal validity. Due to his attempted adherence to such ideals of natural science, Izenberg claims, Freud falls short of a 'phenomenological' approach which demands that behaviour 'be described in its own terms, as seen from the perspective of the agent and using his own criteria'.[41] Izenberg even explicitly states that Freudian symbolism is not literary. He cites the example of Freud's equation of a horse with Little Hans's father to demonstrate that there is no simile or metaphor in his concept of the symbol.[42] It strikes me that in this case Freud is *more* phenomenological than Izenberg. He has no prejudices about what a symbol should be like; in fact, he prefers the idiosyncratic symbolism created by his patients to 'universal' symbols. It is Little Hans who sees the horse as a symbol for his father, so the lack of apparent similarity does not concern Freud. He interprets his patients' behaviour 'in its own terms'. Freud also seems to fulfil the other criteria Izenberg lays down for a phenomenological hermeneutic. For example, his ideal of empathy means behaviour is indeed considered from the perspective of the agent, whilst his absolute reliance on free associations forces him to use the agent's own criteria to interpret this behaviour. Due to his theories of condensation and displacement, Freud always reads meaning in the *relations* between signifiers, and this meaning is always specifically bound to the highly detailed context of the patient's life. Such a method is semiotic and structuralist, and it respects each object of interpretation as unique. Thus it is Freud's unconscious use of a model of literary response which causes his hermeneutic practice to fall short of the ideals of nineteenth-century science, but also to anticipate some of the criteria of twentieth-century criticism.

The sessions during which Freud gathers his data are intrinsically unrepeatable and unpredictable. Clearly, his method can never fulfil the essential criteria of experimental science. By determinism he does not really imply that the phenomena he studies are causally determined, but simply that they are *meaningful*. For Freud, this meaning is purposive or communicative; it has little to do with the causality which is fundamental to empirical science. As in history, literary criticism, and other 'humanities', it is a meaning which can only be studied *after* it has been generated. By concentrating on such *post hoc* meaning the Freudian concept of determinism remains largely untainted by the mechanistic materialism of his theory of psychic energy. Freud remained uninterested in obtaining any scientific verification of his results. He believed the only way an observer could become convinced of the validity of psychoanalysis was to be analysed himself and see how much *sense* it made. As evinced in concepts such as empathy and transference, Freud was aware of the inescapably subjective and intersubjective nature of his technique. It could never aspire to rigorous scientific standards such as quantifiability and falsifiability.

Even in psychoanalytical theory, the laws which Freud formulates are designed to interpret meanings rather than predict facts. Wittgenstein remarks: 'His explanation does what aesthetics does: puts two factors together.'[43] Although intended as an objection, this insight may represent a partial recognition of the literary-critical paradigm which helps redeem psychoanalysis as a precursor of modern semiology. In practice, the kind of meaning sought by Freud always exists in its own terms, it is constructed in dialogue rather than 'discovered', and it is always only one of many potential meanings. In many such respects it bears a strong resemblance to various twentieth-century conceptions of literary meaning. As we have seen, instead of scientifically verifiable results, Freud sought from his interpretations a certain kind of workable *coherence*, even if this was wholly grounded in the criteria of the patient's own fictional creations. Richard Wollheim sees nothing amiss in Freud's apparent indifference towards the distinction between fiction and reality. He excuses Freud for treating Norbert Hanold in Jensen's *Gradiva* as if he were a real patient on the grounds that the interpretation *works*.[44] This is not just a critic's revision of Freud's own standards of interpretative corroboration. For Freud, internal agreement between the elements of a text and the elements of its reconstruction as an interpretation represents an *ersatz* scientific validation. His constructions are not falsifiable, but their relative merits can be judged in terms of which makes the most sense of the most details.

Rieff comes closest to recognizing the literary-critical paradigm when he writes: 'The task of the Freudian science remains a kind of literary criticism, the discovery of equivalences of symbols and actions through perceptual analogies.'[45] Certainly Freud's love of the meaningful ambiguities generated by word-play in complex networks of signifiers, his feel for symbols and metaphors which, with an aesthetic indirectness, reveal and conceal meaning, and his sensitivity towards the meaning that can, in its own terms, be inscribed in fictional discourse are amongst the specifically literary qualities which he tries to account for in the framework of the rules and theory of a strict discipline. Like literary criticism, psychoanalysis is somewhere between a science and an art. Trilling suggestively calls it 'a science of tropes, of metaphor and its variants, synecdoche and metonymy',[46] although, like Rieff, he believes that the unconscious mind just happens to employ such 'poetic' mechanisms, and the phenomenon does not need to be explained with any reference to the legacy of Freud's own literary culture.

Surely, though, Freud's method of treating neurosis proved to be versatile so far beyond the field of clinical psychiatry precisely because it was itself derived from a purely interpretative sphere. Hermeneutics is not concerned with facts as such, it attempts to establish procedures whereby meaning can be read from ambiguous and symbolic texts. Although the term was originally associated with religious scholars, Freud's pre-psychoanalytical familiarity with such texts owes little to the Bible or the Talmud. Marcus may characterize Freud's conviction that everything is interpretable as a kind of religion of meaning,[47] but Freud was converted to this religion by his reading of secular, literary texts. It was here he learnt to make subtle connections in order to construct multiple layers of meanings for enigmatic texts. He himself admits that his assumption that every psychical creation has a meaning amounts to a 'prejudice' (XI, 86). This conviction led him to his basic 'scientific' insight, which was simply to read what were previously dismissed as meaningless – symptoms, dreams, slips – as if they were complex signifiers. His literary culture causes him to perceive these signifiers in specific ways: they are always ambiguous, simultaneously revealing and concealing a metaphorical meaning, and they always tell a dramatic story of a dynamic conflict. It is hardly surprising that this mode of reading could be 'applied' to literary discourse so felicitously – it was his wide experience of literary texts which conditioned its very development.

To be sure, it is difficult to prove that the literariness which Freud reads into psychic texts is a consequence of his own literary cultivation and is not necessarily immanent in the texts themselves. In certain rare but revealing cases, however, Freud's rage for interpretation can be seen causing him to read literary qualities of his own invention into texts where they demonstrably do not exist. The most notable such example is his reading of Leonardo da Vinci's only recorded childhood memory. Freud believes Leonardo has written about a vulture pressing its tail into his mouth when he was an infant. He considers the memory to be fabulous (märchenhaft) (XI, 82), but its fictionality only renders it even more in need of interpretation. In order to construct a meaning for the memory, Freud draws on such sources as Egyptian hieroglyphics (in which a vulture represents 'mother'), an ancient Christian legend (according to which the vulture is emblematic of the immaculate conception), the biblical account of the virgin birth, his own theory of sexual symbolism (according to which a tail in the mouth can be read as phallic), and his own account of the infantile sexual theory of the 'phallic mother'. He elucidates this vulture fantasy over twenty-four pages, reading Leonardo as a 'vulture-child' who is intensely attached to his mother and symbolically admits: '"It was through this erotic relation with my mother that I became a homosexual"' (XI, 106).

As I have already explained, Freud's logocentric transcription of this 'screen memory' into rational discourse does not necessarily mean his reading is not literary. It is, in fact, a source study of an extremely elaborate fictional construction, and it is wholly dependent on a symbolic mode of interpretation. Furthermore, it would be absurd to describe as reductionist Freud's twenty-four-page elucidation of a memory which is itself only thirty words long, a ratio between text and interpretation which one would expect only from critiques of the most sophisticated poetry. The problem with his construction is, rather, that there is no vulture in Leonardo's childhood memory. The German translator of Freud's copy of the Merezhkovsky novel simply mistranslated *nibio*, actually a kite.

Freud's famous mistake is usually dragged into the light by hostile critics who wish to demonstrate that the whole of psychoanalysis is corrupt. Of course, nothing of the sort is revealed. Not only does this mistake reveal what a formidable literary critic Freud would have made had he restricted himself to *bona fide* literary fictions, but by itself it invalidates neither his pathography of Leonardo nor even his speculations about vultures and mothers. All that is lost is the symbolic link between the two in the case of Leonardo da Vinci. It does, however, demonstrate how Freud actively *creates* complex and profoundly meaningful symbolic connections where they patently do not exist. He does not simply follow threads, he unravels them and weaves them together with others spun by himself to create a whole new fabric. The elaborate nexus of signifiers which makes up the 'vulture fantasy' is not Leonardo's, but Freud's own creation, and for breathtakingly erudite and seamlessly intricate symbolism it matches many a novella by Thomas Mann.

*

Imbued as it is with his literary expectations, Freud's respect for the intricate fabric of psychic textual structures is, if anything, excessive. His favourite image for this fabric comes from Goethe, it is the 'weaver's masterpiece' with its thousands of interlocking connections. Freud may have a voyeuristic desire to unravel the threads and denude some other 'truth', but this never causes him to underestimate the complexity of the material he is handling – something which cannot be said of many of his followers, who, coming to psychoanalysis from medicine, lacked the redeeming qualities of a literary-critical paradigm. Critics are wrong, therefore, to assume that Freud's literary criticism *must* be reductionist because it is derived from a paradigm of psychotherapy. They crucially fail to recognize that Freud's therapeutic hermeneutic itself was not simply developed in clinical isolation and then 'applied' to literary texts; rather, it was established in a complex dialectical relationship in which literary expectations played an active role.

Felman has argued that psychoanalysis attempts to subordinate literature in a master/slave dialectic, literature producing the necessary goods, but only for psychoanalysis to claim dominion over them. She demands instead a 'real *dialogue*' between the two.[48] My hypothesis of Freud's literary-critical paradigm may be seen as a contribution to this dialogue: Freud does not imply that poets are quasi-neurotic, he assumes, rather, that neurotics are meaningfully creative like poets, and he elevates all aspects of their behaviour, including dreams and slips, to the status of literary texts, whose thematic and formal elements he interrogates for meaning. Psychoanalysis cannot, therefore, imperialistically annex the territory of literature; on the contrary, it must recognize that it developed as a colony of literary criticism, and its assumptions and methods become less valid the more distant it becomes from this mother country. Equally, though, it would be incautious to argue that psychoanalysis 'belongs' to literary criticism. My reading of Freud as a covertly 'literary' critic focuses on only one of his many facets. Freud the biologist of the mind, the 'moral' philosopher, the structuralist linguist, and the 'strong' poet, are all equally convincing readings produced by Sulloway, Rieff, Lacan, and Bloom respectively, and there are many others. Bloom expresses the complexity best when he says psychoanalysis is 'on the border between all prior disciplines'.[49] Literary criticism, however, is a prior discipline of particular significance. The most valuable evidence that it was a dominant influence on Freud's hermeneutic is not only the fact that his technique transfers so well to literary discourse, but also that this was where it was to find its widest acceptance. Whereas psychoanalysis is often reduced to a footnote in psychiatric encyclopaedias, whole chapters are devoted to it in accounts of twentieth-century literary criticism.

In *The Question of Lay Analysis* Freud admits that a 'college of psychoanalysis' would have to teach the humanities as well as medicine, and his syllabus includes 'the science of literature'. His only direct hint at his own literary-critical paradigm is given when immediately he adds: 'Unless he is well at home in these subjects, an analyst can make nothing of a large amount of his material' (XX, 246). Although such frankness can no doubt be attributed to the context, an anti-medical polemic, it serves as a reminder that the concept of the 'return of the repressed' must be used metaphorically here, rather than in the full-blooded psychoanalytical sense. Nevertheless, it is worth reiterating just how useful this metaphor is. Literary texts were the earliest and the most attractive objects of interpretation for Freud, and yet he seems to have suppressed his indulgence in this pleasure. Ultimately, however, literary criticism gradually returned to and even came to engulf his science of psychoanalysis. Most interestingly of all, the first site of the return of the repressed was the very scientific methodology with which Freud had tried to discipline his literary tendencies. What he conceived of as the most scientific aspects of his mode of analysis were, from their very inception, surreptitiously pervaded by a literary mode of reading. This sheds light on many of the paradoxes of Freud's hermeneutic – why his interpretations are often so ingenious and yet simultaneously so dubious; why his analogies between dreams, even neurotic symptoms, and literature are, in practice, never reductionist; why what he conceived of as a scientific method found a cool reception amongst fellow scientists and yet revolutionized the practice of literary criticism; why literary critics are more interested in his texts which are *not* about literature than they are in his literary criticism; and why a nineteenth-century rationalist came to be championed as a pioneer of deconstructive criticism.

It is possible that Freud was perfectly aware of the lineage of his hermeneutic but discreetly hushed up its illegitimate origins. As we have seen, Rieff, for one, believes that Freud 'kept his humanist literacy under wraps'.[50] This would explain why he kept a tight rein on his urge towards literary criticism much more convincingly than any flippant oedipal interpretation that he was avoiding 'mother' country. At his most honest, for example in his letter to the secretary of the Goethe Prize fund, who to Freud's astonishment has guessed the 'secret, personal intentions' behind his life's work (XXI, 207), he implicitly acknowledges that his interpretative method was always intended to effect a gradual return to his first love, the interpretation of cultural objects. This was the 'regressive development' in his life's work, and the reading of literary texts was both the point of departure and the ultimate destination of Freud's circuitous intellectual odyssey.

CHAPTER FOUR

The frustrated Dichter:
literary qualities of Freud's text

FREUD AS STYLIST: ARTFUL REVELATIONS

In chapter 3 certain confusions arose regarding Freud's precise role in
his treatment of various 'texts'. In his Leonardo study, for example, he
is patently no mere 'literary critic' analysing the text of a childhood
memory; he is, rather, the *creator* of a wholly new kind of text. It is tempting to expand the scope of this insight to embrace not only Freud's therapeutic constructions and dream interpretations, but also his more
abstract theoretical works. Such a radical reappraisal of Freud – as a
writer, in a literary sense of the term – has been attempted by a few
critics, such as Stanley Hyman and Patrick Mahony, and in this chapter
I shall draw on their conclusions. Principally, though, I intend to follow
my own path, starting from the most superficially 'writerly' aspects of
Freud's texts and developing towards a fundamental reassessment of the
very status of his oeuvre. The chapter will cover three main areas. Firstly,
I shall examine Freud as a stylist, concentrating mainly on his expository
skills and his use of imagery. Next, I shall consider him as a creator, both
in therapy and theory, of 'fictional' narratives. Finally, I shall view his
work from the most radically literary perspective of all: as the obliquely
autobiographical product of a – frustrated or suppressed – would-be
Dichter.

It is customary for Freud critics to pay at least passing tribute to the
quality of his prose. They tend, however, to say very little, often limiting
themselves to cursory praise for its lucidity. This alone would at least be
valuable evidence that Freud took great care over the written presentation of his theories. He was perhaps more sensitive than most authors
about the need for clarity. In his book on parapraxes he remarks: 'A clear
and unambiguous manner of writing shows us that here the author is at
one with himself' (VI, 101). That Freud successfully adhered to this
crucial stylistic principle is widely acknowledged. Alfred Döblin writes

most trenchantly on the subject: 'Note the simple lucid style, it is not even a style; he says, without affectation or empty phrases, what he means; thus speaks a man who knows something.'[1] In addition to acknowledging this quality, critics also commonly make passing reference to the fact that Freud was awarded the Goethe Prize in 1930 for his merits as a writer. Most fail to mention, though, that in 1964 the Deutsche Akademie für Sprache und Dichtung inaugurated an annual Sigmund Freud Prize for outstanding scientific prose.

Admittedly, there is little scope here for a reappraisal of Freud as a *Dichter*. The emphasis on scientific prose, unambiguity, the 'absence' of a style, and so on all tend rather to undermine the case for any specifically literary dimension in Freud's writing. In the very act of lavishing praise on Freud's style Stefan Zweig seems explicitly to negate any such suggestion:

totally unostentatious, strictly objective, a Roman or Latin prose style, it never skirts poetically around its subject-matter, but simply expresses it firmly and robustly.[2]

Nevertheless, florid elaboration is neither a sufficient nor a necessary element of literary writing, as Freud himself, an ardent admirer of the restrained, classical Goethe, would no doubt have argued. Indeed, in the above quotation Zweig may well be flattering his subject's aspirations to emulate the later Goethe. Conversely, there is much more to Freud's written style than mere terse objectivity and scientific precision. Indeed, James Strachey's English translations of Freud, widely acknowledged to be more 'scientific' in style than the original German, are often criticized for falling short of Freud's richer, more humanistic use of language. Bettelheim is most vocal about the stylistic distortions Freud has suffered; he describes the translated works as 'abstract, depersonalized, . . . erudite, and mechanized'.[3] Bettelheim argues at length that Freud preferred emotionally charged words, like *Ich* and *Seele*, terminology drawn from charmingly familiar mythical narratives, and metaphorical language vibrant with multiple connotations – for instance, *Besetzung*, for which Freud suggested 'interest', but which Strachey infelicitously renders as 'cathexis'. Even the more dispassionate Mahony complains that Strachey tends to make Freud's present tenses past, his active constructions passive, and his personal pronouns neutral.[4] Something is lost when Freud's unique style is homogenized into standard scientific prose, and there is evidently much more to be said for him as a stylist than just that he writes clearly.

Fundamental to Freud's lucidity – and to his expository skill as a whole – is his remarkable capacity to visualize and identify with his reader. Walter Muschg, the first critic to appreciate Freud primarily as a writer, comments that his intensive relationship with a vividly imagined audience is by itself proof of Freud's 'natural vocation as a writer'.[5] The quality is most evident in his mastery of prolepsis, his sensitivity in anticipating, articulating, and disarming most of his reader's potential objections. When writing for a live audience, this rhetorical tendency becomes even more overt; for example, in his 1896 lecture 'The Aetiology of Hysteria' he asks:

Shall I put before you the actual material I have obtained from my analyses? Or shall I rather try first to meet the mass of objections and doubts which, as I am surely correct in supposing, have now taken possession of your attention? (III, 203)

Characteristically, he chooses the latter; in fact, his countering of anticipated objections constitutes almost half of the entire lecture. Freud seems to be acutely aware not just of potential objections, but of *all* his reader's responses, and he is anxious for us positively to enjoy reading his works. When, in the afterword to his Dora case history, he apologizes for not having simultaneously portrayed the structure of Dora's hysteria as well as his own analysis of it, he explains that not only would this have been practically impossible to write, it would also have been unenjoyable to read (eine sicher ungenießbare Lektüre) (VII, 112). Clearly the first reason suffices perfectly, revealing just how much weight he accords to the second.

As I pointed out in chapter 1, Freud is guided by a constant sensitivity towards his readers' expectations, resistances, and levels of interest. He often tells us that 'we' are confused, relieved, impatient, astonished, and so on, and this repeated use of the first-person plural form is more than just a device, it is symptomatic of his entire approach. He likes to speak personally to and *for* his readers, and – more remarkably – to have them speak back to him. This dialogic aspect of his style, drawing on a literary tradition he probably first encountered in Plato, is most conspicuous in two texts he wrote in the mid-twenties. *The Question of Lay Analysis* of 1926 is subtitled 'Conversations with an Impartial Person' and does indeed take the form of a dialogue. Freud deftly manipulates this fiction; for example, whilst addressing the interlocutor in the second person (Sie), he continues to refer to the reader in the first-person plural – 'Our Impartial Person cannot be either so ignorant or so perplexed as we thought to begin with'

(XX, 189), and so on – as if the reader, already in Freud's camp, is being offered collusive asides. In *The Future of an Illusion*, written the following year, Freud again creates an interlocutor, and again the primary function is polemical. The 'objections' in section IV, for example, are a series of Aunt Sallies which Freud knocks down with ease. However, by section IX the 'opponent' has become more aggressive, and clearly vents a genuine tension within the author. Section X actually begins with a two-page-long attack on Freud's professed faith in scientific progress, which forces him to acknowledge that this faith may stem from his own 'illusions' (XXI, 53). Ultimately, then, there is a genuine dialogue in the text.

This kind of dialogue is present, albeit often covertly, throughout much of Freud's work. It rises to the surface when his tone becomes polemical, as for example in *Civilization and its Discontents* when, imagining an angry reader, Freud voices this reader's lengthy objection to his own arguments (XXI, 131). Equally, though, the whole of the final section of this work consists of what are really answers to a series of unvoiced objections, much in the style of his dialogue technique. The only reason this technique is so explicit in *The Question of Lay Analysis* and *The Future of an Illusion* is that these texts are energetically directed against specific targets, namely doctors and priests. Freud's awareness of his reader is at its most intense here, and he spontaneously creates an interlocutor. The dialogue with an imagined reader, however, runs through his works at least from 1896 onwards, when he began using anticipated objections to determine the very structure of his texts.

When considering Freud's penchant for writing in dialogue form, it is worth remembering that his favourite works of literature consist entirely of dialogue. He rarely refers to lyric poetry or descriptive prose, and his favourite works – *Oedipus, Faust, Hamlet, Macbeth* – are all dramas. When he quotes from prose, he tends to quote dialogue, and it is well known that he could enjoy music only when it was accompanied by a libretto. For Freud, dialogue is essential to literature, a fact which should be borne in mind not only when considering that he was the first to raise clinical dialogues to the status of 'texts', but also when acknowledging that his own texts so readily adopt – subliminally or overtly – a dialogue form.

Given such proclivities, it is not surprising that when he made his most decisive bid to popularize his science, Freud chose the form of a series of lectures, the *Introductory Lectures on Psycho-Analysis*, which he delivered in person between 1915 and 1917. He improvised each lecture, and he insisted on meeting each member of the audience personally. Not surprisingly, then, his awareness of their presence in these lectures is acute.

Not only does he constantly forestall their potential objections, he even offers them imaginary debates in dialogue form. When he wrote the *New Introductory Lectures on Psycho-Analysis* in 1932, he knew perfectly well that the surgical interventions on the cancer in his jaw made any delivery of these lectures quite impossible. Nevertheless, all through them he continues to refer to the audience as if it were physically present before him; thus he begins the first lecture: 'Ladies and Gentlemen, – If, after an interval of more than fifteen years, I have brought you together again' (XXII, 7), and so on. In the foreword to the lectures he admits this is 'only an artifice of the imagination', but it is one which serves a purpose he took very seriously: 'it may help me not to forget to bear the reader in mind' (XXII, 5). Freud scarcely needs the prompt; his ability to envisage his audience and thus simulate a concrete, even intimate relationship with them had always been a crucial element of his style. He told Lou Andreas-Salomé that his technique in lectures was to single out and address one member of his audience, and he admitted that she was the focal point of many of his – much-admired – lectures to the Vienna Psychoanalytical Society, to the extent that he felt lost when one week she did not attend.[6] In all his texts, though, it seems that Freud singles out one reader, real or imaginary, hence his often personal, conversational tone, his sensitivity towards the reader's responses, and his predilection for dialogue. As he needed to connect with only one member of his audience, his magnum opus, *The Interpretation of Dreams*, written in the face of indifference from both the public and the scientific establishment, still manages to retain his unique, sensitive, often intimate style, being addressed, as he often liked to remark, to an audience of one, his closest friend of those years, Wilhelm Fliess.

Freud was, of course, well aware that the majority of his readers would not be as sympathetic as, say, Fliess or Lou Salomé. The reader he most commonly envisages is open-minded but certainly no convert to the cause. Indeed, the salient function of Freud's efforts to empathize with the reader is to facilitate the reception of his texts not intellectually, but *emotionally* – or, as he would say, dynamically. He is eminently aware that his findings arouse resistance, and Freud – like any literary writer – uses *stylistic* features to manipulate and circumvent this powerful impeding force. For example, before listing the clues which point to Dora's repressed memories of infantile masturbation, he writes:

He that has eyes to see and ears to hear may convince himself that no mortal can keep a secret. If his lips are silent, he chatters with his finger-tips; betrayal oozes out of him at every pore. (VII, 77–8)

When anticipating the most intense objections, then, Freud heightens his rhetoric, resulting here in graphic imagery, carefully poised syntax, and a subtle literary allusion (to the Midas story in Ovid's *Metamorphoses*). His style is informed by his own dynamic theory of aesthetic function. At one point in his Schreber case history he employs his favourite stylistic device of a brief debate between himself and a hypothetical reader. Tellingly, the passage follows on the heels of his claim that Schreber's second breakdown was caused by a surge of homosexual libido, a hypothesis which he anticipates will arouse 'a storm of remonstrances and objections' (XII, 43). This technique of identifying with the indignant reader – he even calls his own hypothesis about Schreber 'an act of irresponsible levity, an indiscretion and a calumny' – and of allowing this reader a voice is clearly an aspect of Freud's psychoanalytically-informed style. It slows the pace of his revelations, offers a vent for frustrated indignation, and eases the reader's own identification with Freud.

Similar factors influence Freud's considerations of structure. As is evident from a work such as 'The "Uncanny"', his favourite method of introducing his topic is to survey its baffling, apparently contradictory complexities. This initial confusion undermines the reader's assumptions and prejudices, thus making Freud's arguments harder to resist. *The Interpretation of Dreams* is certainly structured along these lines. Freud's recurring metaphor for the book is that of a guided journey, moving first through a dark forest, on to a concealed narrow pass which leads, suddenly, to the summit and a panoramic overview. Freud commonly assumes the role of guide in relation to his readers. For example, he writes in *Civilization and its Discontents*: 'Having reached the end of his journey, the author must ask his readers' forgiveness for not having been a more skilful guide' (XXI, 134). He is, furthermore, a much more skilful guide than he cares to admit. Hyman, for example, demonstrates the shrewdness underlying the structure of *The Interpretation of Dreams*. Starting with the confusion of his survey of the literature on dreams, moving on to the irresistible simplicity of his wish-fulfilment theory, next explaining the distortions caused by repression and the complexity caused by overdetermination, Freud has his theory that a dream is the disguised fulfilment of a repressed infantile wish gradually unfold over hundreds of pages.[7] This approach has been carefully thought out by Freud, as is clearly revealed on a close second reading. For instance, he 'dismisses' his own wish-fulfilment theory very early on as an 'unjustifiable generalization . . . which it is easy to disprove' (IV, 134). Having thus voiced the reader's protests, he goes on, of course, to assert the absolute universality of this very theory. Clearly, when in this same text Freud extols Sophocles, as we have seen, for his gradually escalating and artfully delayed revelation of the crimes of Oedipus, at least some of the praise is subtly directed at his own exposition.

Most of Freud's major works are structured with similar sensitivity to his reader's resistances. For example, the first of the *Three Essays on the Theory of Sexuality* deals with adult perversions, the second tackles the much more controversial theory of infantile sexuality, whilst the explosive Oedipus complex theory is not broached until the final essay. His introductory lectures are intended for an even broader audience, and, correspondingly, Freud takes pains to ensure that the first four lectures deal only with the most harmless area of psychoanalytic theory, namely parapraxes. He has no intention of hiding any of his theories from the public, but he is aware that the manner and pace of his presentation is crucial.

Freud's most brilliantly structured work is 'The Return of Totemism in Childhood', the fourth essay of *Totem and Taboo*. He begins by plunging the reader into a confusing patchwork of quotations from the existing literature which is without apparent organization or direction – although he is actually dropping subtle hints to his own solution throughout. His readers lose confidence in any previously held assumptions about even the basics of totemism, and Freud explicitly 'sympathizes':

My readers will, I am sure, be astonished to hear of the variety of angles from which attempts have been made to answer these questions, and of the wide divergences of opinion upon them put forward by the experts. (XIII, 108)

Then he adds a footnote quoting Frazer's 'lovely' remark that the candid enquirer should, like a chameleon, shift colours with the shifting ground on which he treads. Having, as Mahony correctly surmises,[8] thereby induced even further receptivity in the reader, Freud's first hint of dramatic revelation is itself communicated in a simple but dramatic image: 'Into this obscurity one single ray of light is thrown by psycho-analytic observation' (XIII, 126). For added impact, this sentence is even given its own paragraph. Most of the remainder of the essay is then devoted to building up a vivid narrative of the murder of the primal father, and Freud does all he can to intensify the eidetic impact of this account, often explicitly, as when he suggests: 'Let us call up the spectacle of a totem meal of the kind we have been discussing' (XIII, 140). By virtue of such techniques, his bizarre hypothesis becomes, at least during the reading of the essay, almost irresistible. It will also be remembered how Freud slyly concludes the essay with an account of the weaknesses of his reconstruction, only to turn these dramatically to his advantage with the aid of striking quotations from Goethe. In all, the essay is a *tour de force*, and, fittingly, it is most eloquently appreciated by a *Dichter*. For Thomas Mann, *Totem and Taboo* is

without doubt, in purely artistic terms, Freud's most outstanding work; a masterpiece which, in its structure and its literary form, is related to and belongs to the greatest examples of the German essay.[9]

Several critics offer more detailed appreciations of the skill demonstrated by Freud in his exposition of theory. Schönau, for example, contrasts the method of dogmatic exposition – merely conveying stable conclusions – with that of genetic exposition, which retraces the author's own cognitive processes. He recognizes that Freud prefers the latter, and even asserts that he learnt the technique from Lessing.[10] Mahony is the most astute commentator on this quality. He describes Freud's style as 'processive', that is, constantly shifting ground, picking up and dropping threads, and questioning prior assumptions.[11] Freud, unlike many of his followers, does indeed like to qualify, modify, and gradually develop his theories *within* his texts, often thereby guiding the reader through his own thought processes. He avoids blunt statement and rigid closure, and he enjoys expressing doubts, objections, and even self-criticism, hence his preference for conversation and argument over monologue. Although these features of his style bring advantages far beyond merely inducing receptivity in his audience, it is not implausible to suggest that his crucial intellectual fluidity results primarily from his sensitivity towards the emotional responses of a vividly imagined reader. Muschg somewhat underestimates Freud when he praises him for answering potential objections, painstakingly covering the existing literature, recapitulating his own theories, and so on. He ascribes these qualities simply to Freud's exemplary patience.[12] In truth, however, they are all aspects of his sophisticated approach to overcoming resistances in his reader, and as such they are all, at least in the psychoanalytical sense of the term, *aesthetic* techniques.

IMAGERY AND DYNAMISM

Freud's powers of visualization were by no means limited to his ability to invoke an almost concrete reader. In his 1893 obituary for Charcot he describes his old mentor as having 'the nature of an artist . . ., a *"visuel"*, a man who sees' (III, 12), and it seems that Freud himself shares something of this gift. Not only does his relationship with his reader bear witness to a vivid imagination, his intensely visual dreams were an important spur to his decision to submit them to an analysis, and his memory was, at least in his youth, almost photographically faithful. More importantly, many of Freud's most abstract cognitive processes appear to depend wholly upon strong images. The idea that he was himself an *Augenmensch* may well have unsettled the empirical realist in Freud, but it cannot, for one very good reason, have been entirely uncongenial; he was no doubt aware that he shared this attribute with his great idol, Goethe, who wrote, for example:

whenever I philosophized about things in my own way, I did so with an unconscious naivety and actually believed I could see my opinions before my eyes.[13]

One of the earliest critics to appreciate the crucial eidetic dimension in Freud's writing was Thomas Mann, who states: 'Freud in general writes a highly graphic [höchst anschauliche] prose.'[14] Muschg concurs with this judgement, but attributes Freud's predilection for visually graphic (anschauungsstarke) words simply to his fondness for playing the role of tour guide to his reader.[15] More far-reaching in his assessment of Freud's reliance on metaphors is Schönau, who even considers that 'On Transience', the anecdotal essay of 1916, is based not on a real event, but is, rather, a concretization of Freud's recurring metaphor of the leisurely walk. His contention that the essay represents 'the externalization of an inner dialogue in the form of a fictional discussion'[16] is certainly consonant with Freud's imaginative dialogic tendencies, but even more suggestive is the significance Schönau here imputes to metaphor in Freud's work. His most important insight in this respect is that metaphors are often not merely Freud's *Darstellungsmittel*, but also his *Vorstellungsmittel*,[17] that is, images do not only express Freud's thoughts, he often *thinks* in images.

It could be argued that Freud's almost unparalleled scope as a thinker is due in some part to his ability to understand a phenomenon by means of metaphor. (I use the term 'metaphor' quite loosely here, to refer to a whole range of figurative devices through which Freud perceives X in terms of Y.) Many of his theories take as their point of departure *analogies* between the neurotic, the dreamer, the child, the primitive, the poet, and so on, and these parallels then provide him with the impetus for further theorizing. Thus Freud writes in *Jokes and their Relation to the Unconscious* that his analogy between the joke and the dream is not a proof, but a hypothesis allowing him to venture into uncharted territory, or as he puts it, 'one single, short and uncertain step forward into the unexplored region' (VIII, 178). Individual images used by Freud often provide the basis for developing his theories. In *The Interpretation of Dreams*, for example, Freud uses an analogy between the repressed dream-thought and the political writer fearing censorship in order to draw inferences about the dynamics of dream-distortion:

The fact that the phenomena of censorship and of dream-distortion correspond down to their smallest details justifies us in presuming that they are similarly determined. We may therefore suppose that dreams are given their shape in individual human beings by the operation of two psychical forces (or we may describe them as currents or systems); and that one of these forces constructs the wish which is expressed by the dream, while the other exercises a censorship upon this dream-wish and, by the use of that censorship, forcibly brings about a distortion in the expression of the wish. (IV, 143–4)

Like many of his most vivid analogies, this one takes on a life of its own (Freud goes on to imagine a complex political conflict between a populace, their autocratic ruler, and his officials) and thereby underpins further speculation.

Any claim that metaphorization – which so closely resembles the unconscious primary process of condensation – is a vital element of Freud's own theorizing could be seen as a slur on the purely rational derivation of his theories. Freud, however, at least in his letters to Fliess, was not afraid to confess to this 'primary' factor. Whilst working on the final metapsychological chapter of *The Interpretation of Dreams*, he writes:

The psychology is proceeding in a strange manner; it is nearly finished, *composed as if in a dream* and certainly, in this form, not fit for publication, nor intended for it, as the style shows.[18]

Freud's stylistic ideal of giving prior consideration to the reader is clearly being offended, but in a subsequent letter to Fliess, accompanying a draft section of *The Interpretation of Dreams*, he again underlines the *primary* creativity involved in the writing:

It completely follows the dictates of the unconscious. . . . I did not start a single paragraph knowing where I would end up. It is of course not written for the reader; after the first two pages I gave up any attempt at stylization.[19]

Fascinatingly, this 'unconsciously' written seventh chapter of *The Interpretation of Dreams* is quite saturated with elaborate imagery. For example, Freud claims the tenuous connections between the dream's manifest content and the latent dream-thoughts are due to censorship, as when a flood in the mountains blocks the main roads, so that the steep and rocky footpaths have to be used instead (V, 530). He then says of the infantile wishes underlying the dream:

[They] remind one of the legendary Titans, weighed down since primaeval ages by the massive bulk of the mountains which were once hurled upon them by the victorious gods and which are still shaken from time to time by the convulsion of their limbs. (V, 553)

Next he distinguishes between the superficial day residues and these crucial underlying unconscious wishes by comparing them with an entrepreneur, who has the initial idea, and a capitalist, without whose backing nothing can happen (V, 561). A page later he produces another simile to highlight a different aspect of this relationship:

the position of a repressed idea resembles that of an American dentist in this country: he is not allowed to set up in practice unless he can make use of a legally qualified medical practitioner to serve as a stalking-horse and to act as a 'cover' in the eyes of the law. (V, 563)

These colourful analogies are not restricted to mere details of dream mechanisms; for example, he says of the dream as a whole: 'It is like a firework, which takes hours to prepare but goes off in a moment' (V, 576). Even the mind itself is described as an instrument, like a microscope or a camera, which contains virtual localities (V, 536). Clearly, in the very chapter in which Freud – not for the reader's, but for his own sake – is grappling to come to terms with the metapsychology of dreams, a prominent role is being played by imagery.

In this same chapter Freud apologizes for his predilection: 'I hope I may be forgiven for drawing analogies from everyday life' (V, 563); but his striking imagery is, in fact, one of his salient strengths as a writer. In a 1920 footnote to the *Three Essays on the Theory of Sexuality*, for example, he claims that neurotic anxiety is to libido what vinegar is to wine (VII, 224n.), and, although a few years later he retracts this oversimple equation, his image remains far more powerful than his revision. Jones reports that Freud strove to avoid clichés even in relaxed conversation,[20] and his imagery does indeed bear witness to great originality, as, for example, when he describes fantasies as areas in the mind like Yellowstone Park, set aside 'for reservation in their original state and for protection from the changes brought about by civilization' (XII, 222n.). Not only are they novel and memorable, his images are often elaborately developed. The most striking example is perhaps the 'Note upon the "Mystic Writing-Pad"' of 1925, which consists of a five-page-long analogy between the reusable writing block, made of wax and celluloid, and the structure of the psyche. The outer celluloid sheet is a protective shield allowing only so much stimulus through; the wax paper beneath is the system of perceptual consciousness, sensitive to incoming stimuli but capable only of retaining them temporarily; and the wax block below is the unconscious, which is permanently but invisibly imprinted. Freud even uses this analogy to offer a concrete image illustrating his conception of the temporal functioning of human consciousness (XIX, 232).

However apt and original Freud's images are, they are not essentially distinct from the utilitarian analogies used by any other scientific writer. Nevertheless, many of them seem to have a uniquely personal dimension which enriches his texts. Commenting in *Civilization and its Discontents* on the sophistication of modern man, with his engines, microscopes, cameras, and telephones, he claims: 'Man has, as it were, become a kind of prosthetic God.' As he wrote this, Freud was himself in constant pain from an ill-fitting oral prosthesis, and this suffering seeps into his image when he adds: 'but those organs have not grown on to him and they still give him much trouble at times' (XXI, 91–2). Similarly, his own deeply personal fantasy of conquering Rome surfaces in his description of dream interpretation as the *via regia* to a knowledge of the unconscious (V, 608). Schönau convincingly argues that most of Freud's favourite extended metaphors have just such a personal dimension. For example, images of a conquistadorial expedition, an act of decipherment, and an archaeological excavation – all privileged metaphors in Freud's writing – can be traced back to powerful identifications with Columbus, Champollion (who deciphered the Rosetta stone), and Schliemann.[21] Even without such speculation, there are many choice examples of the immediately personal, vivid, and original nature of Freud's images. One which simultaneously reveals his constant awareness of his audience is to be found in the second of his *Five Lectures on Psycho-Analysis* delivered in the USA in 1909. Here Freud imagines a noisy interrupter being expelled from the lecture theatre by three or four of the stronger members in the audience, who then keep him outside by pressing their chairs up against the door (XI, 25). Freud thus turns his own audience into a metaphor for the conscious, the unconscious, and the processes of repression and resistance – and he no doubt simultaneously secures its attention for the rest of the lecture.

However ingenious they are, individual images such as these are mere *Darstellungsmittel*, means of representation. Freud's most important metaphors are present, often subliminally, throughout his entire oeuvre, serving primarily as *Vorstellungsmittel*, his actual means of conception. The most crucial quality of these images is their ability to convey something of Freud's *dynamic* conception of the mind. They must incorporate tension, conflict, movement, and change. These criteria are admirably fulfilled by his principal metaphor for libido, namely flowing water. In the *Three Essays on the Theory of Sexuality* libido is a river which runs up against the dams of inhibitions, leading to build-ups and breakthroughs, whilst neuroses and perversions are collateral channels resulting from a blocked main bed, and so on. Freud later problematizes this metaphor when he claims that some of the 'sources' of infantile sexual arousal flow both ways (VII, 205), but he never ceases to trust in his fluidity imagery. Even after the enormous revision of libido theory catalysed by his new concept of narcissism, he retains the fundamental metaphor, now speaking of narcissistic libido as 'the great reservoir' (VII, 218). Indeed, other metaphors such as that of electricity or of an economy are themselves probably favoured by Freud because of their capacity to convey a sense of fluidity.

More dynamic, and at least as prevalent, are Freud's images of conflict. He uses countless military metaphors – battles, outposts, front lines – and he himself recognizes that essential terms, such as 'to repress', are 'derived from a set of ideas relating to a struggle for a piece of ground' (V, 610). Even when a 'battle' has been won, he manages to capture a sense of ongoing tension, as in his description of the super-ego as 'a garrison in a conquered city' (XXI, 124). However, the conflict does not always have to be military. When illustrating the fate of olfactory stimuli in human sexuality, once all-powerful but now a source of repugnance, he recycles one of his favourite analogies: 'the gods of a superseded period of civilization turn into demons' (XXI, 99n.). A decade earlier in 'The "Uncanny"', when he first used the metaphor, he admitted it was borrowed from Heine's *Die Götter im Exil* (XVII, 236n.). However, more important here than the question of originality is the fact that it so perfectly conveys Freud's conception of dramatic conflict and development. Rieff has good reason, then, to proffer the following extenuation: 'Beneath the mechanist trappings of hydraulics (as of electricity), Freud's metaphors of mental activity are always reliably dialectical and dynamic.'[22]

Freud is quite explicit about the need for dynamic imagery. One of his most protracted analogies is to be found in *Civilization and its Discontents*, where he has us suppose that Rome is not a city but a psychical entity, a 'flight of imagination' on which he elaborates for a full two pages. The

fantasy leads to 'things that are unimaginable and even absurd', but this
is precisely his point: 'It shows us how far we are from mastering the
characteristics of mental life by representing them in pictorial form'
(XXI, 69–71). This extended analogy, then, serves the sole purpose of
demonstrating the inadequacy of static imagery. Later in the same text,
writing about the connection between the development of the individual and that of the whole of humanity, he offers a much more dynamic
image:

> Just as a planet revolves around a central body as well as rotating on its own axis,
> so the human individual takes part in the course of development of mankind
> at the same time as he pursues his own path in life.

Nevertheless, Freud is again primarily drawing a distinction between the
rigidity of the image and the dynamism of the process he wishes to
describe, and he continues:

> But to our dull eyes the play of forces in the heavens seems fixed in a never-
> changing order; in the field of organic life we can still see how the forces contend
> with one another, and how the effects of the conflict are constantly changing.
> (XXI, 141)

His scrupulous endeavour to avoid misrepresenting the elusive nature of
mental processes with excessively inert imagery is nowhere more apparent.

Not only are Freud's metaphors in themselves dynamic, his process of
metaphorization, too, is far from static. His images are constantly shifting, being developed, modified, or superseded, and they are often multi-
faceted, even when retained over decades. His most durable metaphor
for psychoanalysis is probably that of archaeology, which – given his life-
long fascination with a buried human past surviving only in traces – no
doubt contributed materially to his very postulation of an 'unconscious'.
However, more important here is the fact that this image means something different almost every time he uses it. In 1896 the recovery of a
repressed trauma is likened to digging up ancient ruins (III, 192), but in
1905 Freud, still a 'conscientious archaeologist', sees his task more as one
of reconstruction, filling in the gaps between the unearthed fragments
(VII, 12). He greatly expands on this parallel over three decades later, but
this time mainly to draw several *distinctions* between his own constructions and the reconstructions of the archaeologist (XXIII, 259–60). In
1907 there is another subtle shift in emphasis: 'There is, in fact, no better
analogy for repression, by which something in the mind is at once made
inaccessible and preserved, than burial of the sort to which Pompeii fell

a victim' (IX, 40). Thus the same basic metaphor illustrates not only two distinct clinical processes, but also two aspects of repression itself. Most significantly, in the 1927 text *The Future of an Illusion* his imaginary apologist for religion insists:

'Archaeological interests are no doubt most praiseworthy, but no one undertakes an excavation if by doing so he is going to undermine the habitations of the living so that they collapse and bury people under their ruins.' (XXI, 34)

This use of an image drawn from archaeology is almost proof that it is Freud himself speaking, but this should not blind us to his fundamental flexibility here; in the hands of an imagined opponent his favoured archaeology metaphor, already multi-faceted, shifts again, now being marshalled into a coherent argument *against* psychoanalysis. Schönau perfectly illustrates the protean nature of Freud's imagery when he points out that although libido is repeatedly spoken of in terms of a river, this equivalence is never fixed; not only is Freud equally comfortable speaking of libido in terms of electrical charge, he is also happy to use his image of a river to describe, say, Dora's account of her life story, which is 'an unnavigable river whose stream is at one moment choked by masses of rock and at another divided and lost among shallows and sandbanks'.[23] Freud's use of metaphors is itself exquisitely fluid; his images spill into each other and constantly move on, and this incessant flux of metaphorical representation vividly reflects his keen awareness of the elusive dynamics of the mind itself.

Nowadays, of course, Lacan's contention that the unconscious is structured like a language is much more fashionable than, say, Freud's 'reified' image of 'a cauldron full of seething excitations' (XXII, 73). Nevertheless, many critics forget that Freud's attitude to his own metaphors is much less rigid than that of most of his followers. An example of his free-floating approach is at the heart of *Beyond the Pleasure Principle*. Here his entirely fictional 'undifferentiated vesicle' is simultaneously an image for the primal biological organism, for the brain as an anatomical organ, and finally for the mind itself. In 1926 Freud programmatically states the need for such radically multivalent imagery:

In psychology we can only describe things by the help of analogies. . . . But we have constantly to keep changing these analogies, for none of them lasts us long enough. (XX, 195)

He has in mind here his many images for the relationship between the ego and the id, such as a front line, a façade, a cortex, and so on. In *The Ego and the Id* he continually produces new analogies for the systems within the psyche:

Thus in its relation to the id [the ego] is like a man on horse-back, who has to hold in check the superior strength of the horse; with this difference, that the rider tries to do so with his own strength while the ego uses borrowed forces. (XIX, 25)

Or, alternatively:

the ego's position is like that of a constitutional monarch, without whose sanction no law can be passed but who hesitates long before imposing his veto on any measure put forward by Parliament. (XIX, 55)

Within a single page the ego is further described as 'the physician during an analytic treatment: it offers itself, with the attention it pays to the real world, as a libidinal object to the id'; as a 'submissive slave who courts his master's love'; and as 'sycophantic, opportunist and lying, like a politician who sees the truth but wants to keep his place in popular favour' (XIX, 56). Such anthropomorphism, although often criticized, is never static. In fact, the images cannot be systematized; the ego, for example, is both a monarch and a slave! This strategic indeterminacy actually protects Freud from the stagnancy of reification. His descriptions of the psychic agencies are always only metaphors, and these metaphors are always mixed, tangential, and fragmentary, constantly shifting, overlapping, and being replaced.

A crucial difference between Freud and many of his most orthodox followers is his very awareness of the essentially metaphorical status of his theories. He claims, for example, that although the processes he has described in *Beyond the Pleasure Principle* are 'bewildering and obscure [unanschaulich]', he is not concerned:

This is merely due to our being obliged to operate with the scientific terms, that is to say with the figurative language, peculiar to psychology (or, more precisely, to depth psychology). We could not otherwise describe the processes in question at all, and indeed we could not have become aware of them. (XVIII, 60)

Admittedly, he then suggests that such descriptive shortcomings could be avoided if instead he used physiological or chemical terminologies, but he makes it subtly clear that this is no relapse into crass Helmholtzian orthodoxy:

they too are only part of a figurative language; but it is one with which we have long been familiar and which is perhaps a simpler one as well. (XVIII, 60)

Freud clearly prefers his own novel and complex figurative language (Bildersprache) to that of more established sciences; and instead of defending his own dependence on imagery, he points out that even the 'purest' scientific language is – like all discourse, like all *thought* – inherently figurative.

This awareness alone absolves Freud from the charge of scientism. In his descriptions of mental processes he does, of course, tend to draw on the mechanistic terminology of electronics, hydraulics, and so on, but always and only as a source of imagery. Marcus praises this as a kind of negative capability, by virtue of which Freud remains a materialist in metaphor only.[24] Freud is always aware that his descriptions of processes in terms of electrical charge, resistance, hydraulic pressure, inertia, homoeostasis, and so on are purely metaphorical. For example, in *Jokes and their Relation to the Unconscious* he describes his quantitative concepts such as psychical energy and discharge as analogies, or as an 'attempt at picturing the unknown' (VIII, 147–8). These images are not simply the means by which he communicates his ideas to an audience, in many respects they *are* his ideas – in the very same breath he describes his use of them as a habit of thought. Admittedly, he then asserts that the psychic processes will one day be representable in terms of brain anatomy, but he also makes it clear that his interests do not really lie in this direction. Freud's ability to defer indefinitely any anatomically corroborated determinacy demonstrates an awareness of the figurative nature of his theories which was not often shared by his more literal-minded adherents.

Freud's self-aware use of imagery rescues him not only from the Scylla of scientism, but also the Charybdis of mysticism. He fears his death instinct seems too occult precisely because he cannot couch it in visual analogues: 'But this way of looking at things is very far from being easy to grasp [or rather: visualize – *von jeder Anschaulichkeit weit entfernt*] and creates a positively mystical impression' (XVIII, 54). He expresses similar scruples in *Moses and Monotheism* when, to advance his hypothesis of a supra-individual return of the repressed, he needs to assume the existence of something like a collective unconscious. This, however, smacks too much of Jungian mysticism, and Freud rejects it explicitly. Characteristically, he instead asserts: 'For the moment, then, we will make shift with the use of analogies' (XXIII, 132). Thus Freud uses his own theory of repression, drawn from individual psychology and itself essentially figurative, as a *metaphor* for a historical process. By working wholly within this figurative realm, he avoids any need for mystical speculation. Indeed, in *Civilization and its Discontents* he positively checks his own speculative 'psychoanalysis' of entire cultures by reminding himself 'after all, we are only dealing with analogies' (XXI, 144). Generally, however, his emphasis on self-conscious metaphorization contributes substantially to his ability to produce breathtakingly innovative theories whilst tolerating doubts, contradictions, and constant revisions.[25]

Of course, many of the more astute Freud critics fully appreciate such qualities in his texts. David Fisher clearly has them in mind when he describes Freud's writing as 'often literary, metaphorical, evocative, mobile and wandering'.[26] Similarly, Trilling claims not only that Freud demonstrates how 'poetry' is a *method* of thought, but also that it is one Freud himself uses in developing his science.[27] Indeed, Mark Edmundson, following very much in the steps of Harold Bloom, considers that the current sterility of psychoanalysis is primarily due to a fundamental misrecognition of the metaphorical dimension in Freud's writing. Ego and id, Eros and Thanatos, and so on are tropes which have been wrongly literalized and now require a redeeming figurative restitution.[28] As for Freud's awareness of his own use of metaphors, Neil Hertz offers a less sweeping but no less incisive discussion of Freud's comment that Thanatos must be 'tinged' with Eros before it becomes detectable. Hertz discerns here an image from Freud's medical training, that of staining tissues to make them visible under a microscope; and, just as the young Freud distinguished himself with innovations in this laboratory technique, he remained aware that all his metaphors were 'staining agents' used on otherwise imperceptible material. Although they inevitably distort the material, they are, when used self-consciously, indispensable.[29]

As we have seen, Freud is himself perfectly lucid about his own use of imagery. He writes, in his *Outline of Psycho-Analysis*, that although his postulation of a mental apparatus composed of spatially distinct systems appears to put psychoanalysis on an equal footing with, say, physics, he knows that all his insights have to be rendered metaphorically, in 'the language of our perceptions', and he has no illusions that he is empirically describing any 'reality': 'Reality will always remain "unknowable"' (XXIII, 196–7). When, in *The Interpretation of Dreams*, he first embarked on a description of the 'psychical apparatus', he wrote of his use of spatial imagery:

Analogies of this kind are only intended to assist us in our attempt to make the complications of mental functioning intelligible. (V, 536)

Thus he recognizes that his images are actually enabling him to form concepts. He goes on to warn against mistaking these provisional approaches to the unknown for any literal truth – with a characteristically apt metaphor: 'so long as we retain the coolness of our judgement and do not mistake the scaffolding for the building'. The whole 'apparatus', then, is an extended metaphor, and Freud urges us to bear this constantly in mind. It is no fleeting image conjured up to negotiate a theoretical impasse or to communicate his ideas to an audience. The elaboration of this particular metaphor became, to some extent, his life's work. Clearly, figures of speech are not just embellishments for Freud. As Muschg writes: 'He is no coquettish lover of language, he lives with it in wedlock, where sensuality is not everything.'[30]

*

Freud's qualities as a writer, the lucidity of his prose, his vivid empathy with the reader, his 'aesthetic' sensitivity in structuring texts, his original and flexible use of dynamic metaphors, and so on, all testify to the care he took over – and, therefore, to the crucial significance he attached to – the act of writing. This alone demonstrates that he harboured certain specifically literary ambitions, which, although held in abeyance during his medical career, found an outlet in his prodigious written output. Widely scattered but significant pieces of biographical evidence further attest to the existence of such literary ambitions. Perhaps most prominent amongst these is Freud's description, in the 1935 postscript to his *Autobiographical Study*, of the award of the Goethe prize, a primarily literary distinction putting him in the company of, for example, Stefan George, as 'the climax of my life as a citizen' (XX, 73).

Underlying such gratification is, no doubt, Freud's lifelong envy of poets. This envy is generally covert, but, as we have seen, in 'Creative Writers and Day-Dreaming', for example, he freely admits that he is 'intensely curious' to know how poets create, and his knowledge 'that not even the clearest insight . . . will ever help to make creative writers of *us*' (IX, 143) only whets his frustrated curiosity. His own envy and aspirations cast a subtle new light on the plaintive exclamation: 'If we could at least discover in ourselves or in people like ourselves an activity which was in some way akin to creative writing!' or the hopeful assertion: 'creative writers themselves . . . so often assure us that every man is a poet at heart', both made in the very next paragraph. To be a *Dichter* was, it seems, one of Freud's most ardent fantasies. Admittedly, when commenting on his written style, he tends to be critical, as in the following letter sent to Fliess in September 1899:

Somewhere inside me there is a feeling for form, an appreciation of beauty as a kind of perfection; and the tortuous sentences of my dream book, with their parading of indirect phrases and squinting at ideas, deeply offended one of my ideals.[31]

However, as Freud himself indicates, such hypersensitive self-criticism only confirms the presence of lofty aesthetic aspirations on his part. Indeed, the aesthetic ideals of Weimar classicism clearly underlie the following self-castigation, again made to Fliess, again concerning sections of his dream book:

What I dislike about it is the style, which was quite incapable of noble, simple expression and lapsed into facetious circumlocutions straining after metaphors.[32]

Of course, Freud must have been half-aware that such excessive criticism would provoke reassuring blandishments from his confidant specifically about his strength as a writer, which he would no doubt have found particularly gratifying.

The only time Freud positively admits to poetic leanings is in a letter written to his fiancée in 1884: 'You will, I am sure, be astonished to hear that I am feeling poetic stirrings [dichterische Regungen], when previously I myself could think of nothing that was further from me.'[33] Of course, the love-letter context already renders the claim suspect (Freud felt he was competing against artistic rivals who had an unfair head start), and as the 'stirrings' are clearly referred to as anomalous, the document rather confirms the positive lack of literary leanings in the young Freud. Nevertheless, a letter written over a decade earlier, to his school-friend Emil Fluss, reveals that literary fantasies were not alien to the seventeen-year-old Freud:

Incidentally, my professor told me . . . that I possess what Herder so nicely calls an *idiotic* style – i.e. a style at once correct and characteristic. I was suitably impressed by this amazing fact and don't hesitate to disseminate the happy event, the first of its kind, as widely as possible – to you, for instance, who until now have probably remained unaware that you have been exchanging letters with a German stylist. And now I advise you as a friend, not as an interested party, to preserve them – have them bound – take good care of them – one never knows.[34]

Freud may indulge the fantasy in a spirit of jocularity, but the mock advice he gives – to preserve the letters of a great writer – turned out to be prescient.

His German teacher was only the first of many to detect in Freud a 'German stylist'. As early as 1896 the dramatist Alfred von Berger, reviewing the *Studies on Hysteria*, praises both the content and the form of the work, which, he claims, appeals to his 'artistic receptivity'.[35] Plaudits from increasingly prestigious sources were to follow. Although he was never awarded the Nobel Prize, Freud's many distinguished petitioners, including Alfred Döblin, Knut Hamsun, and Arnold Zweig, were as likely to commend him for the Literature as for the Medicine Prize. Perhaps due to the ambiguous nature of his science, Freud rather fell between these two stools; Einstein happily proposed that Freud should be awarded the Literature Prize, but did not feel qualified to sign the petition for the Medicine Prize, whereas Thomas Mann supported the efforts to secure for Freud the prize for medicine, but demurred at signing a petition for the literary award.

In recent decades a number of critics have devoted entire works to examining Freud as a stylist. Hyman was one of the earliest, and although he largely confines himself to quoting long passages from Freud, rather than developing a sustained critique of his own, some of his sweeping statements, such as that *The Interpretation of Dreams* is 'a poem about poetry',[36] prove richly suggestive on further examination. Mahony, the most penetrating critic of Freud's style, similarly goes much further than, say, Schönau, who looks at Freud only as a writer of effective scientific rhetoric. Dismissing such distinctions between the 'scientific' and the 'literary', Mahony claims, for example, that 'Freud's writing *produces* knowledge rather than merely describing it'.[37] Nevertheless, it is not only modern critics who dare to confer literary status on Freud's work. Muschg, for example, produced a detailed appreciation of Freud as a writer as early as 1930. He writes:

Thus already in Freud's beginnings are contained the elements which herald a distinguished prose stylist: a spontaneous instinct for narration, an innate sensual love of words, vivid imagery, tonal und rhythmic sensibilities, and an attachment to literature and the everyday life of language.[38]

I have so far neglected perhaps the most literary of all these qualities, namely Freud's predilection for narrative. My examination in the previous chapter of Freud as an analyst of 'narratives' tells only half the story. Freud is primarily an *author* of narratives, and it is now time to look in detail at this most crucially literary aspect of his own writing.

FREUD AS NARRATOR: THE AESTHETIC CURE

We have seen that Freud's use of dynamic imagery allows him to write – and conceptualize – about elusive mental conflicts and processes.

However, as his Rome analogy in *Civilization and its Discontents* demonstrates, imagery alone is not enough. A sequence of events cannot be portrayed spatially, and Freud's favoured mode of explanation is, in fact, narrative. In his theories he has a tendency to view everything historically, from libido development to the development of civilization itself; and in therapy he does not simply diagnose and interpret narrative incoherence, he attempts to cure it with master narratives of his own construction. Marcus views Freud not just as a stylist, but as a writer, precisely because, as he claims:

[Freud] addresses parts of experience through creating structures in written language that purport to represent, analyze and make sustained coherence out of those experiences by means of their translation or transposition into such constructions of exposition, narrative, analysis, argument, or case history as he finds appropriate.[39]

Freud describes phenomena in terms of *Entwicklungsgeschichten*, developmental narratives of dynamic conflicts, all of which are variants of 'the history of desire in its great debate with authority'.[40] I have already alluded to some of these agonistic, developmental narratives, for example Freud's account of the evolution of the tendentious joke from play through jest and the harmless joke, in the face of adversaries such as reason, criticism, and inhibition. The most prominent, of course, is his narrative of libidinal development, which begins with autoeroticism, comprising oral and anal-sadistic phases, progresses to narcissism, the phallic phase, the oedipal phase, through the castration complex and resulting latency period, and finishes with puberty and its non-incestuous, heterosexual object-choices. Of course, aberrations are not excluded from the schema; indeed, Freud explains them wholly in terms of this narrative, using temporal concepts such as arrested development, regression, and fixation. And, as we have seen, this chronology plays a salient role in therapy, hence Freud's conclusion of, for example, the Wolf Man case history in the form of a fourteen-page summary of a variant of this master narrative.

Freud considers a case concluded when 'we have before us an intelligible, consistent, and unbroken case history' (VII, 18), that is, on production of a linear, omniscient narrative. In the previous chapter I suggested merely that he played the role of literary critic to neurotic narratives, or editor to the patient's own authorship of a new, 'healthier' narrative. Nevertheless, the urge to narrativization is so central to all of Freud's writing, not just his case histories, that he must also be considered the *author*. Freud certainly is, in many respects, a 'reader' – of the transference,

of dreams, of slips, and so on – but since the advent of reception theory
it has become customary to regard the reader as a creator of textual
meaning, and Freud indeed creates not only the 'nineteenth-century
realist' narratives of his cures, but also – by his imputing of significance
to them – the poetry and symbolic drama of his patients' symptoms and
dreams.[41]

In both theory and therapy, then, Freud is a creator of narratives.
Such an appraisal, which tends to confirm that he was something of a
frustrated *Dichter*, is most crucially underpinned by Freud's own increasing emphasis on what he called 'historical truth'. This notion of truth
has less to do with facts than with the meaningful coherence of an adequately constructed *fiction*. In his 1927 book *The Future of an Illusion* he
makes one of his earliest uses of the concept to explain that his 'social
contract' account of the prohibition against murder is only a 'rationalistic construction' and, as such, is devoid of historical truth (XXI, 41–2).
By 1935 he all but apologizes for his negative evaluation of religion, and
he acknowledges that its compulsive power 'lies in the truth which it contains', adding that this is 'not a material but a historical truth' (XX, 72).
Freud comes to believe, then, that the essence of the prohibition against
murder is better conveyed by the religious fiction of divine intervention
than by his own rationalistic account.

Admittedly, Freud came late to a recognition of the importance of historical truth, but his narratives, theoretical accounts, and reconstructions had long been implicitly based on the notion. Donald Spence has
many perceptive comments to make about these constructions; for
example, he writes that Freud's therapeutic interpretations are a kind of
artistic product whose effect is primarily aesthetic,[42] an observation I
shall presently examine in more detail. Nevertheless, when he claims
that Freud never realized 'narrative truth' was more important to
therapy than historical truth, he is misrepresenting Freud's own concept
of *historische Wahrheit*. Whilst he acknowledges that Freud knew about
narrative truth, Spence insists that, because he only valued it for its
kernel of historical truth, he failed to respect its autonomy, and instead
privileged the less significant 'actual' past.[43] Here Spence seems unaware
that for Freud, 'historical truth' is crucially distinct from 'material truth'.
It is certainly not the complacently scientistic notion of 'actual' truth
Spence assumes it is; in fact, it could itself accurately be described as narrative truth. Freud believes a fictional construction can be both
significant and therapeutic, but it cannot be just any fiction. It has to be
an adequate synthesis of fragments of symbolic truth in the raw

material. The resulting – self-consciously hypothetical – construction is not objectively factual. Its truth is 'narrative' or 'poetic', contained only in the *structure* of the story, which is already marked out as a fiction by its very coherence and linearity. If the patients can stably re-invest their repressed energies in this new account, though, its factuality is as good as irrelevant.

Freud no doubt feared this subtle notion could provoke ridicule from a scientific establishment founded on strictly materialist traditions, and he rarely emphasized it. In his final decade, however, he dared to become increasingly explicit. In the 1938 preface to *Moses and Monotheism* he again states that religious doctrines are powerful 'by force of the historical truth of their content' (XXIII, 58), and this book itself represents his most sustained foray into the area. Indeed, the fact that the penultimate section of his last published work is entitled 'Historical Truth' bears eloquent testimony to his increasing dependence on the concept. However, he makes his most telling reference to it in the 1937 essay 'Constructions in Analysis'. Having first stated, by way of an allusion to *Hamlet*, that inaccurate constructions are nonetheless effective in recovering repressed memories – 'we often get an impression as though, to borrow the words of Polonius, our bait of falsehood had taken a carp of truth' (XXIII, 262) – he then claims:

The delusions of patients appear to me to be the equivalents of the constructions which we build up in the course of an analytic treatment – attempts at explanation and cure . . . Just as our construction is only effective because it recovers a fragment of lost experience, so the delusion owes its convincing power to the element of historical truth which it inserts in the place of the rejected reality. (XXIII, 268)

Freud thus admits to crucial similarities between his own therapeutic narratives and the very delusions they attempt to cure. It is not so much that one delusion supplants another, but more a case of a fiction being rewritten – primarily by Freud himself – in a more functional genre. Steven Goldberg, recognizing these foundations of Freud's therapeutic practice, actually describes psychoanalysis as 'science fiction', both a science of the fictions produced by patients, and a science which itself produces fictions, with less emphasis on accuracy than on narrative closure.[44]

Such tendencies are, of course, by no means restricted to therapy. Freud's creative misprisions of poets, for instance, can usefully be viewed in terms of him 'rewriting' the literary texts he analyses. Indeed, Kofman views his interpretations of texts by Hebbel,

Hoffmann, and Jensen as 'analytic novels', and she even suggests that Freud should have described himself as a novelist to prevent his adherents from misrepresenting his works by attempting to reduce them to dogma.[45] Cixous is more critical of Freud, but her emphasis is the same when she demonstrates how he utterly restructures 'The Sand-Man', creating a narrative which is linear, logical, and unambiguous in a way that Hoffmann's original systematically is not.[46] Freud's summary of the novella's plot is indeed tendentiously selective, constructed in terms of its own 'future' (actually prior) interpretation. In Freud's defence, however, it could be argued that he is essentially writing his *own* narrative – fully aware of its constructedness – and that his arrogance, therefore, has less to do with scientist authoritarianism than with his sovereignty as an author. When, in his analysis of *Gradiva*, Freud needs to maintain that the crass coincidences by which Jensen contrives to link Zoë Bertgang with Gradiva are not completely arbitrary, he makes an unusual remark: 'We might be tempted here to allow the play of *our own phantasy* to forge a link with reality' (IX, 42, my emphasis). And indeed, he goes on to imagine Zoë as a Germanic descendant of the Greek girl who originally modelled for the bas-relief. Although he soon checks this somewhat absurd speculation, he has already told us far more about his own intellectual proclivities than about the congruity of Jensen's poetic imagination.

Normally, of course, Freud treats suggestions that his own imagination plays any role in his interpretative constructions with brusque disdain. It will be remembered that in his Dora analysis of 1905 he positively challenges any idea that his portrayal of her 'fine poetic conflict' resembles a literary text – though, tellingly, not before having imagined what he *would* do 'if I were a man of letters engaged upon the creation of a mental state like this for a short story' (VII, 59). At the outset of the same work he makes an even testier admonition to his readers not to view it as 'a *roman à clef* designed for their private delectation' (VII, 9). Then, just two pages later his keen imagination conjures up a reader dismissing the whole case history as the product of an over-imaginative author (eines für phantastisch erklärten Autor) (VII, 11). The notion that he has played an active, *imaginative* role in the case history clearly makes him uncomfortable, yet he himself keeps alluding to the possibility. In the passage in the *Studies on Hysteria*, written in 1895, where he claims to find it strange that his case histories read like novellas, he actually goes on to defend this similarity. Neuropathological details about the patients turn out to be irrelevant, whereas:

a detailed description of mental processes such as we are accustomed to find in the works of imaginative writers enables me . . . to obtain at least some kind of insight into the course of that affection. (II, 160–1)

Freud was soon to begin denying this very correlation, and a key factor here may have been his distress at the famous episode, a year after the publication of the *Studies on Hysteria,* in which Krafft-Ebing dismissed Freud's seduction theory of neurotic aetiology as 'a scientific fairy tale'.[47] Whatever the reason, Freud became even more deeply ambivalent about the contribution his own powerful imagination was making to his science, and this is at the root of his oversensitive denials of the 'literary' dimensions of psychoanalytical theory and practice.

Despite Freud's touchiness about the role played by his imagination, he never ceases to strive to establish contexts in which he can legitimately unleash its powers. Although in 1934 he firmly cautions Arnold Zweig against attempting a biography of Nietzsche, he does add an important qualification:

Where in history and biography a hopeless chasm yawns, here the poet may go in and try to guess what took place. He may colonize the uninhabited land with the creatures of his imagination.[48]

Although it is intended for a poet, Freud often took his own advice. For instance, he allowed himself to speculate at great length about the identity of Shakespeare, no doubt excited primarily by the gaps which he felt existed in what was known of the bard's life. It could, moreover, be argued that Freud had always surreptitiously craved gaps such as these precisely because they permitted him to elaborate on his own imaginative creations. Perhaps the 'phallocentrism' of his desire to fill in textual gaps has less to do with the logocentrism of nineteenth-century science than with his need to find outlets for his stifled creative urges.

In *Moses and Monotheism* he makes a similar point to the one he had earlier made to Zweig, but this time he adopts the poet's perspective:

If all that is left of the past are the incomplete and blurred memories which we call tradition, this offers the artist a peculiar attraction, for in that case he is free to fill in the gaps in memory according to the desires of his imagination and to picture the period which he wishes to reproduce according to his intentions. (XXIII, 71)

This passage is striking not just because of its sustained sexual imagery, but also because, with very few modifications, it could be read as a cryptic account of his own approach to *therapy*. Freud considers it axiomatic that all that remains of a patient's past is fragmented and distorted, and that his patients are incapable of telling their own story without leaving crucial gaps. This is a most convenient assumption for a frustrated *Dichter* to make; it legitimizes his own desire to fill these gaps and rewrite their stories. Indeed, the very notion of the 'unconscious' – which can only ever be known via coherent fictions constructed to fill the gaps occurring in conscious discourse – is ideally congenial to the would-be poet.

Whilst it would be extremely rash to claim that Freud actually invented a form of therapy based on rewriting gap-ridden life stories – or, indeed, invented the unconscious itself – for the sole purpose of satisfying his suppressed literary tendencies, it is rather more plausible to suggest that these covert tendencies enabled Freud to develop a theory of the human subject which was far more subtle than the materialist orthodoxy of his day would have allowed. Fascinatingly, his first biographer, Fritz Wittels, recounts an anecdote in which Freud apparently admitted to literary leanings precisely with regard to the retelling of his patients' stories:

Stekel informed me that Freud told him he even wanted to become a novelist [Romanschriftsteller] one day, in order to pass on to the world the stories his patients had told him.[49]

Even Ernest Jones, a more judicious commentator and a much more intimate acquaintance of Freud's, alludes to similar off-the-record remarks.[50] Of course, the most significant evidence is in Freud's own texts, where it spans at least a forty-year period, from his comparison of his case histories to novellas in his first major work, *Studies on Hysteria*, to the aborted title of his final major work, 'Moses the Man: a Historical Novel'.

Spence disputes the accuracy of Freud's explanations and constructions precisely because of their persuasive aesthetic appeal,[51] but he thereby misses the most crucial point. Freud's emphasis on symbolic parallels, narrative coherence, and self-conscious fictionality all indicate that his constructions are primarily aesthetic products. Spence does indeed claim this, but he considers it an heretical attack on Freudian orthodoxy. Freud, however, explicitly states that more important than the truth content of a construction is the manner and timing of its mediation. It must be communicated gradually, often indirectly, and always with sensitivity to the patient's resistances. Often it still does not gain the ultimate sanction of reactivating repressed memories, but this hardly matters:

Instead of that, if the analysis is carried out correctly, we produce in him an assured conviction of the truth of the construction which achieves the same therapeutic result as a recaptured memory. (XXIII, 265–6)

In other words, the 'aesthetic' conveyance of the construction to the patient is more important than its factuality. Ultimately, what matters is the patient's suspension of disbelief in the analyst's authoritative narrative.[52]

Freud took great pains over the presentation of his results not only to the patient, but also to the *reader* of his case histories. When he is about to offer his interpretation of the Wolf Man's dream – as a symbolic re-enactment of his witnessing his parents performing *coitus a tergo* – he painfully senses the reader's impending outrage: 'I am afraid it will also be the point at which the reader's belief will abandon me' (XVII, 36). He continues:

I can assure the reader that I am no less critically inclined than he towards an acceptance of this observation of the child's, and I will only ask him to join me in adopting a *provisional* belief in the reality of the scene. (XVII, 38–9, Freud's emphasis)

Freud, then, literally asks his reader to suspend disbelief, thereby circumventing much potential resistance and crucially delaying full acceptance of his construction. Of course, he will ultimately demand this full acceptance, although not because he believes the construction is necessarily factual – he points out that the 'primal scene' may be a fantastic invention – but because it makes most *sense* of the dream.

Freud is equally preoccupied with the reader's reception of his Rat Man case history. He repeatedly expresses the fear that it will be found unsatisfyingly incoherent: 'The crumbs of knowledge offered in these pages, though they have been laboriously enough collected, may not in themselves prove very satisfying' (X, 157). He anticipates even more anxiously the reactions to his patient's sexual fantasies. Thus, for the key episode in which the Rat Man describes the oriental rat torture with which he has become obsessed, Freud adopts his most overtly novelistic tone. The section opens with direct dialogue from the Rat Man:

'I think I will begin to-day with the experience which was the immediate occasion of my coming to you. It was in August, during the manoeuvres in ——.' (X, 165)

The apparently unnecessary narrative detail continues for over a page. It is interrupted when the Rat Man begs not to have to describe the torture itself, but Freud persists and – again apparently unnecessarily – lists all the various reasons he gave why the patient should continue, including the axiom that the overcoming of resistances is a law of the treatment. It also appears to be a rule of Freud's writing of case histories, as is evident from the passage in which the details finally emerge:

Was he perhaps thinking of impalement? – 'No, not that; . . . the criminal was tied up . . .' – he expressed himself so indistinctly that I could not immediately guess in what position – '. . . a pot was turned upside down on his buttocks . . . some *rats* were put into it . . . and they . . .' – he had again got up, and was showing every sign of horror and resistance – '. . . *bored their way in* . . . .' – Into his anus, I helped him out. (X, 166)

Freud could simply have described the torture a page earlier, instead he repeatedly delays the bizarre climax of the description. He deliberately intensifies curiosity and suspense, expending considerable descriptive power – as when he describes the Rat Man's facial expression of horror at his own unknown pleasure – and he sweeps the reader's resistance aside with sheer narrative force.

Such skill and sensitivity evolved gradually. Freud was, for example, not happy with his Dora case history, and when he finally published it in 1905 it was not well received. Fascinatingly, the next piece Freud wrote after this disappointment was the unpublished essay 'Psychopathic Characters on the Stage', whose very theme is the aesthetic sensitivity a writer requires in order to present an abnormal character to an audience without arousing resistance. Here he writes: 'It would seem to be the dramatist's business to induce the same illness in *us*; and this can best be achieved if we are made to follow the development of the illness along with the sufferer', and he refers to the all-important 'dramatist's skill in avoiding resistances and offering fore-pleasures' (VII, 310). Once again, Freud's advice to the poet could equally be directed at himself; or rather, he is the *Dichter*, cryptically resolving to pay more attention to the 'aesthetics' of his case histories. Admittedly, when referring to a doctor who was shocked by Schreber's uncensored *Memoirs of a Nerve Patient*, Freud ridicules the idea that a case history should exhibit '"aesthetic" charm' (XII, 37n.). Nevertheless, he clearly uses the term 'aesthetic' ironically here, as a synonym for 'tasteful'. He certainly makes aesthetic demands of his own case histories – precisely as a means of enabling him to avoid alienating his audience whilst writing about what is most distasteful.

Several critics have commented on the artfulness of Freud's case histories. Fish, for example, claims the Wolf Man account is structured with the overriding purpose of engendering in the reader a false sense of conviction.[53] Fish's evidence is indeed cogent, but it could be viewed from a less damning perspective, namely as the result of Freud's own 'aesthetic' principles of avoiding resistance. Timms's analysis of the parallels between the Freudian case history and the novella as systems of narrative organization is more sympathetic. He demonstrates how Freud structures his narratives around central symbolic motifs, not simply to make them as compelling as novellas, but out of an awareness of the symbolizing tendencies inherent in the psyche itself, which, moreover, Freud was able to explore precisely because of his familiarity with the novella.[54] The most influential 'literary' reading of Freud's case histories, however, is probably Marcus's analysis of 'Dora'. He claims this text is, in its density and richness, a masterpiece of literature, pointing to such literary strategies as the novelistic framing action, the involuted narrative, Freud's foregrounding of his role as narrator, his imagery and rhetorical questions, the Ibsen-like drama, especially of the dialogue, and the Proustian complexity of his handling of time.[55] All such critics have a different axe to grind, but the single point that emerges most sharply is that Freud was a consummately skilled narrator who took great care over the aesthetic presentation of his narratives.

It is precisely the aesthetic integrity of some of his most dubious hypotheses that caused Freud to cling to them in the face of all opposition. Of his death instinct he writes that, although biology may blow away his entire 'artificial structure of hypotheses', he nonetheless values it for its 'analogies, correlations and connections' (XVIII, 60). Similarly, he defends his primal parricide hypothesis on the grounds that 'a number of very remarkable, disconnected facts are brought together in it into a consistent whole' (XXI, 23). He was by no means as impervious to the beauty of his theories as he often pretended. When Einstein wrote telling him he was delighted that such a beautiful conception as the theory of repression should prove consonant with reality, Freud replied drily, but somewhat disingenuously, that he could not understand what there was to be admired in a doctrine apart from its measure of truth.[56] In *Civilization and its Discontents*, however, he discusses the possibility of achieving a lifetime's satisfaction by appreciating 'the beauty . . . of natural objects and landscapes and of artistic and even scientific creations' (XXI, 82). As he often admitted to gaining intense pleasure from the first three, it is hard to imagine him being unreceptive to the fourth, especially as he was himself the creator of theories which Einstein himself considered beautiful. Once again the Fliess letters offer a glimpse of the passions Freud endeavoured to keep hidden from his public. For example, in one letter – written, incidentally, less than a fortnight before his celebrated announcement of the universal subtext of *Oedipus* and *Hamlet* – he enthuses: 'I cannot convey to you any idea of the intellectual beauty of this work.'[57] This aesthetic sense was both a prime motive force and a trusted guide in his establishment of a new science, and it is not surprising that he largely kept it to himself. His work was to be repeatedly criticized as 'unscientific' for the rest of his life, and many of his critics were – and still are – made suspicious by its very symbolic ingenuity, aesthetic coherence, and narrative power.

BETWEEN SCIENCE AND FICTION: PSYCHOANALYTICAL MYTHOPOEIA

So far in my analysis of Freud as a narrator, I have concentrated on his clinical work, that is, his therapeutic constructions and his case reports. Narrative structures, however, are also at the heart of many of his most important theories, which, like his constructions, often have a fundamentally fictional status. We have already seen that Freud self-consciously employs various anthropomorphic metaphors to describe the agencies within the psyche. The ego in particular is often treated as a fully rounded character, as in *The Ego and the Id*, for example, where it is portrayed 'in its strengths and in its weaknesses' (XIX, 55). Here Freud sketches the character of an almost epic or tragic hero, confronted with multiple adversaries and herculean tasks in its 'progressive conquest of the id':

we see this same ego as a poor creature owing service to three masters and consequently menaced by three dangers: from the external world, from the libido of the id, and from the severity of the super-ego. (XIX, 56)

He even extends the anthropomorphism to include dialogue. For example:

When the ego assumes the features of the object, it is forcing itself, so to speak, upon the id as a love-object and is trying to make good the id's loss by saying: 'Look, you can love me too – I am so like the object.' (XIX, 30)

Indeed, in *Moses and Monotheism* the super-ego could be said to take human form in the guise of Moses. Even when Freud discusses it as a purely theoretical concept, he still does so in terms of human relationships:

When the ego has brought the super-ego the sacrifice of an instinctual renunciation, it expects to be rewarded by receiving more love from it. The consciousness of deserving this love is felt by it as pride. (XXIII, 117)

In *The Ego and the Id* the super-ego, too, is given its own dialogue:

Its relation to the ego is not exhausted by the precept: 'You *ought to be* like this (like your father).' It also comprises the prohibition: 'You *may not be* like this (like your father) . . .'. (XIX, 34)

Well before this Freud was using dialogue to give simple but vivid demonstrations of psychological mechanisms, in his Schreber analysis, for example, when he summarizes the aetiology of various symptoms of paranoia. The basic fact of male homosexuality: '"*I* (a man) *love him* (a man)"', can, when pathologically denied, variously lead to delusions of persecution: '"I do not *love* him – I *hate* him, because HE PERSECUTES ME"', erotomania: '"I do not love *him* – I love *her*, because SHE LOVES ME"', delusional jealousy: '"It is not *I* who love the man – *she* loves him"', and delusions of grandeur: '"I love only myself"' (XII, 63–5).

Even when he does not resort to such overtly fictional techniques as dialogue and characterization, many of Freud's theories are, as he acknowledges, still 'fictions'. For instance, his basic distinction between primary and secondary processes seems to imply a chronological sequence, but in *The Interpretation of Dreams*, he admits that a psyche functioning by primary processes alone is a 'theoretical fiction' (V, 603). However fictional such hypotheses are, they enable Freud to theorize about the unknown and the unknowable. In fact, his metapsychology has no physiological basis whatsoever. Freud never imagines he is 'discovering' real entities within the mind; he knows he is merely constructing – and constantly modifying – fictions which offer a coherent account of his observations. He admits, for example, that his 'psychical topography' has nothing to do with anatomy, and that his assumptions about it 'set out to be no more than graphic illustrations' (XIV, 175). These illustrations may even be positively false; for example, the distinction between the conscious and the unconscious is, he admits, not spatial but functional. A functional distinction, though, is 'less plastic, less easy to manipulate', and Freud insists on retaining the more overtly fictional spatial mode of representation.

It is difficult to overestimate the significance of these fictions in psychoanalytical theory; Freud even describes the 'normal ego', the *telos* of therapy, as an 'ideal fiction' (XXIII, 235). He was well aware that his emphasis on this aspect of theory could provoke resistance, and in *The Question of Lay Analysis* he has the interlocutor attack the very idea of the psychical apparatus on the grounds that it does not exist. Freud, who once remarked that the elaboration of this apparatus constituted his entire life's work (XXI, 208), naturally defends his creation:

What do you expect? It is a hypothesis like so many others in the sciences . . . 'Open to revision' we can say in such cases. It seems to me unnecessary for me to appeal here to the 'as if' which has become so popular. The value of a 'fiction' of this kind (as the philosopher Vaihinger would call it) depends on how much one can achieve with its help. (XX, 194)

The term 'fiction' only appears in quotation marks here because Freud wants to distance himself from any philosophical debate about the epistemological status of his science. He generally uses the term quite freely, far more so, at least, than his literal-minded followers, who were perhaps somewhat uncomfortable at the thought that the master devoted his entire life to creating a fiction.

In his most radical speculations, such as *Totem and Taboo*, *Beyond the Pleasure Principle*, and *Moses and Monotheism*, Freud fuses such metaphorical or fictional aspects of theory with his predilection for narrative. He then produces what is perhaps best described as scientific *myth*. By 'myth' I do not mean something at the opposite pole from any privileged 'reality', but rather a self-consciously fictional narrative, often dealing with pseudo-historical origins, but whose significance is actually *structural*. Freud was well aware that such mythopoeia contributes even to the most objective disciplines, and conversely he had always respected the structural significance of mythology itself. In 1901 he writes:

In point of fact I believe that a large part of the mythological view of the world, which extends a long way into most modern religions, *is nothing but psychology projected into the external world*. (VI, 258)

Mythology consists of projections not just of the unconscious mind, but of the mind's attempts at constructing explanations, hence Freud's use of the term 'psychology' here, implying that myth, like literature, is a form of proto-analysis.

Although he had always respected myth as significant, Freud's own mythopoeia did not really begin to surface until the latter half of his career. I have already examined how myths such as those of Oedipus, Narcissus, and Eros came to exercise an increasing influence on his formulation of theory. A corollary of this was a growing tendency for Freud to create myths of his own. His descriptions of, say, Eros and Ananke as 'the parents of human civilization' (XXI, 101), or of the conflict between Eros and Thanatos as a 'battle of the giants' (XXI, 122) already indicate something of his mythopoeic tendencies. Of course, he was, and always remained, a relentless demythologizer: the sovereign ego, childhood innocence, normal sexuality, a paternal God, these are just a few of the precious cultural myths which he infamously deconstructed. And I use the anachronistic term 'deconstructed' advisedly here. Freud does not simply dismiss what he dismantles. He rather illustrates how, for example, abnormal sexuality is structurally contained within the 'normal', or how religious narratives tell 'fictional' truths which are in many respects similar to the kinds of truth extolled by more rational disciplines. In this sense, he could be said to prefigure the 'postmodernist' received wisdom that truth consists in dwelling knowingly among fictions.[58] Consequently, he was just as apt to create new myths as he was to unravel existing ones.

In the opening sentence of *The Future of an Illusion*, Freud describes his critique of civilization as an attempt to find out 'what its origins were and along what path it has developed' (XXI, 5). His mythopoeic narratives do indeed tend to account not only for developments, but also for origins – of totemism, of fire, of clothing, of civilization, and so on. At his most daring, in *Beyond the Pleasure Principle*, he even vies with the Book of Genesis when, consolidating his speculation about the death instinct, he narrates the origins of life itself:

The attributes of life were at some time evoked in inanimate matter by the action of a force of whose nature we can form no conception. . . . The tension which then arose in what had hitherto been an inanimate substance endeavoured to cancel itself out. In this way the first instinct came into being: the instinct to return to the inanimate state. . . . For a long time, perhaps, living substance was thus being constantly created afresh and easily dying, till decisive external influences altered in such a way as to oblige the still surviving substance to diverge ever more widely from its original course of life and to make ever more complicated *détours* before reaching its aim of death. These circuitous paths to death, faithfully kept to by the conservative instincts, would thus present us to-day with the picture of the phenomena of life. (XVIII, 38–9)

The impossibility of any material verification of this account does not trouble Freud; it is a quasi-poetic vision whose narrative structure makes sense of the death instinct. In fact, this instinct itself has not been 'discovered', but *constructed* to make a coherent whole out of disparate fragments of evidence. This bold constructedness is quite typical of Freud's mythopoeia. It allows him an essential freedom from the constrictions of verifiability, and enables him to develop some of his most extravagant hypotheses.

In *Civilization and its Discontents* Freud produces two such 'myths', quite casually, in footnotes. The first is his account of how man originally tamed fire. He suggests that primal man generally extinguished any naturally occurring flame by urinating on it, gaining pleasure from the potent sexual symbolism of the act. The first man to resist this pleasure was able to control fire and make the great cultural stride forward. Freud even suggests that women then became the guardians of the domestic hearth because of their anatomical inability to yield to this temptation (XXI, 90n.). Although he does not explicitly admit to any mythopoeic dimension in this construction, he does hint at his own active imaginative contribution when he concedes that the hypothesis is 'fantastic-sounding'. Even more revealing is his use of two grammatical equivalents of 'as if': he opens the section about the urinary habits of primal man with 'als wäre' and the passage about the role of women with 'als hätte' (both meaning 'it is as though'). Most telling of all, though, is the fact that when he expands on this hypothesis, two years later in the 1932 essay 'The Acquisition and Control of Fire', he uses as his prime source of supporting evidence *other myths*, mainly the Prometheus myths, but also those of Servius Tullius, the Phoenix, and the Hydra.

The other psychoanalytical 'myth' outlined in *Civilization and its Discontents* concerns the origins of civilization as a whole. Freud traces this back to man's adoption of an erect posture:

From that point the chain of events would have proceeded through the devaluation of olfactory stimuli and the isolation of the menstrual period to the time when visual stimuli were paramount and the genitals became visible, and thence to the continuity of sexual excitation, the founding of the family and so to the threshold of human civilization. (XXI, 99n.)

Striking here is Freud's effortless creation of an astonishingly dense narrative despite his utter lack of material evidence. Even more important, though, is the structural similarity to the previous account. In both cases an act of instinctual repression – of homoerotic pleasure, of olfactory stimuli – leads to cultural progress. This pattern is the only 'truth' contained in these narratives. In the story of how man tamed fire, Freud even makes this 'moral' explicit with an epigrammatic metaphor: 'By damping down the fire of his own sexual excitation, he had tamed the natural force of fire' (XXI, 90n.).

Although such flights of fancy often made his more scientifically-minded followers uncomfortable, many critics respect such flexible creativity. Kofman writes that self-conscious myth is positively preferable to scientific theory because it recognizes that the 'primary' is a construct, entirely dependent upon the always already present 'secondary'.

Therefore, even when Freud attempts to pin narratives down to historical 'origins', he remains a structuralist.[59] Most such critics ascribe Freud's use of myth to some kind of precocious postmodernism. A less reverential – and more dynamic – explanation, though, could be that they arise simply from the partial re-emergence of Freud's suppressed creative and literary urges. He certainly did not need future generations of critics to elucidate the role played by mythopoeia in psychoanalysis. In a letter written to Einstein in September 1932, later published as part of 'Why War?', he writes:

It may perhaps seem to you as though our theories are a kind of mythology . . . But does not every science come in the end to a kind of mythology like this? Cannot the same be said to-day of your own Physics? (XXII, 211)

The rhetorical questions here are defensive; Freud does not want his science to be seen as fundamentally distinct from physics. However, even in a text intended for the broadest public, the *New Introductory Lectures on Psycho-Analysis*, written at the same time, he acknowledges: 'The theory of the instincts is so to say our mythology. Instincts are mythical entities, magnificent in their indefiniteness' (XXII, 95).

The most striking of Freud's narrative 'myths' is his account of the prehistoric murder of the tyrannical primal father by his outcast sons. Through their subsequent remorse, their institution of taboos against murder and incest, and their creation of an *ersatz* father in the form of a totem, this murder becomes the founding act of all social organization, all morality, and all religion. Ellenberger writes:

To Freud, it did not matter whether the murder of the primordial father had actually been perpetrated or not, no more than it did concern Goethe whether the *Urpflanze* actually existed as a botanical species.[60]

Actually, Goethe was rather nettled when Schiller said of his 'primal plant': '"That is not an experience, it is an idea"', and he responded with not quite gentle irony: '"I am very glad that I can have ideas without knowing it and can even see them in front of my eyes."'[61] Freud was similarly defensive about his 'primal father', whose murder he had no doubt seen equally vividly in his mind's eye. As I have pointed out, though, he granted that what really mattered was the coherent, meaningful structure of his account. Certainly the critics who respect the primal parricide hypothesis do so only on these latter terms. Goldberg writes that it is 'defensible not as empirical anthropology but as a dramatization of the social contract',[62] and Rieff considers it to be a moral parable, illustrating that rebellion fails whereas renunciation works.[63] Lacan, with characteristic aplomb, is less apologetic about Freud's construction, describing it as the sole example of a fully-fledged myth to have emerged in the modern age.[64] Similarly, Lévi-Strauss probably has it in mind when he writes: 'The principal merit of Freud is in having "thought in the form of myths".'[65]

Freud was himself aware that his account was mythopoeic at least in its dramatic condensation of events which could only have unfolded over millennia. In different contexts he describes the hypothesis in a variety of ways which fully reflect his somewhat ambivalent awareness of its non-real status. In *Totem and Taboo* itself he acknowledges that it is:

a hypothesis which may seem fantastic but which offers the advantage of establishing an unsuspected correlation between groups of phenomena that have hitherto been disconnected. (XIII, 141)

The word *phantastisch* was an uncomfortable one for Freud (*Phantasie* being German for 'imagination'), but rather than contesting it, he sidesteps the issue of his own imaginative contribution by deeming it less important than the satisfying coherence of his construction. Decades later, in *Moses and Monotheism*, he strongly denies that his account of the primal parricide is 'purely imaginary' or 'wholly fabricated' (XXIII, 84), but he then goes on to describe it in literary terms, as 'the prehistoric tragedy' (XXIII, 86). In fact, it is precisely here that he chooses to present his second theory of classical tragedy, namely that it is a re-enactment of the heroic deed and tragic guilt of the parricidal son (XXIII, 87). His first, quite different theory of tragedy, in which the hero represents the doomed *father*, is, of course, to be found in *Totem and Taboo* itself (XIII, 155–6). It seems that whilst discussing his own dramatic construction of heroic deeds, Freud can hardly suppress his ardent fascination with *literary* tragedy.

Freud uses various other literary terms to describe his construction. For instance, he has the angry reader of *Civilization and its Discontents* protest:

'Either it is not true that the sense of guilt comes from suppressed aggressiveness, or else the whole story of the killing of the primal father is a fiction [Roman].' (XXI, 131)

Of course, Freud can easily counter this superficial objection, but the 'Roman' epithet was less easily dismissed, and it was to return less than five years later in the title of his first draft of *Moses and Monotheism*, itself essentially an elaboration of the primal parricide hypothesis. At his most relaxed, Freud does not even contest this literariness. In the 1921 work

Group Psychology and the Analysis of the Ego, he refers back to his hypothesis of the primal horde and casually adds: 'a "Just-So Story", as it was amusingly called by a not unkind English critic' (XVIII, 122). Rather than, as was his wont, dismissing such a designation as a form of resistance, he seems rather charmed by the comparison with Kipling. Most telling of all, though, is Freud's choice of opening words for his narrative reconstruction: 'Eines Tages' – a German equivalent of 'Once upon a time' (XIII, 141). Admittedly, he inserts, immediately after the word 'Tages', a disclaiming footnote, betraying his acute unease with this classic narrative formula. Nevertheless, he lets the fairy-tale wording stand – and tell its own story.

As usual, in private Freud admitted more freely to the imaginative nature of his hypothesis. Speaking with Lou Andreas-Salomé in 1913, before he had even written the final essay of *Totem and Taboo*, he forthrightly called his construction a 'fantasy'; and in her journal Andreas-Salomé astutely remarks that it is more ingenious than Freud usually *permits* himself to be.[66] Even in print, Freud allows himself an uncharacteristic freedom when describing this particular theory. In his *Autobiographical Study* he does not quite admit that it is more a creative than a scientific product, but when he mentions the 'hypothesis' he corrects himself: 'or, I would rather say, vision' (XX, 68), acknowledging the role played by his powerfully visual imagination. Again, Freud did not need future critics to redeem his theory by trading its mythopoeic qualities off against its scientific credentials. In *Group Psychology and the Analysis of the Ego* he offers the best definition of his own creation when he frankly calls it a 'scientific myth' (XVIII, 135).

Fascinatingly, it seems this scientific myth was itself only a fragment of a much larger – unpublished – mythopoeic narrative. In 1924 Freud recommends Ferenczi's *Versuch einer Genitaltheorie*, in which individual sexual development is viewed as an ontological recapitulation of biological evolution. Freud describes the book non-committally, as 'no doubt fantastical but nonetheless ingenious' (eine gewiß phantastische, aber überaus geistreiche Schrift) (VII, 229n., translation amended). This description, however, better applies to his own work, not least because the impetus for the pupil's book came from the master himself. Jones reports that in a letter written to Ferenczi in 1915, that is, almost a decade before the publication of the latter's book, Freud outlined a narrative of the prehistory of mankind which simultaneously accounted for the primal aetiology of all the varieties of neurosis. In this breathtaking schema, anxiety hysteria corresponds with the hardships of the glacial period, conversion hysteria with the subsequent internalization of these privations, compulsion neurosis with the horde phase under the tyrannical primal father, dementia praecox with the sons' enforced relinquishment of sexual objects, paranoia with their homosexual reorganization, and finally, manic depression with the triumph and grief of the primal parricide.[67] The vivid, dramatic mythopoeia of the final essay of *Totem and Taboo* may be rare in Freud's works – not least in the extent to which he was willing to admit its status as a product of his imagination – but it may very well have been the tip of an iceberg.

*

A quarter of a century after producing his account of the primal parricide, Freud admits that it suffers from a significant distortion:

The story is told in an enormously condensed form [in großartiger Verdichtung], as though it had happened on a single occasion, while in fact it covered thousands of years. (XXIII, 81)

The use of the term *Verdichtung* here to describe his fantastical distortion of reality may be quite fortuitous, but it could equally be read as an 'overdetermined' ambiguity, betraying a covert *primary* element in his own thought processes. Freud, especially in his later years, makes various remarks to this effect, notably the explicit parallel he draws between his own constructions and the delusions of his patients. In the same year, 1937, when referring to the difficulty of forming a conception of how the ego 'binds' drive energy, he admits: 'Without metapsychological speculation and theorizing – I had almost said "phantasying" – we shall not get another step forward' (XXIII, 225). Although this is his most unequivocal acknowledgement of the 'primary' imaginative basis of his speculative and theoretical thinking, such an admission is already implicit in his use of terms such as fiction, vision, fantasy, and mythology to describe his own theories.

For Freud, fantasies and myths are varieties of waking dream and, as such, are governed by the processes elucidated in *The Interpretation of Dreams*. We have already seen that his own extensive use of analogy and metaphor does indeed reveal something akin to the primary processes of condensation and symbolization at the heart of his formation of theory. If his narratives are viewed from the same perspective, it could be argued that their characteristic tendency towards various kinds of unity – synthesis of disparate elements, causal coherence, narrative closure, and so on – bears a marked resemblance to secondary revision, the process by

which fragments of dream content are fused into an apparently meaningful sequence. It will be remembered, for example, that Freud considered the redeeming advantage of his uncomfortably fantastical primal
parricide hypothesis to be that it offered him an unsuspected unity
between hitherto disconnected groups of phenomena (XIII, 141). His
wording could, with very little modification, be taken as a text-book
definition of secondary revision.

Mahony notes that Freud wrote relatively poorly when working to a
commission as he preferred abandoning himself creatively to unconscious impulses.[68] Even Jones remarks that Freud preferred to wait passively for inspiration to visit him before writing.[69] However, few critics
explore the ramifications of such insights, or even cite the revealing
textual evidence which suggests that Freud was quite aware of his own
approach. For example, Freud often comments that the very act of
writing has led him in a direction alien to his initial intentions. Even in
such a confident exposition of well-established theory as the *Introductory
Lectures on Psycho-Analysis*, he finds his material has led him astray, and he
apologizes for this 'artistic fault':

But one cannot always carry out one's reasonable intentions. There is often
something in the material itself which takes charge of one and diverts one from
one's first intentions. Even such a trivial achievement as the arrangement of a
familiar piece of material is not entirely subject to an author's own choice; it
takes what line it likes. (XVI, 379)

Freud's more speculative texts are, of course, even less consciously controlled. *Beyond the Pleasure Principle*, for example, appears at times to be
structured by nothing more than Freud's own free associations. It
wanders over astonishingly wide fields, and arrives at conclusions which
disturb even its author. Moreover, some of these conclusions are, as I
have demonstrated, at least partly determined by 'unconscious' factors,
namely suppressed literary and philosophical influences. In other speculative texts very different 'unconscious' factors are at work, and I shall
examine these in detail in the final part of this chapter. One such text is
Moses and Monotheism, towards the end of which Freud admits:

Unluckily an author's creative power does not always obey his will: the work
proceeds as it can, and often presents itself to the author as something independent or even alien. (XXIII, 104)

Perhaps Freud's most valid defence against the charge that he
degrades poets by declaring their most profound intentions to be unconscious is that he would himself often write by ceding a certain amount

of control to his unconscious processes. In the letter in which he criti-
cizes the seventh chapter of *The Interpretation of Dreams* for failing to find
a 'noble, simple expression', he continues: 'I know that, but the part of
me that knows it and knows how to evaluate it is unfortunately the part
that does not produce.'[70] He admits, then, not only to having a conscious
aesthetic sense, but also to relying on more intuitive thought processes in
order to be able to make genuine innovations. When asked by Joseph
Wortis for the influences on his written style, he replied that his model
was Lessing, and there is indeed much of Lessing's clarity and sobriety
in Freud's prose. Nevertheless, he knew perfectly well that the issue was
not so simple, and his initial response to the question was: 'Conscious or
unconscious?'[71]

Lou Andreas-Salomé was the first to evaluate the more 'primary'
aspects of Freud's work. She considered that a kind of artistic *synthesis*
was just as crucial as 'analysis', and she deemed this work to be creatively
narcissistic, a theory with which she persisted despite constant protests
from Freud. In 1915 he wrote to her:

I so rarely feel the need for synthesis. The unity of this world seems to me so
self-evident as not to need emphasis . . . In short, I am of course an analyst, and
believe that synthesis offers no obstacles once analysis has been achieved.[72]

Once when he casually mentioned that he neither was, nor had any
desire to be, an artist, Andreas-Salomé retorted that this was a denial of
his actual inclinations.[73] Occasionally, Freud would admit that there was
some element of creative synthesis in his work, but only after projecting
responsibility for it onto Andreas-Salomé herself. He repeatedly refers to
her as the graceful restorer of all he crudely dissects, or as the provider
of poetry to his prose.[74] In a 1930 letter he concedes more than usual,
but he still acknowledges only a minimum of creative activity on his part:

I strike up a – mostly very simple – melody; you supply the higher octaves for
it; I separate the one from the other, and you blend what has been separated
into a higher unity.[75]

Andreas-Salomé – the poet of psychoanalysis, as Freud called her –
clearly compelled him to reflect, albeit reluctantly, on the creative
aspects of his own practices.

Many critics have since described Freud as an 'artist', and moreover
for reasons far more comprehensive than merely his expertise as a stylist.
Immediately after commenting on Freud's highly vivid prose, for
instance, Thomas Mann adds: 'he is an artist of thought'.[76]
Contemporary critics corroborate this in detail. Marshall Edelson writes:

The psychoanalyst's skill in interpreting a presentation depends upon his sensitivity to the possibilities of metaphor, his responsiveness to resemblance and particularly his readiness to perceive the unexpected similarity, and his capacity to detect patterns, arrangements, and significant form. If these are the characteristics of a poet, then at least to this extent the psychoanalyst must be a poet.[77]

For very different reasons, post-structuralist critics who seek to rescue Freud from the disrepute of logocentric science also view his work as literary. Derrida, for example, concentrates on the self-conscious and self-reflexive figurativeness of some of Freud's writing, and its refusal to determine 'essence'.[78] Bersani pursues these suggestions in detail and describes Freud's more 'troubled' texts – such as 'The "Uncanny"', *Beyond the Pleasure Principle, Civilization and its Discontents* – as 'aesthetic' in that they cause all systems of knowledge, including psychoanalysis itself, to collapse. Bersani views such writing as the 'coming-into-literature' of a failed meta-discourse.[79]

As well as a self-deconstructing postmodernist, Freud can equally be seen as a creator of mythopoeic narratives, an introspective Romantic, a nineteenth-century bourgeois realist, a modernist experimenting with stream-of-consciousness technique, and as many variations on this theme as there are critics. The most suggestive commentator on Freud's works *as art*, though, is probably Harold Bloom. He reads Freud's later works as literary writing about literary writing; for instance, he describes Freud's opposition of life and death drives as 'a great writer's Sublime interplay between figurative and literal meanings'.[80] He insists that all of Freud's most essential concepts – the unconscious, the drives, even 'science' itself – are nothing more than tropes, and he implies that Freud subtly acknowledges this in later texts such as *Beyond the Pleasure Principle, Inhibitions, Symptoms and Anxiety*, and 'Negation', all of which demonstrate that the 'primary' can only ever be created by the negation of the already present secondary. For Bloom, this insight constitutes nothing less than a model for a theory of creativity. In all, he considers Freud to be a 'prose-poet of the Sublime', in that he strongly misreads not only his precursors, but also his *own* earlier discourse as literal and scientific in order to emphasize that he now inhabits only the figurative language of tropes and rhetoric.[81]

This 'literary' reading of Freud is, of course, quite distinct from Freud's own view of literature, and Bloom would, for instance, certainly reject the 'early Freud' orthodoxy of my own loose equation of 'primary' and 'creative' processes. However, unlike other critics of his generation,

Bloom retains one aspect of Freud's conception of literature: the biographical factor. His view of the autobiographical nature of Freud's
work is again rigorously postmodernist; for example, he considers *Beyond
the Pleasure Principle*, one of Freud's 'High Romantic crisis-poems', to be
autobiographical only in that it is about the dynamics and paradoxes of
its author's own speculation.[82] Nevertheless, Bloom is not afraid, for
example, to ascribe the crisis underlying Freud's writing of *The
Interpretation of Dreams* to the death of his father and his problematic relationship with Fliess; indeed, he considers this aspect of personal crisis to
be 'the book's most literary quality'.[83] Following on in this vein (although
drawing – for reasons of phenomenology rather than psychoanalytical
orthodoxy – on Freud's own insights rather than on Bloom's revisions),
I shall devote the remainder of this chapter to an analysis of some of
these 'unconscious' autobiographical pressures. They can be seen to
influence and even impel much of Freud's work, shifting it away from
objective science towards the status of a quasi-literary 'working through'
of Freud's own most intimate concerns and conflicts.

FREUD AS *DICHTER*: IDENTIFYING WITH THE HERO

At least to the extent that it sometimes employs quasi-primary processes,
then, some of Freud's writing can be viewed as analogous to fantasies,
poetic fiction, and dreams. This 'primary' factor may account for the
covert autobiographical element in many of his works. Freud himself
writes:

Dreams are completely egoistic. Whenever my own ego does not appear in the
content of the dream, but only some extraneous person, I may safely assume
that my own ego lies concealed, by identification, behind this other person. (IV,
322–3)

Admittedly, Freud did not relish writing directly about himself, but on
closer analysis his ego – in various 'decentred' guises – can be seen to
pervade a surprising number of his works. His tendency to shift the
accent from his own person onto apparently neutral objects of study is
not, in itself, unduly problematic. It is essentially a form of 'displacement', the fundamental primary process. This form of displaced
identification is perhaps most evident in Freud's works of art criticism.
He usually displays some kind of personal affinity with the characters he
analyses, hence Jack Spector's claim that Freud's choice of subjects in
the aesthetic field has 'less to do with central aesthetic questions than

with his own personal needs and obsessions'.[84] It is no accident, for example, that Freud, the self-styled archaeologist of the mind, should choose for his longest piece of literary criticism a work which has an archaeologist as its hero, Norbert Hanold of *Gradiva*. Freud was, indeed, particularly enchanted by Pompeii, which he had visited shortly before writing the piece. He also identifies with the character of Zoë, who, as he sees it, effects a psychoanalytic cure correct to the last detail. Spector has good reason, then, to term Freud's tendency to project himself into the heroes of the works he analyses the '*Gradiva* principle'.[85]

Freud also readily identified with non-literary heroes. His fantasies about Rome, for example, stem from an identification with Hannibal so overpowering that for years it prevented him from visiting the city. This affinity had deeply personal roots, including his Jewishness, his dissatisfaction with his father, and his own fantasies of conquest. Freud admits to much of his Rome 'complex' in *The Interpretation of Dreams*, a work in which many other aspects of his fantasy life are, albeit reluctantly, revealed. These fantasies tend to be powerfully heroic and are often elaborate, despite being subtly disguised. In one passage he explains that one improbably detailed and coherent dream of the French revolution reported by Maury must have drawn on a prior unconscious fantasy, as if the dream-work were thinking: '"Here's a good opportunity of realizing a wishful phantasy which was formed at such and such a time in the course of reading"' (V, 496). This is, of course, another example of Freud's use of figurative dialogue, but in this instance the words could be his own. Although he claims only to be imagining what sort of fantasy *Maury* must have had, he goes on to describe it in suspiciously elaborate and coherent detail for over twenty lines, clearly betraying Dantonesque fantasies of his own:

How tempting for a young man to plunge into all this in his imagination . . . to take the place of one of those formidable figures who, by the power alone of their thoughts and flaming eloquence, ruled the city . . . and who prepared the way for the transformation of Europe. (V, 497)

Freud was quite prone to such fantastic identifications, often to the extent that they would override his usual sceptical rationalism. For example, he retained powerful identifications with biblical heroes many decades after he had rejected the Bible itself. Most notable among these was, of course, Moses (of whom more later); but a conversation he had with Thomas Mann in 1936 reveals, for example, an equally protracted identification with the biblical Joseph.[86]

Not surprisingly, though, Freud was most profoundly affected by *literary* heroes. A letter to Martha written in 1882 illustrates just how peculiarly susceptible he was to his similarities with characters from literature. Referring to a photograph of his fiancée which he always carried with him, he remembered that the tale of which this reminded him was to be found in *Wilhelm Meister*:

For the first time in years I took down the book and found my suspicion confirmed. But I found more than I was looking for. The most tantalising, superficial allusions kept appearing here and there, behind the story's every feature lurked a reference to ourselves.[87]

Freud was so overcome that he eventually threw the book down in exasperation, but this alertness to multiple connections is quite typical of him. His essay 'The Theme of the Three Caskets', for example, focuses on the themes of impending death and of a choice between three women, the third of which is the most attractive. In 1913 Freud was himself in the grip of a superstitious conviction that he, like Lear, was dying, or at least had only four more years to live. Moreover, he admitted to Ferenczi that another 'subjective determinant' of the essay was the fact that he also had three daughters, and he even directly compared his favourite, Anna, to Cordelia.[88] More important than Lear, of course, were his lifelong identifications with the characters of Hamlet and Oedipus, but again these are by no means limited merely to shared parricidal and incestuous desires. There is, for example, a strong element of identification with Oedipus the conqueror of the Sphinx in Freud's compulsive desire to solve riddles; and, aged over sixty, he presented yet another facet of this identification when, in a letter to Ferenczi, he referred to Anna as 'my faithful Antigone', the daughter who tended the blind Oedipus in his final years.[89] His relationship with characters from literature was no mere transient response to his reading, it was bound up with his very sense of his own identity, and his pieces of literary criticism, at least, cannot be fully appreciated without reference to this subjective dimension.

Admittedly, one of Freud's strongest literary identifications was with the hero of a work about which he published no specific study. His entire written output, though, is permeated with references to Goethe's Faust. Many such references, especially when they involve Freud's own identification with the character, only exist between the lines. In his Dora case history, for example, he writes:

No one who, like me, conjures up the most evil of those half-tamed demons that inhabit the human breast, and seeks to wrestle with them, can expect to come through the struggle unscathed. (VII, 109)

His image of conjuring up demons and his use of the term *Brust* for the unconscious here strongly suggest that Freud is seeing himself in terms of Goethe's Faust. As I have shown, most of his allusions to *Faust* actually indicate a covert, but nonetheless powerful, affinity with Mephistopheles, but his relationship to Goethe's play was sufficiently complex to sustain such a contradiction. Perhaps surprisingly, Freud was equally reluctant to admit to his identification with the more noble of the two characters, which may account for his failure to publish any analysis of what was easily his favourite work of literature. At the age of eighty he was still concealing his identification with Faust. In 'Analysis Terminable and Interminable' of 1937 he finally admits to having much in common with Empedocles, a 'many-sided personality' whose work ranged from painstaking scientific research to 'cosmic speculations of astonishingly imaginative boldness', but this identification with a historical figure certainly 'screens' a literary one, as is evident when Freud notes of Empedocles: 'Capelle compares him with Dr. Faust "to whom many a secret was revealed"' (XXIII, 245). Indeed, it was Faust the striver for secret knowledge that had the most defining effect on Freud's self-image. When writing to Stefan Zweig in 1932, he describes Anna O.'s declaration, half a century earlier, that she was pregnant by Breuer as a key moment in the history of psychoanalysis:

At this moment he held in his hand the key that would have opened the 'doors to the Mothers', but he let it drop. With all his great intellectual gifts there was nothing Faustian in his nature.[90]

The implication here that it would actually take a Faust – that is, himself – to create psychoanalysis is unmistakeable.

At least as enduring as his identification with Faust was one with Goethe himself. As well as an ambivalent father-figure, the *Dichter* is something of an *alter ego* for him; thus, as we have seen, his praise for poets is often disguised self-praise. He must be aware, for example, when he claims the poet possesses 'a sensitivity that enables him to perceive the hidden impulses in the mind of other people, and the courage to let his own unconscious speak' (XI, 165), that such a passage can hardly be read without evoking his own achievements. As he sees it, genuine poets acknowledge the unconscious, suspend repression, analyse disguised wish-fulfilments, and can even cure neurosis. This cannot be ascribed solely to his Bloomian strong misprision of his precursors; Freud clearly draws great strength from *identifying* with these poet-analysts. Most revealing in this respect is his correspondence with Arthur Schnitzler. As early as 1906 he wrote to the author:

For many years I have been conscious of the far-reaching conformity existing between your opinions and mine on many psychological and erotic problems.[91]

Schnitzler similarly admired Freud, but by 1922 the two Viennese had still not met. Finally, Freud made the 'confession that strikes me as too intimate':

I think I have avoided you from a kind of reluctance to meet my double [Doppelgängerscheu] . . . Your determinism as well as your scepticism – what people call pessimism – your preoccupation with the truths of the unconscious and of the instinctual drives in man, your dissection of the cultural conventions of our society, the dwelling of your thoughts on the polarity of love and death; all this moves me with an uncanny feeling of familiarity . . . Indeed, I believe that fundamentally your nature is that of an explorer of psychological depths, as honestly impartial and undaunted as anyone has ever been, and that if you had not been so constituted your artistic abilities, your gift for language and your creative power would have had free rein and made you into a writer of greater appeal to the taste of the masses.[92]

It is fascinating to conjecture that Freud could again be speaking about *himself* here. Particularly striking in this respect is his use of the word *Doppelgängerscheu*. In 'The "Uncanny"' he explains that a *Doppelgänger* embodies 'all the unfulfilled but possible futures to which we still like to cling in phantasy, all the strivings of the ego which adverse external circumstances have crushed' (XVII, 236). Freud's admission that his own *Doppelgänger* was a novelist and playwright certainly suggests he harboured fantasies that he could have enjoyed a similar vocation.

It could, of course, be argued that Freud rather views Schnitzler as a scientist in order to *avoid* seeing himself as a *Dichter*. However, in his most powerful identifications – that is, with Leonardo and, especially, Goethe – Freud implicitly challenges the distinction between artist and scientist. Goethe, with his work in optics, anatomy, botany, and so on, certainly considered scientific and artistic activities to be of a piece, and Freud acknowledges this in his acceptance speech for the Goethe Prize when he states that the award conjures up before him 'the figure of the great universal personality'. This in turn reminds him of Leonardo 'who like him was both artist and scientific investigator' (XXI, 208). It is difficult to ascertain which of the two Freud most identifies with here – Leonardo, in whom the scientist stifled the artist, or Goethe, who, unlike Leonardo, took an interest in 'everything erotic, and hence psychology too'. He certainly reserves special admiration for Goethe's ability to reconcile scientific with literary achievements, but this may again be read as concealed self-praise; after all, Freud is here accepting a literary award for scientific writings. Although in the speech itself he rather sidesteps the theme he was asked to address, 'My inner relations as a man and a scientist to Goethe', in his letter to the Prize secretary, Alfons Paquet, he does admit: 'There is something about [the award] that especially fires the imagination' (XXI, 207). Perhaps the theme Paquet had asked him to address was simply too intimately connected to his fantasy life. A letter Freud wrote to Arnold Zweig a month later would seem to suggest so:

I do not deny that I am pleased about the Goethe Prize. The fantasy of a closer relationship with Goethe is all too tempting.[93]

Certainly, when in 1915 Ferenczi compared Freud to Goethe, Freud rejected the comparison as too flattering, although not before pointing out that he shared Goethe's brand of courageous independence from conventions and, more interestingly, his mode of production: boldly roving imagination followed by ruthlessly realistic criticism.[94] When Ferenczi persisted with the comparison, Freud deflated him in customary dry fashion: they had indeed both visited Karlsbad, he retorted, but he had little in common with any man who did not smoke. Freud was most reluctant, as Jung found out to his cost, to allow pupils to pry into such personal concerns. This was no doubt a legacy of his experience with Fliess, to whom he had freely admitted intimate details of his self-analysis, and with whom he certainly did not play down his affinity with Goethe. At a climactic point in his self-analysis in 1897, he wrote:

I am gripped and pulled through ancient times in quick association of thoughts; my moods change like the landscapes seen by a traveler from a train; and as the great poet, using his privilege to ennoble (sublimate), puts it:

> Und manche liebe Schatten steigen auf;
> Gleich einer alten, halbverklungenen Sage,
> Kommt erste Lieb' und Freundschaft mit herauf.

> (And the shades of loved ones appear;
> With them, like an old, half-forgotten myth,
> First love and friendship.)[95]

These lines from the dedication of *Faust* were probably the epigraph which Freud wanted for *The Interpretation of Dreams* before Fliess advised against them. At the key point in his self-analysis, though, Freud is clearly identifying with Goethe who, on taking up *Faust* exactly one hundred years earlier, had also had to conjure up memories that were decades old. Freud, who was born 107 years after Goethe (and died 107 years after him), was quite aware of parallels such as these. In a letter to Fliess, for example, he called the period in which he wrote his first major work, *Studies on Hysteria*, his 'Sturm und Drang period'.[96] And in 1901 he made a pivotal trip to Rome, after which he entered his own 'classical' phase, becoming a professor, leaving Fliess behind, and founding a movement of his own. In this respect, he overcame his limiting Hannibal identification by emulating Goethe. Admittedly, there is no evidence that he saw this turning point specifically in terms of Goethe's own Italian journey, but it seems likely. Whilst holidaying in Italy the previous September, Freud had sent Fliess a postcard on the front of which was not any Italian landscape or work of art, but a portrait of the German poet.

Similarly, the young Freud was inspired by the sentiments of the young Goethe, as recorded by Tobler in the apocryphal fragment 'Nature'. The central metaphor for Nature in this text is that of a mother granting to her favourite children the pleasure of exploring her bounteous secrets. This imagery, especially in lines such as: 'Her children are without number . . . but she has favourites',[97] touched on some of the most crucial aspects of Freud's identification with Goethe. Both men were the first-born son of a very young mother who was married to a much older man. Amalie Freud continued all her life to refer to her eldest son as 'mein goldener Sigi',[98] and Freud always assumed that Goethe enjoyed the same privileged status. His essay 'A Childhood Recollection from *Dichtung und Wahrheit*' is yet another of his works ostensibly about an artist, but which actually treats of deeply subjective material. It focuses unerringly on the similarities between Freud and Goethe: the condition of being the first-born son, the death wishes against subsequent siblings, and the heroic courage and success resulting from the mother's favouritism:

if a man has been his mother's undisputed darling he retains throughout life the triumphant feeling, the confidence in success, which not seldom brings actual success along with it. And Goethe might well have given some such heading to his autobiography as: 'My strength has its roots in my relation to my mother.' (XVII, 156)

Again Freud could easily be speaking about himself. His insight into the significance of enjoying the mother's exclusive favour was certainly important to him; it can also be found in his own *Dichtung und Wahrheit – The Interpretation of Dreams*:

I have found that people who know that they are preferred or favoured by their mother give evidence in their lives of a peculiar self-reliance and an unshakeable optimism which often seem like heroic attributes and bring actual success to their possessors. (V, 398n.)

So far it may seem that I have failed to distinguish between Freud's identifications with heroes, literary characters, and poets. This 'confusion', however, is actually present in Freud's own thinking. He equated poets with heroes both in his 'biographical' approach to analysing literary characters and in his attitude towards poets themselves. He often claims, for example, that the poet is a frustrated fantasist who, when successful, 'actually becomes the hero . . . he desired to be' (XII, 224). And the poet offers a similar exaltation to his audience. The reader is, Freud writes in 1905, a '"poor wretch to whom nothing of importance can happen"', but who harbours heroic fantasies of his own:

he longs to feel and to act and to arrange things according to his desires – in short, to be a hero. And the playwright and actor enable him to do this by allowing him *to identify himself* with a hero. (VII, 305)

As Freud sees it, then, literature is quintessentially 'heroic', the hero being simultaneously the central character, the poet, and the reader. He even believes that epic poets created the first heroes before any historical hero had actually emerged. He conjectures that one of the brothers in the prehistoric horde aspired to usurp the position of the primal father:

He who did this was the first epic poet; and the advance was achieved in his imagination. This poet disguised the truth with lies in accordance with his longing. He invented the heroic myth. The hero was a man who by himself had slain the father. (XVIII, 136)

This homology between 'heroism' and literature is most relevant to any consideration of Freud as a frustrated poet, not least because he harboured such intense heroic fantasies of his own. In an extraordinarily revealing letter to his fiancée, written in 1886, Freud speaks of his defiance and passion, and – no doubt disinhibited by a considerable dose of cocaine – he adds:

I have often felt as though I . . . could gladly sacrifice my life for one great moment in history. And at the same time I always felt so helpless and incapable of expressing these ardent passions even by a word or a poem. So I have always restrained myself.[99]

A quarter of a century later, this time writing to Pfister, he touches on this again when explaining why he avoids public disputes about psychoanalysis. He admits that he could easily write to vent his own passions, but, as he is incapable of artistically modifying his indignation to make it pleasurable to others, he chooses to hold his peace.[100] This modesty is, of course, somewhat disingenuous. Freud often writes polemically about psychoanalysis, and, tellingly, his favourite approach is to narrate the history of its development. His *Autobiographical Study* of 1925, for example, is a singularly impersonal autobiography. In it Freud claims he has already published too much about his personal involvement, and his brief autobiographical sketch soon gives way to an objective exposition of psychoanalytical theory. The tone does become personal again when he starts to speak of the isolation brought about by his theories, but he then stifles this by proceeding to narrate the history of the psychoanalytical movement as a whole. Ultimately, his autobiography is actually about psychoanalysis, but its themes are no less epic for this; indeed, they range from fortitude, conflict, and rebellion to fame and triumph. In the postscript added in 1935 he writes:

Two themes run through these pages: the story of my life and the history of psycho-analysis. They are intimately interwoven. (XX, 71)

On the same page he describes psychoanalysis as 'the whole content of my life', and it is in the public sphere of psychoanalytical politics that some of his most private heroic fantasies were actually played out.

In a similar narrative, *On the History of the Psycho-Analytic Movement* published in 1914, Freud says that, looking back, his early period of isolation in a hostile environment 'seems like a glorious heroic age' (XIV, 22). Admittedly, he does then go on to repeat his familiar disavowal of any attempt to vent his own passions in written form:

I can be as abusive and enraged as anyone; but I have not the art of expressing the underlying emotions in a form suitable for publication [literaturfähig] and I therefore prefer to abstain completely. (XIV, 39)

However, this work, written shortly after the defections of Jung and Adler, can hardly avoid the theme of quasi-parricidal revolt, and within twenty pages Freud has not only attacked Jung for fleeing from the truth, he has also more or less annihilated Adler. Adlerian theory is dismissed as 'a remarkably good example of "secondary revision"' (XIV, 52); and, less than five pages after promising not to comment on the truth content of rival theories, Freud further describes this pupil's work as 'empty and unmeaning' (XIV, 57). When narrating psychoanalytical history, Freud thus departs from his account of the primal horde, in which the father is only *posthumously* triumphant, when the remorseful sons have reinstated his commandments. In both stories, however, the epic themes are identical. In 1905 Freud writes: 'Epic poetry aims chiefly at making it possible to feel the enjoyment of a great heroic character in his hour of triumph' (VII, 306), and in many respects, his own epic is the history of psychoanalysis itself. Freud is not only its poet – declaring on the first page of its *History* 'psychoanalysis is my creation' (XIV, 7) – but also its triumphant hero.

Freud's need to narrate the history of psychoanalysis in his own terms is nowhere more strikingly apparent than in his scorn for his potential biographers. Even Arnold Zweig, whom he greatly respected, was given short shrift when he suggested a biography to the then eighty-year-old Freud:

Whoever becomes a biographer commits himself to lies, to concealment, to hypocrisy, to whitewashing, and even to the concealment of his own lack of comprehension, because biographical truth is not to be had, and even if it were, we still could not use it.[101]

Over fifty years earlier, in 1885, Freud had destroyed most of his notes, letters, and manuscripts, and described with delight to Martha the difficulties this would cause his future biographers, who would now have to conjecture about '"The Development of the Hero"'.[102] In 1907, when he was a much more likely potential subject for biographers, he once again destroyed most of his private papers. Sulloway considers these to be acts of deliberate mystification, and, correspondingly, he detects a great many mythopoeic traits in early psychoanalytical history: the call to adventure from Breuer, the temporary refusal, the new guide in Charcot, the perilous journey of his self-analysis, the dangerous temptations of the seduction theory, the secret helper in Fliess, the reconciliation with his father, the emergence from dark realms with new powers of analytical technique, the initial hostile reception, the ultimate reward of fame, and so on.[103] Sulloway exaggerates the heroism of this account rather more than Freud ever did, but his relentless demythologization is otherwise scrupulously executed. He catalogues no less than twenty-six major myths surrounding Freud, only about a third of which derive from Freud himself, but all of which make of him a lone, heroic, and absolutely original pioneer facing universal hostility, a mythology which Sulloway contests on all counts.[104]

Whether or not Freud deliberately fostered his own heroic legend, he certainly did all he could to thwart potential biographers. This does not, however, prevent his works themselves being read for their scattered and distorted autobiographical traces. If literature is, to some extent, a sphere in which wishful, heroic fantasies can be played out, and if

Freud's works were for him a kind of *ersatz* literary outlet, then they may be re-examined as quasi-autobiographical texts – fragments of a great confession, so to speak – which are shaped not only by his clinical observations and abstract theorizing, but also by the exigencies of his own heroic and literary aspirations.

THE PSYCHOANALYTICAL NOVEL

The most intimate of Freud's works is, of course, *The Interpretation of Dreams*. He points out in the foreword to the first edition that he has, quite unwillingly, had to use his own dreams for the bulk of his material:

> But if I was to report my own dreams, it inevitably followed that I should have to reveal to the public gaze more of the intimacies of my mental life than I liked, or than is normally necessary for any writer who is a man of science and not a poet. (IV, xxiii–iv)

Again Freud only feels able to draw a parallel with a poet when it is safely negated, but he does at least admit to a similarity, if only in the extreme subjectivity of his material. This consists not only in his reported dreams as such, but also in his writing of the book as a whole. Freud did not fully grasp its personal meaning for him until he had finished work on it, and in the foreword of the 1908 edition he writes:

> For this book has a further subjective significance for me personally – a significance which I only grasped after I had completed it. It was, I found, a portion of my own self-analysis, my reaction to my father's death – that is to say, to the most important event, the most poignant loss, of a man's life. (IV, xxvi)

Freud admits, then, that he not only dreams, but actually *writes* in a way that allows such autobiographical traces to be registered unconsciously in his texts. The emphasis on his grief at his father's death suggests, furthermore, that in the book's most famous passage he identifies not only with Oedipus and Hamlet, but also with Shakespeare himself. As Freud remarks, the poet wrote *Hamlet* directly after the death of his own father, 'under the immediate impact of his bereavement and, as we may well assume, while his childhood feelings about his father had been freshly revived' (IV, 265). These revived feelings were clearly also Freud's own; and *The Interpretation of Dreams* is, like *Hamlet* in Freud's reading, a work in which the author creatively – and not quite fully consciously – works through his reaction to his father's death.

The autobiographical aspects of *The Interpretation of Dreams* have been too well documented to merit yet another detailed analysis. The work reveals not only the most intimate details of Freud's relationship with his father, but also his professional ambitions, his guilt and self-justifications, his fantasies, even his sexual desires. Just before his paradigmatic analysis of the dream of 'Irma's Injection' he writes:

And now I must ask the reader to make my interests his own for quite a while, and to plunge, along with me, into the minutest details of my life. (IV, 105–6)

Many critics consider such intense subjectivity to be more proper to a work of literature. Hyman, for example, calls *The Interpretation of Dreams* 'a relentless and unsparing *Confessions*',[105] and Ronald Thomas describes it as an autobiographical *Bildungsroman*. He analyses the book's recurrent themes of writing and authorship, and he uncovers an entire subplot relating to how Freud became the author of this, his life story. He connects this urge for authorship with Freud's oedipal fantasies by viewing it as a desire for self-procreation in defiance of the father.[106] Such studies are certainly valuable, not least for their recognition of the literary and autobiographical aspects of Freud's writings. However, a detailed analysis of the subjective elements in *The Interpretation of Dreams* would not, in itself, quite support my case that his work bears traces of a quasi-literary working-through of his own personal conflicts. It is with some justification that Freud writes in the 1908 preface: 'To my readers, however, it will be a matter of indifference upon what particular material they learn to appreciate the importance of dreams and how to interpret them' (IV, xxvi). The 'autobiography' in *The Interpretation of Dreams* does indeed exist primarily in its raw material, rather than in the resulting theories as such. In this respect, it is less significant than other texts in which autobiographical pressures appear to influence Freud's treatment of ostensibly *neutral* objects of study. Only texts of this latter kind really support the case that his scientific writings provided him with a vent for frustrated literary aspirations.

Freud certainly avoided ever repeating such intimate revelations. In the postscript to his *Autobiographical Study* he expresses positive regret at having been 'more open and frank' than most other writers, and he recommends such candour to no one (XX, 73). Even in *The Interpretation of Dreams* itself Freud never pursues an interpretation of one of his own dreams to its absolute conclusion. He had intended to include at least one whole analysis, if only to demonstrate the beauty of a complete interpretation, but he gave in to pressure from Fliess who considered this to be excessively indiscreet. As it is, Freud only reveals as much as is necessary to clarify any relevant area of theory. Nevertheless, his voluminous output offered him many outlets for more subtle forms of self-revelation. In fact, it was perhaps impossible for him to write so much without his ongoing self-analysis seeping into his works, and this could be true even of his most theoretical texts. In 1912, writing about the limitations of any analyst who has not himself been analysed, he warns:

He will easily fall into the temptation of projecting outwards some of the peculiarities of his own personality, which he has dimly perceived, into the field of science, as a theory having universal validity. (XII, 177)

It would, of course, be unfair simply to have this criticism backfire on Freud himself. Even if its objectivity was not assured by any external analyst, his painstaking and sober self-analysis could hardly be described as dim self-perception. Nevertheless, Freud's personal conflicts do appear to exist in a complex dialectic with the subject matter of his works, especially his more speculative texts about the artists and heroes with whom he identified so strongly. It now remains to trace some of the threads of this displaced autobiography through some of his most problematical works.

Freud's 1910 book *Leonardo da Vinci and a Memory of his Childhood* is an obvious point of departure. Commentators from Jones onwards recognize that Freud identifies with his subject in this work. The parallels are most evident when he describes Leonardo's scientific career. For example, he writes:

In an age which was beginning to replace the authority of the Church by that of antiquity and which was not yet familiar with any form of research not based on presuppositions, Leonardo – the forerunner and by no means unworthy rival of Bacon and Copernicus – was necessarily isolated. (XI, 65)

Even apart from the emphasis on isolation brought about by scientific research which was ahead of its time, there is a subtle personal note in that Freud specifically saw himself as the Copernicus of psychology, relegating consciousness to the periphery of the system of which it was supposed to be the centre. He repeatedly extols Leonardo not only for his unconventionality and independence as a thinker, but also because of the way this ardent scientific integrity derived from sublimated libido:

His affects were controlled and subjected to the instinct for research; he did not love and hate, but asked himself about the origin and significance of what he was to love and hate . . . He had merely converted his passion into a thirst for knowledge. (XI, 74)

This factor alone would be enough to indicate a strong identification, but Freud further underlines the point when he adds that it caused

Leonardo to be called 'the Italian Faust' (XI, 75). He traces the tendency back to the infant's 'untiring love of asking questions' in response to the threat of an unwanted sibling (XI, 78). As is often the case when Freud writes about the traumas of childhood, he shows an uncommon degree of empathy with the infant's experience. Here he describes its jealousy and disappointment, and the profound depression caused when its precocious research founders. In many similar passages he writes with empathy about, for example, the agonies accompanying the 'downfall' of infantile sexuality, which include disappointed love, insecurity, jealousy, sexual humiliation, and corporal punishments which 'show him at last the full extent to which he has been *scorned*' (XVIII, 21, Freud's emphasis in the original German). Tellingly, such accounts are usually recounted from the male perspective, indeed, specifically from the perspective of the first-born son, the only one to experience and lose the parents' exclusive love. In these passages Freud is clearly somehow working through his own childhood traumas, and his reconstruction of Leonardo's infancy appears to belong to this ongoing process.

Leonardo may have been a particularly apt subject for Freud's displaced self-analysis because of his sublimation of libido into scientific research, but this is not the only element of his identification. Freud is most fascinated by the 'universal genius' (XI, 63). Naturally, he gives Leonardo's scientific work priority over his artistic achievements, but the parallel with the artist can be detected for example in Freud's remark about Leonardo's attitude to his paintings: 'There is no doubt that the creative artist feels towards his works like a father' (XI, 121). Freud knows this primarily because it is his attitude to his own works, as is evident from various remarks, such as his comment on his 'The Moses of Michelangelo': 'My relationship to this work is something like that to a love-child . . . Not until much later did I legitimise this non-analytical child.'[107] Freud's artistic leanings may have been buried deep beneath his official identity as an exact scientist, but his fantasy that he had the potential to be productive as an artist was certainly a prime factor in his choice of Leonardo as a subject for a speculative biography.

Particularly relevant in this respect is the fact that the Leonardo study itself is, in Freud's own opinion, his most artistic work: 'the only truly beautiful thing I have ever written'.[108] Its prose is exceptionally highly polished, and I have already examined other broadly literary features such as its exquisitely intricate symbolism and its essentially fictional basis. Admittedly, Freud considers the work ultimately to have failed because of the 'fragmentary nature [Lückenhaftigkeit] of the material' about Leonardo (XI, 135), but, as we know, this factor is perfectly consonant with his fiction-writing tendencies. He positively dwells on how great are the gaps in our knowledge about Leonardo, knowing that precisely this permits him to unleash his imagination. Thus it is most significant that in this very text he chooses to add a thirty-line footnote recapping his analysis of Goethe's childhood memory (XI, 84n.). This latter work has many features in common with the Leonardo analysis, not only in its decentred working through of Freud's own childhood traumas via his identification with an artist-scientist, but specifically in its 'fictional' qualities. Freud likewise justifies his Goethe analysis by pointing out in the opening paragraph that the poet 'relates in fact only one *single* event' from his earliest childhood (XVII, 147, Freud's emphasis in the original German). Thus he establishes another of those legitimate gaps which he needs before allowing himself to write fiction. Perhaps the most strikingly fictional feature of the Goethe analysis, though, is that Freud dares to give the poet a soliloquy:

'I was a child of fortune: destiny preserved my life, although I came into the world as though dead. Even more, destiny removed my brother, so that I did not have to share my mother's love with him.' (XVII, 156)

And, of course, the essay actually concludes with Freud giving his poet-hero yet more dialogue: 'My strength has its roots in my relation to my mother' (XVII, 156). Fascinatingly, the central conclusion of his Leonardo analysis is itself presented in the form of imagined dialogue ascribed to the 'hero': 'It was through this erotic relation with my mother that I became a homosexual' (XI, 106). Striking here is not just the necessarily fictional status of such dialogue, but the fact that it allows Freud to use the first-person form.

The Leonardo study is much fuller than the Goethe essay, and it has room for Freud's favourite 'literary' feature: a constructed narrative of the hero's entire development from childhood onwards. After having presented this he admits:

If in making these statements I have provoked the criticism, even from friends of psycho-analysis and from those who are expert in it, that I have merely written a psycho-analytic novel, I shall reply that I am far from over-estimating the certainty of these results. (XI, 134)

Instead of disputing, then, that this is a literary account, he simply reassures his readers that he does not consider his own conclusions to be necessarily factual. Indeed, in one letter he openly admitted that the study

was 'partly fiction' (halb Romandichtung).[109] In the text he even inti-
mates why he has written this 'novel':

Like others I have succumbed to the attraction of this great and mysterious
man, in whose nature one seems to detect powerful instinctual passions which
can nevertheless only express themselves in so remarkably subdued a manner.
(XI, 134)

Thus Freud does not even try to defend himself against the – normally
vexing – claim that he has produced an artistic fiction; he simply points
out that he was driven to write by a deep fascination with his subject.

It is, however, somewhat naive to attribute Freud's affinity with
Leonardo to *unconscious* identification; his approach to his subject is much
more sophisticated than mere wishful fantasy. When apologizing for the
pathographical elements in the work, he positively attacks biographers
who are emotionally enthralled by their subject:

biographers are fixated on their heroes in a quite special way. In many cases
they have chosen their hero as the subject of their studies because – for reasons
of their personal emotional life – they have felt a special affection for him from
the very first. (XI, 130)

Freud, on the other hand, believes he has presented us with 'a human
being to whom we might feel ourselves distantly related', and the 'distantly' here is just as important as the 'related'. Freud is certainly quite
careful to establish various *distinctions* between himself and his subject.
When discussing the fate of the infant's love of asking questions, for
example, he offers only three possible outcomes: firstly, total repression
and a concomitant inhibition of the intellect; secondly, sexualization of
the act of thinking itself, which becomes an unsatisfying compulsive activity; and finally, 'the rarest and most perfect' outcome: sublimation.
Leonardo clearly belongs to this third category, but surprisingly Freud
does not, as he makes clear when he adds that this sublimated drive for
knowledge always then bears a hallmark of sexual repression 'in that it
avoids any concern with sexual themes' (XI, 80). Freud is thus utterly
excluded from the whole scheme. Indeed, he expands on Leonardo's
extreme chastity at great length (XI, 70). Admittedly, Freud is himself
strangely chaste in this text. On this very page he makes his first reference
to Eros 'the preserver of all living things', whereas elsewhere he explicitly
rejects the term 'erotic' as an unnecessary concession to prudery (XVIII,
91); and on the next page he refers to Leonardo's virginity with an uncharacteristically delicate circumlocution: 'It is doubtful whether Leonardo
ever embraced a woman in passion' (XI, 71). Despite such unwonted gen-

tility, Freud is clearly establishing a certain distance between himself and his rather prudish subject, and this may have been crucial to his purposes. Gay, for one, considers that Freud was actively dealing with his own personal problems in this text – specifically, his homosexual attachments.[110] When discussing Leonardo's homosexuality, Freud takes care to point out that homosexual object choices are, at least unconsciously, universal (XI, 99n.), and he always recognized that he had had strong homosexual feelings for Fliess. In 1910, moreover, he was well aware that Jung was something of a revenant of this earlier intimate. Freud, then, was certainly not simply denying any homosexual feelings. He may, however, have been achieving a crucial *distance* from them. It could be that, instead of repeating his past mistakes, he was writing about Leonardo as a homosexual with whom, because of profound similarities, he could fully empathize, but about whom, due to essential differences, he could have superior insight. This technique of working out conflicts by achieving a critical distance from a recognizably autobiographical, but distinctly 'other' character actually comes close to Freud's own conception of the process of genuine literature as he had understood it at least since 1897, when he had admired Goethe for 'curing' himself by means of his Werther.

In 1914 Freud wrote an essay about the work of another Renaissance master, but 'The Moses of Michelangelo' again appears to be more concerned with his own personal conflicts than with art criticism as such. One difference is that in this text he appears to identify less with the artist than with the *subject*, but this distinction soon proves to be superficial. Even Jones acknowledges Freud's identification with Moses,[111] and Fuller fleshes this out, remarking that in 1913 Jung was the faithless son returning to earlier idolatry, whilst Freud, about to undertake the massive revisions provoked by his theory of narcissism, felt he was losing his own grip on the tables of the law.[112] Indeed, the autobiographical element is so blatant that it probably accounts for Freud's initial decision to publish the work anonymously. He had started planning it shortly before his break with Jung in January 1913; however, even when relations with Jung had been ideal, Freud had still seen himself as Moses. In a 1909 letter to Jung he writes: 'if I am Moses, then you are Joshua and will take possession of the promised land of psychiatry, which I shall only be able to glimpse from afar'.[113] By October 1912, just after he had first conceived of the Michelangelo essay, he had utterly revised his opinion of Jung, but his fundamental identification remained, and he told Ferenczi that regarding Jung he was not Michelangelo's self-possessed Moses but the irate Moses of the biblical account.[114]

In the essay itself this pronounced identification is never made explicit, but it does leave conspicuous traces. At one point the statue is described as:

the image of a passionate leader of mankind who, conscious of his divine mission as Lawgiver, meets the uncomprehending opposition of men. (XIII, 221)

Admittedly, Freud is here quoting a previous critic, but this is just the screen he needs before he can indulge in the autobiographical resonances. His choice of this particular passage, with such ideally overdetermined words as *Führer, gesetzgebend,* and *Widerstand,* is patently motivated by his self-projection into his material. Freud is primarily reminding himself that he, too, is on a mission, and his priority must be the new laws he is bringing to his own select group – which, after the loss of Jung, was now more exclusively Jewish than ever. Under the cloak of anonymity, Freud describes psychoanalysis rather grandly as 'our work in the service of a great cause' (XIII, 234, translation amended), thus bringing the parallel into even sharper focus. He depicts Moses with remarkable empathy for his rage, his sense of mission in the name of a higher truth, and his pain at the betrayal by his own followers. However, as he is primarily trying to master his anger towards Jung, his interpretation centres on Moses' own 'frozen wrath' (XIII, 229), by virtue of which the tables of the law are saved. As Marianne Krüll astutely points out, Michelangelo actually sculpted the self-composed Moses on his second descent from Sinai, but Freud, for his own purposes, *needed* a Moses still struggling with his rage against his followers.[115] Thus, for him, the statue has to represent the precise moment at which the hero inhibits his wrathful passions. Freud does indeed describe this feat in suitably heroic terms, as 'the highest mental achievement that is possible in a man' (XIII, 233).

Like the Leonardo study, this essay is a quasi-literary working through of Freud's own conflicts, and correspondingly 'writerly' elements are not difficult to detect. Although it is an essay about sculpture, Freud's own creative urge is exclusively literary. On the opening page he admits that he is enormously receptive to works of art, 'especially those of literature and sculpture' (XIII, 211). Thus, even in an essay about a sculpture, literature comes first. This quickly becomes evident as Freud continues. For example, he asks:

But why should the artist's intention not be capable of being communicated and apprehended in *words*, like any other fact of mental life? (XIII, 212)

This faith in the power of language may be the arrogance of a philistine scientist, but it could equally be an echo of the suppressed *Dichter* in Freud. At one point he actually speaks of the statue's meaning as a 'script in the stone' (XIII, 215); and, highly characteristically, he does indeed translate the statue into an elaborate narrative. He begins by asking:

Did Michelangelo intend to create a 'timeless study of character and mood' in this Moses, or did he portray him at a particular moment of his life and, if so, at a highly significant one? (XIII, 215)

Of course, only this latter – dynamic, dramatic – reading could really capture Freud's imagination, and accordingly he decides that Moses has just seen the golden calf. Typically, he then produces an *Entwicklungs-geschichte* of how the statue's posture arose, presented in the form of *three* sketches and, more significantly, a twenty-line account of the dramatic events narrated in the historic present tense (XIII, 224–5). Moses is initially sitting peacefully, but on hearing his followers' idolatrous worship he turns his head and realizes what has happened. He wants to leap up in anger to smite the sinners, but he can only clasp his beard in frustration. Suddenly, a change comes over him. He feels the stone tablets beginning to slip, and the would-be punitive hand draws back, pulling his beard with it, to rescue the commandments from destruction. Like all of Freud's narratives, it makes sense of the wealth of details he has painstakingly enumerated, but it is ultimately another – not quite plausible – 'just-so story'.

Freud actually prefaces his narrative with the words: 'In imagination we complete the scene', thus all but admitting its fictional status. As with the Leonardo study, its real significance lies less in its objective plausibility than in the insight it affords into Freud's quasi-literary imagination. He had been obsessed by the Moses statue since his first visit to Rome in 1901, and he had repeatedly visited it, making measurements and even drawings of it. Then, of course, it had had a very different meaning for him, as he admits at the beginning of the essay:

How often have I . . . essayed to support the angry scorn of the hero's glance! Sometimes I have crept cautiously out of the half-gloom of the interior as though I myself belonged to the mob upon whom his eye is turned. (XIII, 213)

This unease seems to relate to his oedipal Rome complex, and in 1901 Moses was clearly an imago of Jakob Freud, a terrifying avatar of the super-ego. Over the course of the next twenty pages, however, Freud creatively rewrites Moses as an exemplary *ego*, his passions harnessed in the service of the reality principle. At such a critical stage in the history of the psychoanalytical movement, this is evidently Freud's admonition to himself. He at least considers that the statue is *Michelangelo's* attempt to rise above his resentment of the Pope he was supposed to be honouring:

And so he carved his Moses on the Pope's tomb, not without a reproach against the dead pontiff, as a warning to himself, thus, in self-criticism, rising superior to his own nature. (XIII, 234)

As this is the final sentence of the essay proper, it appears that Freud, rather than simply indulging in an 'unconscious' identification with Moses or Michelangelo, has once again consciously manipulated the story of a fantastical, but semi-autobiographical character in order to gain insight into his own dilemma. By writing Moses as an ideal self, he has 'rewritten' not only Michelangelo's statue and, of course, the biblical narrative, but also his *own* reading of Moses as Jakob Freud. It could therefore be argued that his most fundamental identification in this essay is not with Moses, but with Michelangelo, who, as Freud sees it, has creatively rechannelled his aggressive drives by means of an imaginative work of revisionary story-telling.

Over twenty years later Freud returned to the subject of Moses and produced a book as deeply personal as anything he had written since *The Interpretation of Dreams*. *Moses and Monotheism* is also arguably the most imaginative and, indeed, the most 'literary' of all his works, if not the most stylistically polished. In effect, he wrote it twice. The first time he resolved to leave most of it unpublished, but, he explains, 'it tormented me like an unlaid ghost' (XXIII, 103). Not only does this suggest that the book was written in anything but an objective state of mind, it even hints at the function of such a quasi-autobiographical work: to exorcize his own ghosts and demons. He certainly admits to a strong emotional need to give the work a full airing: 'I had scarcely arrived in England before I found the temptation irresistible to make the knowledge I had held back accessible to the world' (XXIII, 103). In fact, his desire to see the English translation published became his most urgent dying wish.

Moses and Monotheism is, to some extent, the sequel to another work of great imagination, the final essay of *Totem and Taboo*. Although Freud defends the methodology of his primal parricide construction in this later work, a remarkable letter written to Jung in December 1911 reveals just how unscientific his approach had been even then. Here Freud complains that the background reading for *Totem and Taboo* is meaningless to him because he already possesses the truths he is trying to prove. This alone is telling, but he goes on to reveal much more:

I can see from the difficulties I encounter in this work that I was not cut out for inductive investigation, that my whole make-up is intuitive, and that in setting out to establish the purely empirical science of ΨA I subjected myself to an extraordinary discipline.[116]

Most surprising here is Freud's admission that he worked by intuition, which he usually disparaged as blindly solipsistic, for example:

It is once again merely an illusion to expect anything from intuition and intro-spection; they can give us nothing but particulars about our own mental life. (XXI, 31–2)

If he admits that speculative works such as *Totem and Taboo* are actually based on 'intuition', he must accept that they may themselves be read for insights into his own psyche. Many critics have done just this. Gay, for example, writes that *Totem and Taboo* is 'a round in his never-finished wrestling bout with Jacob Freud'.[117] If Freud is the 'hero' of *Totem and Taboo*, it could indeed only be in identification with the parricidal sons. As he writes in *Moses and Monotheism*: 'A hero is someone who has had the courage to rebel against his father and has in the end victoriously overcome him' (XXIII, 12). In his account of the parricide Freud's empathy is exclusively reserved for the rebel sons. With each set of circumstances he describes their emotional responses – ambivalent love, jealousy, defiance, brotherly feelings, remorse, and so on – whereas the father and the women enjoy no such privilege. Freud wrote 'The Return of Totemism in Childhood' in a state of elation, but on completing it he was plagued with doubts. Jones pointed out that this followed the pattern of the sons' emotions in the essay, and he put it to Freud that he had himself experienced the excitement of killing the father and that his doubts were only a manifestation of his subsequent remorse.[118] This would certainly be strong evidence that *Totem and Taboo* is yet another of the works in which Freud continued his self-analysis by identifying with essentially imaginary heroic characters.

There are equally cogent grounds for viewing *Moses and Monotheism* as a continuation of this self-analytical process. The doubts Freud had about *Totem and Taboo* certainly returned to trouble this later work, which was written and published in agonized fits and starts between 1934 and 1939. In fact, the themes of the two works are virtually identical: the murder of a powerful father-figure, and, via the perpetrators' remorse, the eventual re-establishment of his laws. Other details of Freud's coming to terms with his father recur; for example, the theme of castration, which appears in his emphasis on Moses' introduction of the custom of circumcision – the 'symbolic substitute' for castration (XXIII, 122) – as a token of filial submission. Not surprisingly, then, critics have viewed *Moses and Monotheism* in terms of Freud's relationship with Jakob. Krüll calls it his 'final confrontation with his father' veiled behind the symbolic language of psychoanalytical theory, and she asserts that '*his* fiction, *his* Moses myth was a cover for his own family romance'.[119] Marthe Robert also emphasizes this fictionality, describing Freud's book as 'the novel of his life'. She, too, primarily has his relationship with Jakob in mind, hence she calls it 'the son's last protest and bulwark against the inevitable return of the fathers'.[120]

Such lucid recognition of the literary and autobiographical elements in Freud's work is extremely valuable, but both Krüll and Robert offer a too narrowly oedipal reading of this text. By the 1930s Freud hardly still saw himself as a parricidal son. On the contrary, he positively identifies with Moses as a father-figure, a transition he had crystallized decades earlier by the very act of writing 'The Moses of Michelangelo'. His most vivid concern now is the fate of his 'child', psychoanalysis, and *Moses and Monotheism* is perhaps best understood as a veiled history of the psycho-analytical movement. Many details of Freud's speculative account of monotheism seem to resonate with the epic legend of psychoanalytical history. He writes, for example, that Akhenaton's teachings were gradu-ally distilled 'under the influence of . . . violent opposition' (XXIII, 22), and that at first the religion was not popular; 'it had probably remained restricted to a narrow circle surrounding the king's person' (XXIII, 23). However, Moses then makes his 'heroic attempt to combat destiny' (XXIII, 28) by choosing to lead a select group of Jews, a move which Freud describes with uncharacteristic enthusiasm: 'Eine weltgeschicht-liche Entscheidung!' (Strachey rather tones the German down by remov-ing the dramatic ellipsis, the exclamation mark, and the 'world-' prefix, leaving just: 'a historic decision'.)

Although he is describing the development of a religion, Freud is par-ticularly careful to present it as intellectually enlightened. Of Akhenaton he writes:

In an astonishing presentiment of later *scientific* discovery he recognized in the energy of solar radiation the source of all life on earth. (XXIII, 59, my empha-sis)

This quasi-scientific progressiveness is an important element of his sus-tained identification with Moses in this text. For example, in order to explain how this religion could be overthrown only to return with renewed force, Freud offers a revealing parallel:

Let us take, for instance, the history of a new scientific theory, such as Darwin's theory of evolution. At first it met with embittered rejection and was violently disputed for decades; but it took no longer than a generation for it to be recognized as a great step forward towards truth. Darwin himself achieved the honour of a grave or cenotaph in Westminster Abbey. (XXIII, 66–7)

The parallels – some of them wishful – with his own career are already quite evident, and they are further underlined when we remember that in addition to Copernicus the one other scientist with whom Freud explicitly compared himself was Charles Darwin (XVI, 284–5). The intermediacy of Darwin here shows just how closely Freud relates to Moses' religion. Thus he repeatedly emphasizes its progressive, intellectual qualities, as, for example, in the section 'The Advance in Intellectuality', in which he praises the absolute priority its followers gave to the written word: 'the Holy Writ and intellectual concern with it were what held the scattered people together' (XXIII, 115). Freud's ardent hopes for the future of his own textual offspring are quite palpable here.

From details such as these it should already be clear that Freud's covert 'history' of his own movement relates less to its past than to a wishfully envisaged future. That the Jews rise up and murder Moses is, of course, a familiar detail from the classic psychoanalytical narrative, but in this text Freud narrates it from a different perspective. He describes the murder not as the sons' triumph against a tyrant, but as the 'fate that awaits all *enlightened* despots' (XXIII, 47, my emphasis). Clearly, he now identifies with the 'father'; in fact, his empathy is reserved for Moses from the very beginning. For example, he describes the hero's distress at the loss of his pharaoh, his exile from Egypt, where he could only have lived as an outlaw or a turncoat, and his encounter with the Semitic tribe: 'Under the necessity of his disappointment and loneliness he turned to these foreigners and with them sought compensation for his losses' (XXIII, 60). Given such insistent privileging of Moses' perspective, it is difficult to imagine that Freud enacts his murder as some kind of oedipal wish-fulfilment. It is, rather, the necessary precondition of a more subtle wishful fantasy, one based on a profound identification with Moses.

In the 1930s Freud considered that Rank and even Ferenczi had succumbed to the same parricidal temptations as Jung and Adler. His greatest fear was that his own approaching death would open the floodgates to a torrent of inferior heterodoxy. After Moses' death Freud describes how the Aton religion is supplanted by the regressive, polytheistic cult of Jahweh – but this is not the end of the story:

The *tradition* of it remained and its influence achieved (only gradually, it is true, in the course of centuries) what was denied to Moses himself. (XXIII, 59)

The shadow of the suppressed but superior doctrine proves far more potent, and it eventually returns with complete authority. On the model of his *Totem and Taboo* construction, a murdered father is more powerful in death than in life.[121] His sons' ambivalent love and inevitable remorse ensure their 'deferred obedience' and ultimately the return of what they have repressed. Freud, dismissing materialist theories of history, then asserts his faith in 'the personal influence upon world-history of individual great men' (XXIII, 52), making quite transparent his own wishful identification with the hero.

A possible objection to this interpretation is that it would imply Freud's own death, an unlikely detail in a scenario of wish-fulfilment. Firstly, however, this simply reflects Freud's knowledge that his jaw cancer had become fatally inoperable. Secondly, his 'parricide' at the hands of his followers is itself positively desirable:

A tradition that was based only on communication could not lead to the compulsive character that attaches to religious phenomena . . . it must have undergone the fate of being repressed, the condition of lingering in the unconscious, before it is able to display such powerful effects on its return, to bring the masses under its spell. (XXIII, 101)

Freud has great faith in the compulsive power of this mechanism, and he illustrates the inevitable return of the repressed father with a rather unexpected example:

and even the great Goethe, who in the period of his genius certainly looked down upon his unbending and pedantic father, in his old age developed traits which formed a part of his father's character. (XXIII, 125)

Marthe Robert reads this as Freud's fear, as a son, that he, too, would come to resemble his rejected father.[122] In the light of his identification with Moses, however, it seems much more likely that Freud is positively defying his followers to resist his *own* paternal authority, confident that, if even Goethe is incapable of such a feat, it is utterly impossible. Freud creatively envisions his imminent death as both heroic *and* necessary for the survival of psychoanalysis. His fantasy of the inevitable immortality of his doctrines is nowhere more apparent than on what, in 1937, he believed would be the final page of his final book. Here, with Schiller, he proclaims:

> Was unsterblich im Gesang soll leben,
> Muss im Leben untergehen.
>
> (What is to live immortal in song
> must perish in life.)   (XXIII, 101)

Via a revised identification, a shift in perspective, and a subtle manipulation of ambiguous narrative detail, then, Freud has rewritten one of his own fictions in order to confront and overcome his two greatest fears: his impending death and – for him a fate worse than death – the overthrow of his teachings.

Moses and Monotheism is often disparaged by critics who fail to appreciate this covert strategy. Although he acknowledges Freud as an imaginative writer, Hyman, for example, calls it his 'one thoroughly bad book', its thesis being 'intrinsically absurd'.[123] Rather than simply dismissing it, though, he should perhaps have considered more carefully *why* it is so problematical. In his analysis of *Gradiva* Freud writes of the hero's temporary lapse of reason:

> But the most important of all the explanatory and exculpatory factors remains the ease with which our intellect is prepared to accept something absurd provided it satisfies powerful emotional impulses. (IX, 71)

Later in the same work Freud comes close to implicating himself in this critique when he mentions the possibility that he may have misrepresented Jensen's novella:

> by introducing into an innocent work of art purposes of which its creator had no notion, and by so doing have shown once more how easy it is to find what one is looking for and what is occupying one's own mind. (IX, 91)

In the light of such comments, *Moses and Monotheism* could be judged not as a plausible and scientifically rigorous hypothesis, but as a work of imagination reflecting Freud's preoccupations and satisfying his most powerful emotional impulses. Ritchie Robertson redeems the book from this perspective, describing it as 'more . . . an imaginative than a scholarly work, one inspired by Goethe and Thomas Mann'.[124] Freud was certainly more galvanized by Goethe's 'Israel in the Wilderness' than by any historian's research. He positively dismisses his own conjecture about actually dating the events he recounts in his book:

> All this, however, is still history . . . Our interest follows the fortunes of Moses and of his doctrines, to which the rising of the Jews had only apparently put an end. (XXIII, 61–2)

The historical questions, then, concern him far less than the essence of the *story* he feels impelled to write.

Privately, Freud was aware of this personal subtext. To Arnold Zweig he wrote that he was haunted by the man Moses and *what he wanted to make of him*.[125] In another letter to Zweig written in the same year, 1934, he even calls the first section of the work 'Moses the Man: a Historical Novel' (Der Mann Moses, ein historischer Roman), although admittedly only after stating his intention never to publish it.[126] It is possible that Freud did not seriously intend to use this title and meant it only as a light-hearted parody of his project. A couple of months later he similarly joked with Eitingon that in future he would leave such works to Thomas Mann.[127] Nevertheless, in 1936 Zweig assured Freud that his approach to Moses was that of a *Dichter*, and Freud was gratified by the comparison.[128] Even if the title was not meant entirely seriously, the hypothesis that Freud's writing became, in various respects, increasingly literary is certainly bolstered by the fact that he considered his final major work a 'novel'.

There are many other passages in the published text which hint at its being a work of creative imagination. At one point in it he actually expresses the fear that age has diminished his 'creative powers' (XXIII, 54), but the very fact that he wrote and extensively rewrote such a long and speculative work without any apparent hope of having it published demonstrates that his creative urge was, if anything, stronger than ever. This does not of itself make the book a work of imagination; again this is only hinted at in various revealing denials made by Freud. At the end of the first section he resolves – in vain – to go no further with his hypothesis:

Even if one accepts the fact of Moses being an Egyptian as a first historical foothold, one would need to have at least a second firm fact in order to defend the wealth of emerging possibilities against the criticism of their being a product of the imagination. (XXIII, 16)

Here Freud is disputing that this work is primarily an imaginative creation, but he simultaneously admits that he could only convince the reader of this if he had more evidence. Yet, although this supplementary evidence never materializes, Freud does not let this impede his speculation in the slightest. In effect, he is admitting that his conclusions are not primarily based on evidence, and he is actually left quite vulnerable to the objection that the work is 'a product of the imagination'. Similarly, a subsequent attempt to deny that his account is a work of heroic fiction again only serves to expose him still further to the initial criticism. He admits that he has imputed an improbable degree of historical significance to one man, and he asks: 'Is not a hypothesis such as this a relapse into the mode of thought which led to myths of a creator and to the worship of heroes?' (XXIII, 107). Rather than actually contesting this fascinating suggestion, however, Freud merely points to 'an important discrepancy between the attitude taken up by our organ of thought and the arrangement of things in the world' (XXIII, 107). He explains:

Our thought has upheld its liberty to discover dependent relations and connections to which there is nothing corresponding in reality; and it clearly sets a very high value on this gift, since it makes such copious use of it both inside and outside of science. (XXIII, 108n.)

Given that he variously acknowledged that his own primal parricide construction was a fantasy, a vision, a 'just-so story', and a myth, it would not be implausible to detect here a veiled admission that we *need* myths and heroes, and we are justified in using them to make sense of the world even if we have to invent them for the purpose.

Like so many of Freud's works, then, *Moses and Monotheism* is on one level a quasi-literary fiction. At least as important as its essential fictionality is the significance Freud attaches to its aesthetic qualities. Admittedly, it is far from being the most elegantly constructed of his works, but its jarring interruptions, repetitions, and contradictions are primarily the result of its protracted and difficult birth. In this text Freud is especially sensitive to such shortcomings, provoking the most vehement stylistic self-criticism he ever published. When about to embark on the repetitious final section, for example, he assures us:

I am aware that a method of exposition such as this is no less inexpedient than it is inartistic. I myself deplore it unreservedly. (XXIII, 103)

However, he goes on to explain that this repetition might after all have practical advantages. All this self-laceration actually reveals, then, is that ideally the work *would* be 'artistic', an epithet he usually claimed to distrust. Similarly, his criticism that the work lacks unity due to its having taken on a life of its own, emerging 'as something independent or even alien' (XXIII, 104), only demonstrates how far his procedure was from the rigours of scientific method and how close it was to imaginative writing.

Some of Freud's most brilliant imagery in this text relates to this tension between scientific and artistic integrity. Mahony particularly admires the image used by Freud when, ever sensitive to his plausibility in the eyes of his readers, he disarms potential criticism by claiming that he is not sure of his own conclusions:

I have already laid stress on the factor of doubt in my introductory remarks; I have, as it were, placed that factor outside the brackets and I may be allowed to save myself the trouble of repeating it in connection with each item *inside* them. (XXIII, 31)

This ingenious use of an image drawn from mathematics simultaneously confers scientific credibility on Freud's procedure *and* gives him the freedom to indulge in profoundly unscientific speculation.[129] Indeed, it is entirely typical of Freud to introduce the most fundamental literary strategy – promoting the suspension of disbelief – under the guise of an image drawn from the purest science. Equally adroit, however, are two images used by Freud to depict the work as a whole. At the outset of the second section he describes it as 'a bronze statue with feet of clay' (XXIII, 17), and in the preface to the third section he calls it 'a dancer balancing on the tip of one toe' (XXIII, 58). Both images are brilliantly strategic. Firstly, they forestall the reader's criticism of the work's most salient flaw, its tenuousness. More importantly, though, both images are drawn from the *arts*, thus they not only turn this weakness into a strength, they also subtly shift the status of the entire work away from objective science towards the realm of the creative imagination. Only in this context can *Moses and Monotheism* receive the appreciation which is its due.

*

Freud only felt able to complete his Moses book after his arrival in England. In a new preface written in exile he expresses great relief:

Here I now live, a welcome guest; I can breathe a sigh of relief now that . . . I am once more able to speak and write – I had almost said 'and think' – as I wish or as I must. (XXIII, 57)

This admission that for him writing was, to some extent, identical with thinking, and resulted from an inner compulsion, is unusually revealing. He certainly did not view writing as a mundane task to be undertaken only in order to communicate the results of his thinking. In 1910 he told Pfister that work and the free play of the imagination were for him one and the same thing,[130] and this was no doubt due to the fact that he undertook both activities at the writing desk. As Mahony puts it, Freud thought with his pen.[131] In *The Interpretation of Dreams* he reveals that even his own self-analysis was based not on dialogue with another person or on free-floating thought, but rather on a kind of automatic writing. Assuring us that the technique of 'uncritical self-observation' is quite simple to achieve, he remarks: 'I myself can do so very completely, by the help of writing down my ideas as they occur to me' (IV, 103). On the very same page he quotes Schiller's recommendation of precisely this technique as the key to *literary* productivity. Of course, Freud claims not to have known about Schiller's letter until Rank pointed it out to him. Nevertheless, he does admit that he knew of the very similar advice offered by Ludwig Börne in his essay 'The Art of Becoming an Original Writer in Three Days'. In chapter 3 I remarked that this made Freud something of a 'literary critic' to the free associations of his patients, but it must equally be remembered that Freud's first analysand was himself. Thus, when he embarked on his self-analysis he chose a method which promised to make of him an 'original writer'. As is evident from the autobiographical subtexts of *Leonardo da Vinci and a Memory of his Childhood*, 'The Moses of Michelangelo', and *Moses and Monotheism*, writing remained for Freud a deeply personal and essentially therapeutic process long after he had completed *The Interpretation of Dreams*. Perhaps most revealing in this respect is his frequent complaint that he had to be somewhat miserable in order to write well.[132]

Of course, Freud was painfully thin-skinned about claims that his texts were subjective or, worse still, autobiographical. Fliess had claimed in 1901: 'the reader of thoughts merely reads his own thoughts into other people',[133] and Freud was so wounded that the comment eventually led to their break. This extreme sensitivity ensured that his 'literary' activities were always elaborately concealed. In his book about Freud as a writer, Schönau begins by pointing out that, fundamentally, Freud was not a *Künstlernatur*, a man of artistic temperament.[134] It would indeed be quite easy to read his entire output and accept this conclusion. His literary aspirations are always heavily screened behind scientific motives and are detectable only in the most subtle tensions and traces. His dependence on metaphor, his predilection for narrative, his theoretical emphasis on fictionality, his identifications with poets and heroes, his creative reworking of his own autobiography in texts about ostensibly neutral subjects – any of these alone would prove little. Only when they are viewed together – and when the scale of their insistent recurrence is acknowledged – do they call for a reappraisal of the very nature of Freud's oeuvre. His texts are not, of course, works of literature in any conventional sense of the word, but they could perhaps only have been the product of Freud's unique and enigmatic fusion of aspiring scientist and frustrated *Dichter*. Trilling writes that Freud was not in the least a 'literary mind' and however much he contributed to our knowledge of it, he always did so from 'outside the process of literature'.[135] I hope at least to have demonstrated that such distinctions are not quite as secure as Trilling imagines. Perhaps a more accurate summary of the situation is offered – albeit unwittingly – by Freud himself when, in his analysis of *Gradiva*, he writes:

Thus the creative writer cannot evade the psychiatrist nor the psychiatrist the creative writer. (IX, 44)

Conclusion

My attempt throughout this book to resituate Freud's writings – clinical, theoretical, and applied texts alike – within the context of his literary culture has given rise to a variety of new perspectives. I have demonstrated not only that authors such as Sophocles, Shakespeare, and Goethe play an active role in Freud's formulation and development of psychoanalytical theory, but also that this depth of intellectual influence is matched by a corresponding profundity in his emotional relationships with great writers. The often underestimated sophistication of his literary analyses suggests that his ambivalence towards poets is by no means the arrogant disdain of a blinkered scientist. Viewed in the context of his appreciation of writers as genuine precursors of psychoanalysis, his 'sublime' ambivalence provides evidence, rather, of fraught emotional undercurrents such as filial reverence, influence anxiety, envy, and creative revolt. Although most would find, say, Harold Bloom's assertion that Freud has essentially rewritten Shakespeare in prose form rather too outlandish, Bloom's main flaw may simply be that he actually neglects Freud's prime precursor, Goethe. *Faust*, for example, constitutes something of an immanence within Freud's writing, present even when it does not surface in the form of an allusion; and Goethe himself emerges as a linchpin of Freud's emotional life: a revered totem, an adored but threateningly powerful father-figure, an invaluable advocate, a hero with whom he ambitiously identifies, and an ideal *alter ego* – the poet-scientist.

The charges of literary insensitivity and reductionism commonly levelled at Freud are further challenged by my postulation of a subliminal paradigm of literary response in his approach to non-literary 'texts' such as dreams and neurotic symptoms. The practice of literary criticism is not just a marginal or secondary application of psychoanalysis, but constitutes an interpretative model which – since psychoanalysis is now widely regarded as essentially a hermeneutic discipline – lies at the very root of Freudian theory and practice. The exigencies of scientific rigour which caused Freud to renounce the pleasures of literary criticism gave rise to his attempt to develop a science of interpretation, but inevitably this itself became the site of the 'return of the repressed' as his technique was – and continues to be – increasingly valued less for its therapeutic than for its literary-critical applications. In the light of this dynamic, Freud's own extreme emphasis on scientific values needs to be reassessed as something akin to a 'reaction formation' against his own repudiated literary desires.

This radical hypothesis is decisively bolstered by the evidence that Freud's most indefatigable tendency is not just to interpret texts, but to generate new ones. Whether these are painstaking clinical reconstructions of a patient's life story, theoretical elaborations of economic, dynamic, or topographical metaphors of the psyche, mythopoeic narratives recounting the evolution of social institutions, or psychoanalytical 'novels' dramatizing the lives of great men, they all tend to suggest that Freud is himself a quasi-literary author, creating aesthetically controlled, fictional narratives that are charged with profoundly personal subtexts. He certainly places increasing emphasis on such features of psychoanalytical theory as figuration, 'aesthetics', narratology, and fictionality, and ultimately these cause his suppressed *Doppelgänger*, Freud the *Dichter*, to emerge uncannily into the foreground of some of his most enigmatic texts.

Despite my own sustained use of Freudian ideas and terminology – deferred action, ambivalence, the return of the repressed – in my account of the dynamic functioning of Freud's literary culture, psychoanalytical doctrine has not been a premise of my investigation. On the contrary, I have found again and again that his literary culture is *prior* to his analytical insights, and accordingly I have handled Freudian theory from a sympathetic but consistently critical distance. My analysis of the crucial literary subtexts of Freud's writing should illustrate precisely why doctrine cannot simply be abstracted from his texts, at least not without stripping it of the tensions and ambiguities that allow us to make sense of his relations with his literary culture. For example, Freud's presumption that the territory of literature will one day be annexed to his psychoanalytical empire emerges as less the obtuse aspiration of a philistine scientist than an attempted revolt by an ambitiously creative writer against his literary forebears. His apparent arrogance is subtly related to his desire to conceal the crucial literary context in which he developed his science; I have sought neither to undermine nor to vindicate psychoanalysis, but merely to restore this specific context.

My use of Freud's own insights as a theoretical framework corresponds, above all, to a sensitive literary-critical approach to his *writing*. For Freud can indeed usefully be viewed as a literary writer transposed – not altogether comfortably – into a foreign culture of positivist science, a cross-fertilization which, whilst tending to alienate 'fundamentalists' in both scientific and literary camps, no doubt contributes to the abiding power of his writing to fascinate, unsettle, and provoke. Despite Freud's own dogged emphasis on developing theories of universal validity, his insights are perhaps best treated as primarily subjective, indeed, penetratingly introspective. Although such a contention may appear largely to undermine the therapeutic pretensions of psychoanalysis, this has not been the focus of my investigation. At his best, Freud teaches the analyst to have endless respect for the minute detail and subjectively overdetermined complexity of any creation of the human mind. My approach has been to turn this interpretative vigour back onto Freud's own writing, viewing it as a body of text which draws heavily on and contributes no less richly to the European literary tradition. If psychoanalysis as therapy is thereby undermined (it is certainly severely challenged), this would not rob Freud's writing of its essential value. Even if, ultimately, his writings were to serve only to illuminate his own personality, this alone would make Freud a unique contributor to a literary tradition which reaches from the Renaissance humanism of Montaigne through the confessional literature of the Romantics and on into Freud's own era, for example in the introspective writings of Nietzsche. In fact, this literary tradition has been continued in the twentieth century by countless modernist writers, such as Kafka, Joyce, and Woolf, who are themselves often in covert debate with Freud.

It is, however, precisely the scale of Freud's impact on twentieth-century culture which suggests that his works are something more than just quasi-literary crypto-autobiography. I myself have found his theories to be irresistibly cogent as a framework for my own analysis. The issue of Freud's literary culture does, after all, centre on a dynamic conflict that is articulated in ambiguous textual form – precisely the constellation which always fascinated Freud himself. This is not simply some variation on Karl Kraus's caustic remark that psychoanalysis is itself the disease for which it purports to be the cure. Although Freudian theory has not been a premise of my work, it has unquestionably provided me – as it provides critics of almost any form of cultural discourse – with a rich stock of powerful and subtle metaphors. In a study which has sought to establish the systematic priority of the literary dimensions of Freud's writing, it is perhaps fitting that I should have made use of psychoanalysis itself purely as a source of metaphor; moreover, this very approach may be an indication of why Freud's works continue to speak to us so urgently.

Although my emphasis on the culturally conditioned, subjectively overdetermined, and emotionally fraught aspects of psychoanalysis raises questions about its pretensions to scientific objectivity, not only is Freud's writing no less richly engaging for this, but equally the very 'literariness' which causes psychoanalysis to fall short of the ideals of natural science seems to have enabled Freud to anticipate some of the twentieth-century currents of thought which have made nineteenth-century scientific positivism itself problematic – his quasi-postmodern appreciation of the inherent fictionality of thought, for example, or his proto-deconstructive awareness of the essential instability of the processes of signification. Even Freud's 'scientism' itself is not simply an unfortunate handicap that he more or less inadvertently managed to overcome. His systematic, taxonomic approach, like his constant aspirations to an impossible objectivity, gave him something of an 'alienated' perspective on material which hitherto had been the reserve of the poets. It thus played its own crucial role in the fertile epistemological ambiguity and sheer intellectual enterprise of his writings. The hybrid result was, for better and worse, Freud's creation of the quintessential mythology of the modern era, for psychoanalysis is not just another series of metaphors, fictions, or narratives. Even – or maybe especially – when it is problematized, revised, or vehemently rejected, its seminal influence persists, and it thus remains one of the most powerful imaginative frameworks by which we make sense of ourselves. Such a singular creation could perhaps only have been the work of a writer possessed of Freud's uneasy but exhilarating fusion of scientific ambition and literary cultivation.

Notes

1 For readings of Freud's works which place psychoanalysis in the broader cultural context of the humanities, see Trilling, *Freud and the Crisis of our Culture* and *The Liberal Imagination*; Ricoeur, *Freud and Philosophy: An Essay on Interpretation*; Rieff, *Freud: The Mind of the Moralist*; and the essays collected in Kurzweil and Phillips (eds.), *Literature and Psychoanalysis*; Meisel (ed.), *Freud: A Collection of Critical Essays*; and Meltzer (ed.), *The Trial(s) of Psychoanalysis*.

2 Postmodernist 'literary' readings of Freud include Lacan's 'The Insistence of the Letter in the Unconscious'; Derrida's 'Freud and the Scene of Writing'; Bloom's 'Freud and the Poetic Sublime'; and Hartman's 'The Interpreter's Freud'. Their approaches have been developed by a great many critics, for example, Brooks, *Reading for the Plot*; Bersani, *The Freudian Body: Psychoanalysis and Art*; Felman (ed.), *Literature and Psychoanalysis. The Question of Reading: Otherwise*; Smith (ed.), *The Literary Freud: Mechanisms of Defense and the Poetic Will*.

3 A useful survey of the history of psychoanalytical approaches to literary interpretation is Berman (ed.), *Essential Papers on Literature and Psychoanalysis*. Practitioners and theorists of Freudian literary criticism include Kris, *Psychoanalytic Explorations in Art*; Brown, *Life Against Death*; Orlando, *Toward a Freudian Theory of Literature*; Skura, *The Literary Use of the Psychoanalytic Process*; Gombrich, 'Freud's Aesthetics'; and Holland, 'Literary Interpretation and Three Phases of Psychoanalysis'.

4 See, for example, Brandell, *Freud: A Man of His Century*; Marcus, *Freud and the Culture of Psychoanalysis: Studies in the Transition from Victorian Humanism to Modernity*; Gedo and Pollock (eds.), *Freud: The Fusion of Science and Humanism*; Horden (ed.), *Freud and the Humanities*; and Bloom, 'Freud: A Shakespearean Reading' in *The Western Canon: The Books and Schools of the Ages*.

5 See Kofman, *The Childhood of Art: An Interpretation of Freud's Aesthetics* and *Freud and Fiction*.

6 Due to the lack of a simple English equivalent, I use the German term *Dichter* throughout this book. It means 'writer' (or 'writers' – *Dichter* is also the plural) in an exclusively literary sense and could otherwise be ade-

quately translated only by a variety of more specific English words, such as 'poet', 'dramatist', and 'novelist'.

7 See Mahony, *Freud as a Writer*; also Muschg, *Die Zerstörung der deutschen Literatur*; Hyman, *The Tangled Bank: Darwin, Marx, Frazer and Freud as Imaginative Writers*; Schönau, *Sigmund Freuds Prosa: Literarische Elemente seines Stils*; Spector, *The Aesthetics of Freud: A Study in Psychoanalysis and Art*; and Marcus, *Freud and the Culture of Psychoanalysis*.

I THE UNCONSCIOUS OF PSYCHOANALYSIS: FREUD'S LITERARY ALLUSIONS

1 *Letters 1873–1939*, letter to Hugo Heller of 1 Nov. 1906, p. 278.
2 All references in this form are to *The Standard Edition of the Complete Psychological Works of Sigmund Freud*, 24 volumes (London, 1953–74).
3 *Letters 1873–1939*, letter to Martha of 8 Nov. 1885, p. 191.
4 Where the *Standard Edition* leaves literary quotations in the original German, giving an English translation at the foot of the page, I have included these translations in parentheses.
5 *Freud/Jung Letters*, letter of 9 Mar. 1909, pp. 210–11.
6 *Ibid.*, letter of 11 Nov. 1909, p. 260.
7 *Freud/Jung Letters*, letter of 25 Feb. 1908, p. 125.
8 'If I cannot bend the Higher Powers, I will move the Infernal Regions'; see *Letters 1873–1939*, letter to Achelis of 30 Jan 1927, p. 376.
9 *Ibid.*, letter to Ferenczi of 4 Feb. 1920, p. 334.
10 Schur, *Freud: Living and Dying*, p. 278.
11 Bersani, *Freudian Body*, p. 108.
12 Mann, 'Freud und die Zukunft' in *Schriften und Reden* 11, pp. 214f., my translation.
13 Admittedly, Freud has been led to the quote by Burdach, one of the scientific authors he is surveying, but the enthusiasm for the poet's 'charming words' is Freud's own.
14 Rieff, *Mind of the Moralist*, p. 254.
15 Trilling, *Liberal Imagination*, pp. 33f.
16 *Letters to Fliess*, letter of 1 Feb. 1900, p. 398.
17 Brown, *Life Against Death*, for example pp. 87, 55.
18 Mann, 'Freud und die Zukunft' in *Schriften und Reden* 11, p. 231, my translation.
19 Bettelheim, *Freud and Man's Soul*, p. 64.
20 Wittels cited in Peters, 'Goethe und Freud', *Goethe-Jahrbuch* 103, p. 87, my translation.
21 Ellenberger, *Discovery of the Unconscious*, p. 773.
22 Brandell concentrates on more contemporary literature and claims, for example, that Ibsen was a 'creative force' in Freud's therapeutic innovations; see, *Man of His Century*, pp. 47 and 37. Gay cites an allusion in which Freud identifies with the hero of *Enemy of the People*, supporting the claim

that Ibsen had an unconscious influence on him; see *Life for Our Time*, p. 27. Of course, Ibsen's characters Nora from *A Doll's House* and Ekdal from *The Wild Duck* surface from Freud's unconscious in his dream about the 'positively norekdal style' (IV, 296).

23 Starobinski, 'Acheronta Movebo' in Meltzer (ed.), *Trial(s) of Psychoanalysis*, pp. 275, 284, 277.

24 *Letters to Fliess*, letter of 15 Oct. 1897, pp. 272f.

25 Eissler cited in Trosman, 'Freud and the Controversy over Shakespearean Authorship' in Gedo (ed.), *Fusion of Science and Humanism*, p. 309.

26 *Letters to Fliess*, letter of 21 Sept. 1897, p. 265.

27 Deleuze, *Anti-Oedipus*, p. 55.

28 *Letters 1873–1939*, letter to Emil Fluss of 16 June 1873, p. 21.

29 *Freud/Arnold Zweig: Briefwechsel*, letter of 4 Apr. 1934, p. 82, my translation.

30 Gay, *Life for Our Time*, p. xviii.

31 Jones, *Life* I, p. 48.

32 Gay, *Life for Our Time*, p. 24.

33 It has, of course, long been recognized that the essay was actually written by the Swiss theologian, Georg Christoph Tobler. Nevertheless, Tobler had recorded the ideas in conversation with Goethe in the 1780s, and Goethe himself later recognized the ideas as his own, even mistakenly including the essay amongst his own collected works. See Goethe, 'Die Natur. Fragment', *Hamburger Ausgabe* XIII, pp. 45–9.

34 Jones, *Life* I, pp. 31f.

35 Ricoeur, *Freud and Philosophy*, p. 72.

36 Gay, *Life for Our Time*, p. 34.

37 Rieff, *Mind of the Moralist*, p. 24.

38 Cranefield, 'Freud and the "School of Helmholtz"', *Gesnerus* 23, pp. 35–9.

39 *Letters 1873–1939*, letter to Stefan Zweig of 19 Oct. 1920, p. 337.

40 Jones, *Life* I, p. 48.

41 Trotter quoted in Galdston, 'Freud and Romantic Medicine', *History of Medicine* 30, p. 505.

42 Ellenberger, *Discovery of the Unconscious*, p. 447.

43 Rieff, *Mind of the Moralist*, p. 21.

44 *Letters to Fliess*, letter of 25 May 1895, p. 129.

45 Jones, *Life* II, p. 479.

46 Ricoeur, *Freud and Philosophy*, p. 313.

47 Trilling, *Liberal Imagination*, p. 34.

48 Ellenberger, *Discovery of the Unconscious*, p. 205.

49 Meisel, *Freud*, p. 7.

50 Letter to Martha of 12 Feb. 1884, cited in Gay, *Life for Our Time*, p. 46.

51 Trosman, *Imaginative World*, p. 23.

52 Edmundson, 'Freudian Mythmaking: The Case of Narcissus', *Kenyon Review* 10, pp. 26ff.

53 Freud voluntarily attended philosophy lectures given by Franz Brentano,

nephew of the Romantic poet, for two years whilst studying medicine. Furthermore, his 1906 list of ten good books includes Gomperz's *Greek Thinkers*, which deals fully with Plato.

54 Santas, *Plato and Freud*, pp. 160ff.

55 Goethe, 'Die Natur. Fragment', *Hamburger Ausgabe* XIII, p. 47, my translation.

56 Jones recognizes that the ideas come from 'some personal and profound source', 'almost as if by free associations', see *Life* III, p. 287; whilst Max Schur speaks with unwonted censure of the book's '*ad hoc* reasoning to prove a preformed hypothesis'; see Gay, *Life for Our Time*, p. 398n.

57 In his texts Freud actually avoids using the term Thanatos, but Jones relates that he did use it in conversation, and it is perfectly in keeping with the spirit of the theory that the name was adopted by those psychoanalysts who accepted the death drive; see Jones, *Life* III, p. 295.

58 Ellenberger, *Discovery of the Unconscious*, p. 204.

59 Ricoeur, *Freud and Philosophy*, p. 536.

60 Bloom, *Agon*, p. 102.

61 *Ibid.*, p. 107.

62 Peters, 'Goethe und Freud', *Goethe-Jahrbuch* 103, p. 99.

63 Goethe, 'Die Natur. Fragment', *Hamburger Ausgabe* XIII, pp. 45f., my translation.

64 *Letters 1873–1939*, letter to Schnitzler of 14 May 1922, p. 345.

65 Trilling, *Crisis of our Culture*, pp. 25f.

66 Ricoeur, *Freud and Philosophy*, p. 86.

67 Cixous, 'Fiction and its Phantoms', *New Literary History* 7/3, p. 537.

68 Jones, *Life* III, p. 307.

69 Trilling, 'The Authentic Unconscious' in Bloom (ed.), *Freud*, pp. 107f.

70 *Letters to Fliess*, letter of 15 Oct. 1897, p. 272.

71 Felman, *Literature and Psychoanalysis*, p. 10, Felman's emphasis.

2 A SUBLIME AMBIVALENCE: FREUD AS LITERARY CRITIC

1 *Letters to Fliess*, letter of 15 Oct. 1897, pp. 272f.

2 *Letters 1873–1939*, letter to Jung of 26 May 1907, p. 261.

3 Fuller, *Art and Psychoanalysis*, p. 37.

4 William Empson refers to Freud several times in his classic account of how ambiguity is absolutely central to literary aesthetics; see *Seven Types of Ambiguity*, for example p. 226.

5 *Freud/Jung Letters*, letter of 24 Nov. 1907, p. 100.

6 Letter to Martha of 5 Oct. 1883, cited in Jones, *Life* I, pp. 190f.

7 Gedo and Wolf, 'Freud's *Novelas Ejemplares*' in Gedo (ed.), *Fusion of Science and Humanism*, p. 91.

8 Orlando, *Theory of Literature*, p. 136.

9 Horden, *Humanities*, pp. 20f.

10 Rieff, *Mind of the Moralist*, p. 139.

11 It may be that Freud is, for once, let down by his use of static metaphors, such as 'disguise' [Witzverkleidung], for what is really a dynamic concept. Ricoeur's metaphor is truer to Freud's own conception; he speaks of aesthetic fore-pleasure as a 'detonator of profound discharges', and goes on to call this 'the most daring insight of the entire psychoanalytical aesthetics'; see *Freud and Philosophy*, p. 167.

12 Holland, 'Literary Interpretation and Three Phases of Psychoanalysis' in Roland (ed.), *Creativity and Literature*, pp. 233–47.

13 Felman, 'On Reading Poetry' in Smith (ed.), *Literary Freud*, p. 133.

14 *Freud/Jung Letters*, letter of 14 Apr. 1907, p. 33.

15 Wollheim, 'Freud and the Understanding of Art' in Bloom (ed.), *Freud*, p. 83.

16 Orlando, *Theory of Literature*, pp. 133 and 129.

17 *Freud/Jung Letters*, letter of 22 Jan. 1911, p. 388.

18 *Letters to Fliess*, 'Draft N', enclosed with the letter of 31 May 1897, p. 251.

19 Ricoeur, *Freud and Philosophy*, pp. 492 and 175.

20 See, for example, Ludwig Marcuse, *Eros and Civilization*, p. 79. For a more accurate view of sublimated libido, see Ernst Kris, *Explorations in Art*, pp. 26f.

21 Auden, 'Psychology and Art Today' in Kurzweil (ed.), *Literature and Psychoanalysis*, p. 120.

22 *Letters to Fliess*, 'Draft N', enclosed with the letter of 31 May 1897, p. 251. The idea that literary creation may, on one level, function as a kind of sophisticated self-analysis is certainly implicit in the psychoanalytically aware approach to Goethe's work taken by Jim Simpson; see his *Goethe and Patriarchy: Faust and th Fates of Desire*.

23 Gay, *Life for Our Time*, p. 322.

24 Brown, *Life Against Death*, pp. 59f.

25 Gay, *Freud, Jews and other Germans*, p. 64.

26 *Letters 1873–1939*, letter to Hugo Heller of 1 Nov. 1906, p. 278.

27 Jones, *Life* II, p. 386.

28 See, for example, *Letters 1873–1939*, letter to Stefan Zweig of 20 July 1938, p. 444, and letter to Abraham of 26 Dec. 1922, pp. 345f.

29 Kofman, *Childhood of Art*, pp. 149ff.

30 Jones, *Life* III, p. 462.

31 Trosman, 'Freud and the Controversy over Shakespearean Authorship' in Gedo (ed.), *Fusion of Science and Humanism*, pp. 325ff. Harold Bloom interprets Freud's 'Looneyism' in terms of a specifically *literary* family romance, based on his anxious relationship with Shakespeare. He considers the English poet to be 'the prime precursor' and even claims: 'Freud is essentially prosified Shakespeare'; see 'Freud: A Shakespearean Reading' in *The Western Canon*, pp. 371–94.

32 Rycroft, *Psychoanalysis and Beyond*, p. 69.

33 Trilling, *Liberal Imagination*, p. 153.

34 Kofman, *Childhood of Art*, pp. 23, 49 and 192f.

35 *Ibid.*, p. 151.
36 *Ibid.*, pp. 6ff.
37 Rycroft, *Psychoanalysis and Beyond*, pp. 69 and 265.
38 Trosman, 'Freud and the Controversy over Shakespearean Authorship' in Gedo (ed.), *Fusion of Science and Humanism*, p. 308.
39 *Letters 1873–1939*, letter to Schnitzler of 8 May 1906, p. 261.
40 Gay, *Life for Our Time*, p. 318.
41 Cixous, 'Fiction and its Phantoms', *New Literary History* 7/3, p. 527.
42 Jones, *Life* I, p. 123.
43 Milner, *Interprétation de la littérature*, pp. 297f. and 303.
44 Wollheim, 'Freud and the Understanding of Art' in Bloom (ed.), *Freud*, pp. 82f.
45 See Cixous, 'Fiction and its Phantoms', *New Literary History* 7/3, pp. 532ff., and Hertz, *End of the Line*, pp. 103ff.
46 Rieff, *Mind of the Moralist*, p. 138.
47 *Letters to Fliess*, letter of 20 June 1898, pp. 317f.
48 Adorno, *Aesthetic Theory*, pp. 11f.
49 Rieff, *Mind of the Moralist*, p. 109.
50 Ellmann, 'Freud and Literary Biography' in Horden, *Humanities*, p. 64.
51 Sachs, *Master and Friend*, p. 103.
52 Cited by Trosman, 'Freud and the Controversy over Shakespearean Authorship' in Gedo (ed.), *Fusion of Science and Humanism*, pp. 311f.
53 See Freud's letter to Alfons Paquet of 3 Aug. 1930, in which he writes: 'I hope it will be acceptable if I thus adapt the theme that has been proposed to me – my "inner relations as a man and scientist to Goethe"' (XXI, 207).
54 *Letters 1873–1939*, letter to Jung of 26 May 1907, p. 262.
55 *Ibid.*
56 *Freud/Arnold Zweig: Briefwechsel*, letter to Zweig of 2 Apr. 1937, p. 150, my translation.
57 *Ibid.*, letter to Zweig of 23 Sept. 1935, p. 120, my translations.
58 *Letters to Fliess*, letter of 15 Oct. 1897, p. 272.
59 Rieff, *Mind of the Moralist*, p. 133.
60 Letter from Jensen to Freud of 13 May 1907, cited in the introduction to the Fischer Taschenbuch edition of 'Der Wahn und die Träume in W. Jensens *Gradiva*' (Frankfurt, 1989), p. 12, my translation.
61 *Letters to Fliess*, letter of 20 June 1898, p. 317, Freud's emphasis.
62 Letter to Martha of 26 July 1883, cited in Jones, *Life* I, p. 192.
63 *Letters 1873–1939*, letter to Stefan Zweig of 19 Oct. 1920, p. 339.
64 Letter to Stefan Zweig of 4 Sep. 1926, cited in Gay, *Life for Our Time*, p. 319.
65 Letter to Jones of 8 Feb. 1914, cited *ibid.*, pp. 167f.
66 *Letters 1873–1939*, letter to Jung of 26 May 1907, p. 262.
67 Kofman, *Childhood of Art*, p. 152.
68 Kofman, *Freud and Fiction*, p. 159.
69 Trilling, *Crisis of our Culture*, p. 22.
70 Adorno, *Aesthetic Theory*, p. 13.

71 *Letters 1873–1939*, letter to Schnitzler of 14 May 1922, pp. 344f.
72 *Freud/Arnold Zweig: Briefwechsel*, letter to Zweig of 12 May 1934, pp. 87f., my translation.
73 Rieff, *Mind of the Moralist*, p. 121.
74 Bloom, *Anxiety of Influence*, pp. 14ff. Elsewhere Bloom himself remarks that Freud 'certainly shared the influence-anxieties and defensive misprisions of all strong writers'; see *Agon*, p. 102.
75 Bloom, *Anxiety of Influence*, p. 8.
76 Rieff, *Mind of the Moralist*, p. 122.

3 THE LITERARY-CRITICAL PARADIGM: SOURCES OF FREUD'S HERMENEUTIC

1 See Bloom, 'Freud and the Poetic Sublime' in Meisel (ed.), *Freud*, p. 225; and Brooks, 'Freud's Masterplot: A Model for Narrative' in *Reading for the Plot*, pp. 90ff.
2 *Freud/Jung Letters*, letter of 8 Dec. 1907, p. 103.
3 See Kofman, *Childhood of Art*, p. 58.
4 Letter to Hale of 3 Jan. 1922, cited in Gay, *Life for Our Time*, p. 554.
5 Timms, 'Novelle and Case History', *London German Studies* 2, p. 125.
6 Hertz, *End of the Line*, pp. 122ff.
7 Ricoeur, *Freud and Philosophy*, p. 193n.
8 Hartman, 'The Interpreter's Freud' in Lodge (ed.), *Modern Criticism*, p. 415.
9 Orlando, *Theory of Literature*, pp. 135f.
10 Lacan, 'Insistence of the Letter in the Unconscious' in Lodge (ed.), *Modern Criticism*, p. 92.
11 Burke, *Philosophy of Literary Form*, p. 277.
12 Bloom, 'Freud and the Poetic Sublime' in Meisel (ed.), *Freud*, p. 225.
13 Orlando, *Theory of Literature*, p. 162.
14 *Freud/Jung Letters*, letter of 10 Oct. 1907, p. 92.
15 Gay, *Life for Our Time*, p. 264.
16 *Freud/Jung Letters*, letter of 30 June 1909, p. 238.
17 *Freud/Lou Andreas-Salomé: Letters*, letter of 23 Mar. 1930, p. 185.
18 Brandell, *Man of His Century*, pp. 56f.
19 *Ibid.*, p. 54.
20 *Ibid.*, p. 74.
21 Suleiman, 'Nadja, Dora, Lol V. Stein' in Rimmon-Kenan (ed.), *Discourse in Psychoanalysis and Literature*, p. 129.
22 Marcus, *Culture of Psychoanalysis*, p. 72.
23 Trilling, 'The Authentic Unconscious' in Bloom (ed.), *Freud*, p. 97.
24 Marcus, *Culture of Psychoanalysis*, p. 248.
25 *Ibid.*, p. 123.
26 Brooks, *Reading for the Plot*, pp. 275ff.
27 Bersani, *Freudian Body*, p. 83.
28 *Ibid.*, pp. 31f., 35 and 40.

29 Bloom (ed.), *Interpretation of Dreams*, p. 5.

30 Kofman, *Freud and Fiction*, p. 8.

31 Eysenck, *Decline and Fall*, pp. 180f.

32 Fish, 'Withholding the Missing Portion: Psychoanalysis and Rhetoric' in Meltzer (ed.), *Trial(s) of Psychoanalysis*, pp. 183–209.

33 Brooks describes the genre as 'an inevitable product . . . of the nineteenth century's . . . pervasive historicism, its privileging of narrative understanding'; see Brooks, *Reading for the Plot*, p. 270.

34 Hartman, 'The Interpreter's Freud' in Lodge (ed.), *Modern Criticism*, pp. 416, 424.

35 Ricoeur, *Freud and Philosophy*, p. 177.

36 Bowie, *Freud, Proust and Lacan*, p. 21.

37 Ricoeur, *Freud and Philosophy*, p. 66.

38 Izenberg, *Existentialist Critique*, p. 4.

39 *Ibid.*, pp. 31f.

40 See Rycroft, 'Causes and Meaning' in *Psychoanalysis and Beyond*, pp. 41–51.

41 Izenberg, *Existentialist Critique*, p. 20.

42 *Ibid.*, p. 201.

43 Wittgenstein, 'Conversations on Freud' in Wollheim (ed.), *Philosophical Essays*, p. 9.

44 Wollheim, 'Freud and the Understanding of Art' in Bloom (ed.), *Freud*, p. 89.

45 Rieff, *Mind of the Moralist*, p. 145.

46 Trilling, *Liberal Imagination*, p. 51.

47 Marcus, *Culture of Psychoanalysis*, p. 18.

48 Felman, *Literature and Psychoanalysis*, pp. 5f., Freud's emphasis.

49 Bloom (ed.), *Freud*, p. 5.

50 Rieff, *Mind of the Moralist*, p. 24.

4 THE FRUSTRATED *DICHTER*: LITERARY QUALITIES OF FREUD'S TEXT

1 Quoted in Schönau, *Sigmund Freuds Prosa*, p. 258, my translation.

2 Stefan Zweig, 'Die Heilung durch den Geist', cited *ibid.*, p. 264, my translation.

3 Bettelheim, *Freud and Man's Soul*, p. 5.

4 Mahony, *Freud as a Writer*, p. 173.

5 Muschg, *Zerstörung der deutschen Literatur*, p. 321, my translation.

6 See, for example, Andreas-Salomé, *Freud Journal*, pp. 44 and 106.

7 Hyman, *Tangled Bank*, p. 312.

8 Mahony, *Freud as a Writer*, p. 28.

9 Thomas Mann, cited in the 'Editorische Vorbemerkung', *Studienausgabe* vol. IX, p. 290, my translation.

10 Schönau, *Sigmund Freuds Prosa*, p. 35.

11 Mahony, *Freud as a Writer*, pp. 118ff.

12 Muschg, *Zerstörung der deutschen Literatur*, p. 320.

13 Goethe, 'Einwirkung der neueren Philosophie', *Hamburger Ausgabe* XIII, pp. 26f., my translation.
14 Mann, 'Freud und die Zukunft' in *Schriften und Reden* II, p. 219, my translation.
15 Muschg, *Zerstörung der deutschen Literatur*, pp. 322f.
16 Schönau, *Sigmund Freuds Prosa*, pp. 215ff., my translation.
17 *Ibid.*, p. 138.
18 *Letters to Fliess*, letter of 20 June 1898, p. 318, my emphasis.
19 *Ibid.*, letter of 7 July 1898, p. 319.
20 Jones, *Life* II, p. 448.
21 Schönau, *Sigmund Freuds Prosa*, p. 176.
22 Rieff, *Mind of the Moralist*, p. 21n.
23 Schönau, *Sigmund Freuds Prosa*, p. 159; for the passage from the Dora analysis see VII, 16.
24 Marcus, *Culture of Psychoanalysis*, pp. 10ff.
25 Mahony, for one, considers that Freud's ability to sustain powerful yet partial, flexible, and undogmatic analogies is an essential corollary of his 'processive style' in general. See *Freud as a Writer*, pp. 109f.
26 Fisher, 'Reading Freud's *Civilization and its Discontents*' in LaCapra (ed.), *Modern European Intellectual History*, p. 276.
27 Trilling, *Liberal Imagination*, pp. 50f.
28 Edmundson, 'Freudian Mythmaking: The Case of Narcissus', *Kenyon Review* 10, p. 22.
29 Hertz, *The End of the Line*, pp. 100f.
30 Muschg, *Zerstörung der deutschen Literatur*, p. 315, my translation.
31 *Letters to Fliess*, letter of 21 Sep. 1899, pp. 373f.
32 *Ibid.*, letter of 11 Sep. 1899, p. 371.
33 Letter to Martha of 1 Apr. 1884, cited in Schönau, *Sigmund Freuds Prosa*, p. 12, my translation.
34 *Letters 1873–1939*, letter to Emil Fluss of 16 June 1873, p. 22.
35 Alfred von Berger in the *Wiener Morgenpresse* of 2 Feb. 1896, cited in Schönau, *Sigmund Freuds Prosa*, p. 257.
36 Hyman, *Tangled Bank*, p. 337.
37 Mahony, *Freud as a Writer*, p. 10.
38 Muschg, *Zerstörung der deutschen Literatur*, p. 314, my translation.
39 Marcus, *Culture of Psychoanalysis*, p. 2.
40 Ricoeur, *Freud and Philosophy*, p. 179.
41 Rieff claims that patients' associations are meaningful, but not in the sense of cause-and-effect determinism. Freud formulates the meaning by shaping this raw material in a way that 'resembles literary creation'; see *Mind of the Moralist*, pp. 117f.
42 Spence, *Narrative Truth and Historical Truth*, p. 37.
43 *Ibid.*, pp. 22ff.
44 Goldberg, *Two Patterns of Rationality*, p. 87.
45 Kofman, *Freud and Fiction*, pp. 3f.

46 Cixous, 'Fiction and its Phantoms' in *New Literary History* 7/3, p. 533.
47 *Letters to Fliess*, letter of 26 Apr. 1896, p. 184.
48 *Freud/Arnold Zweig: Briefwechsel*, letter to Zweig of 12 May 1934, p. 87, my translation.
49 Wittels cited in Schönau, *Sigmund Freuds Prosa*, p. 12, my translation.
50 Jones writes that if Freud had not become a psychologist, he 'might have become a creative writer, perhaps not a poet but a novelist – in fact he said so himself more than once'; see *Life* II, p. 480.
51 Spence, *The Freudian Metaphor*, p. 114.
52 See, for example, Rieff, *Mind of the Moralist*, p. 101.
53 Fish, 'Withholding the Missing Portion: Psychoanalysis and Rhetoric' in Meltzer (ed.), *Trial(s) of Psychoanalysis*, pp. 183–209.
54 Timms, 'Novelle and Case History', *London German Studies* 2, pp. 119ff.
55 See Marcus, 'Freud and Dora: Story, History, Case History' in *Culture of Psychoanalysis*, pp. 42–86.
56 Einstein's letter of 21 Apr. 1936, cited in Jones, *Life* III, p. 217.
57 *Letters to Fliess*, letter of 3 Oct. 1897, p. 269.
58 I take this formulation of the insight from Malcolm Bowie; see his *Freud, Proust and Lacan*, p. 7. He considers it to be the key insight common to the three writers he takes for his subject.
59 Kofman, *Childhood of Art*, pp. 100 and 136ff.
60 Ellenberger, *Discovery of the Unconscious*, p. 204.
61 Goethe, 'Glückliches Ereignis', *Hamburger Ausgabe* X, pp. 540f., my translation.
62 Goldberg, *Two Patterns of Rationality*, p. 111.
63 Rieff, *Mind of the Moralist*, p. 197.
64 Lacan, 'Desire and the Interpretation of Desire in *Hamlet*', in Felman (ed.), *Literature and Psychoanalysis*, p. 42.
65 Lévi-Strauss cited by Starobinski in Meltzer (ed.), *The Trial(s) of Psychoanalysis*, p. 278n., my translation. Lévi-Strauss regarded the whole of psychoanalysis as a modern form of shamanism, the analyst supplanting the patient's private confusion with his own privileged myth; see Skura, *The Literary Use of the Psychoanalytic Process*, p. 23.
66 Andreas-Salomé, *Freud Journal*, p. 104.
67 Letter to Ferenczi of 12 July 1915, cited in Jones, *Life* III, pp. 353f.
68 Mahony, *Freud as a Writer*, p. 162.
69 Jones, *Life* II, p. 447.
70 *Letters to Fliess*, letter of 11 Sep. 1899, p. 371.
71 Joseph Wortis cited in Schönau, *Sigmund Freuds Prosa*, p. 42.
72 *Freud/Lou Andreas-Salomé: Letters*, letter of 30 July 1915, p. 32.
73 *Ibid.*, letter of 27 July 1916, p. 51, or 4 Aug. 1916, p. 52.
74 See, for example, *ibid.*, letter of 13 Mar. 1922, pp. 113–14.
75 *Ibid.*, letter of 23 Mar. 1930, p. 185.
76 Mann, 'Freud und die Zukunft' in *Schriften und Reden* II, p. 219, my translation.

77 Edelson, *Language and Interpretation in Psychoanalysis*, p. 84.
78 See Derrida, 'Freud and the Scene of Writing' in Meisel (ed.), *Freud*, pp. 145–82.
79 Bersani, *The Freudian Body*, pp. 5, 12.
80 Bloom, *Agon*, p. 108.
81 *Ibid.*, pp. 108, and 117f.
82 *Ibid.*, pp. 126ff.
83 Bloom, *Interpretation of Dreams*, p. 2.
84 Spector, *The Aesthetics of Freud*, p. 34.
85 *Ibid.*, p. 53.
86 Schur, *Freud: Living and Dying*, p. 481.
87 *Letters 1873–1939*, letter to Martha of 19 June 1882, p. 26.
88 Letter to Ferenczi of 7 July 1913, see *Studienausgabe* X, p. 182, editor's note and Gay, *Life for Our Time*, pp. 432f.
89 *Letters 1873–1939*, letter to Ferenczi of 12 Oct. 1928, p. 382.
90 *Ibid.*, letter to S. Zweig of 2 June 1932, p. 409.
91 *Letters 1873–1939*, letter to Schnitzler of 8 May 1906, p. 261.
92 *Ibid.*, letter to Schnitzler of 14 May 1922, pp. 344f.
93 *Freud/Arnold Zweig: Briefwechsel*, letter to Zweig of 21 Aug. 1930, p. 18, my translation. In fact, Freud seems to have thoroughly enjoyed playing along with *Jung's* jocular but sustained fantasy of being Goethe's great-grandson. See, for example *Jung/Freud Letters*, letter of 9 Mar. 1909, p. 211.
94 Letters to Ferenczi of 4 Apr. 1915 and 23 Apr. 1915, cited in Jones, *Life* II, p. 205. It could be argued that a scientist of Freud's training could hardly have conceived of anything quite like the *Urvater* without the respectable precedent set by Goethe's *Urpflanze*.
95 *Letters to Fliess*, letter of 27 Oct. 1897, p. 274.
96 *Ibid.*, letter of 25 Apr. 1900, p. 411.
97 Goethe, 'Die Natur. Fragment', *Hamburger Ausgabe* XIII, p. 46, my translation. See chapter 1, n.32.
98 Jones, *Life* I, p. 3.
99 *Letters 1873–1939*, letter to Martha of 2 Feb. 1886, p. 215.
100 *Psycho-Analysis and Faith: Letters of Freud and Pfister*, letter to Pfister of 24 Jan. 1910, p. 33.
101 *Freud/Arnold Zweig: Briefwechsel*, letter to Zweig of 31 May 1936, p. 137, my translation.
102 *Letters 1873–1939*, letter to Martha of 28 Apr. 1885, p. 153.
103 Sulloway, *Biologist of the Mind*, pp. 445ff.
104 *Ibid.*, pp. 489ff.
105 Hyman, *Tangled Bank*, p. 338.
106 Thomas, '*Traumdeutung* as *Bildungsroman*', *Michigan Germanic Studies* 13, pp. 184f.
107 *Letters 1873–1939*, letter to Edoardo Weiss of 12 Apr. 1933, p. 412.
108 *Freud/Lou Andreas-Salomé: Letters*, letter of 9 Feb. 1919, p. 90.
109 *Letters 1873–1939*, letter to Hermann Struck of 7 Nov. 1914, p. 312.

110 Gay, *Life for Our Time*, pp. 274ff.
111 Jones, *Life* II, p. 408.
112 Fuller, *Art and Psychoanalysis*, p. 57.
113 *Freud/Jung Letters*, letter of 17 Jan. 1909, pp. 196–7.
114 Letter to Ferenczi of 17 Oct. 1912, cited in Gay, *Life for Our Time*, p. 317.
115 Krüll, *Freud and His Father*, pp. 186f.
116 *Freud/Jung Letters*, letter of 17 Dec. 1911, p. 472.
117 Gay, *Life for Our Time*, p. 335.
118 Jones, *Life* II, p. 397.
119 Krüll, *Freud and His Father*, pp. 194ff.
120 Robert, *From Oedipus to Moses*, pp. 153, 167.
121 Gay recognizes the wishful element in Freud's speculation here, see *Life of Our Time*, p. 608. Ritchie Robertson elucidates the fantasy element even more fully; see 'Freud's Testament: *Moses and Monotheism*' in Timms (ed.), *Freud in Exile*, pp. 80–9.
122 Robert, *From Oedipus to Moses*, p. 166.
123 Hyman, *Tangled Bank*, p. 421.
124 Robertson, 'Freud's Testament: *Moses and Monotheism*' in Timms (ed.), *Freud in Exile*, pp. 80f.
125 Letter to Arnold Zweig of 16 Dec. 1934, cited in Schur, *Freud: Living and Dying*, p. 456.
126 *Freud/Arnold Zweig: Briefwechsel*, letter to Zweig of 30 Sep. 1934, p. 102.
127 Letter to Eitingon of 13 Nov. 1934, cited in Gay, *Life for Our Time*, p. 606.
128 Letter to Arnold Zweig of 20 Jan. 1936, cited in Schur, *Freud: Living and Dying*, p. 471.
129 Mahony, *Freud as a Writer*, p. 79.
130 *Psycho-Analysis and Faith*, letter to Pfister of 6 Mar. 1910, p. 35.
131 Mahony, *Freud as a Writer*, p. 119.
132 See, for example, Jones, *Life* I, p. 380.
133 *Letters to Fliess*, letter of 7 Aug. 1901, p. 447.
134 Schönau, *Sigmund Freuds Prosa*, p. 8.
135 Trilling, *Crisis of our Culture*, pp. 15f.

Bibliography

I PRIMARY TEXTS

FREUD'S WORKS

Freud, Sigmund, *Gesammelte Werke*, 18 volumes, edited by Anna Freud et al.,
  London, 1946–52
— *Studienausgabe*, 10 volumes with an *Ergänzungsband*, edited by Alexander
  Mitscherlich et al., Frankfurt, 1982
— *The Standard Edition of the Complete Psychological Works of Sigmund Freud*, 24
  volumes, translated and edited by James Strachey, London, 1953–74

FREUD'S LETTERS

Freud, Ernst L. (ed.), *Sigmund Freud / Arnold Zweig. Briefwechsel*, Frankfurt, 1968
— *Letters of Sigmund Freud 1873–1939*, translated by T. and J. Stern, London, 1961
Freud, Ernst L. and Meng, Heinrich (eds.), *Psycho-Analysis and Faith: the Letters of
  Sigmund Freud and Oskar Pfister*, translated by E. Mosbacher, London, 1963
Masson, Jeffrey Moussaieff (ed.), *The Complete Letters of Sigmund Freud to Wilhelm
  Fliess 1887–1904*, London, 1985
McGuire, William (ed.), *The Freud / Jung Letters*, translated by R. Mannheim and
  R.F.C. Hull, London, 1974
Pfeiffer, Ernst (ed.), *Sigmund Freud and Lou Andreas-Salomé: Letters*, translated by W.
  and E. Robson-Scott, London, 1972

II SECONDARY TEXTS

ARTICLES

Amacher, Peter, 'Freud's Neurological Education and its Influence on
  Psychoanalytic Theory', *Psychological Issues*, whole of issue 4/4 (1965)
Anzieu, Didier, 'The Place of Germanic Language and Culture in Freud's
  Discovery of Psychoanalysis between 1895 and 1900', *International Journal
  of Psychoanalysis* 67/2 (1986), pp. 219–26
Auden, W.H., 'Psychology and Art Today', in Kurzweil, Edith and Phillips,
  William (eds.), *Literature and Psychoanalysis* (New York, 1983), pp. 119–31

Barnouw, Dagmar, 'Modernism in Vienna: Freud and a Normative Poetics of the Self', *Modern Austrian Literature* 23/2 (1990), pp. 71–88

Bloom, Harold, 'Freud and the Poetic Sublime', in Meisel, Perry (ed.), *Freud: A Collection of Critical Essays* (New Jersey, 1981), pp. 211–23

— 'Freud: A Shakespearean Reading', in *The Western Canon: The Books and Schools of the Ages* (New York, 1994), pp. 371–94

Calhoon, Kenneth S., 'The Education of the Human Race: Lessing, Freud and the Savage Mind', *The German Quarterly* 64/2 (1991), pp. 178–89

Carroll, David, 'Freud and the Myth of the Origin', *New Literary History* 6/3 (1975), pp. 512–28

Cixous, Hélène, 'Fiction and Its Phantoms: A Reading of Freud's "Das Unheimliche"', *New Literary History* 7/3 (1976), pp. 525–48

Cranefield, Paul F., 'Freud and the "School of Helmholtz"', *Gesnerus* 23 (1966), pp. 35–9

Derrida, Jacques, 'Freud and the Scene of Writing', in Meisel, Perry (ed.), *Freud: A Collection of Critical Essays* (New Jersey, 1981), pp. 145–80

Edmundson, Mark, 'Freudian Mythmaking: The Case of Narcissus', *The Kenyon Review* 10/2 (1988), pp. 17–37

Ellmann, Richard, 'Freud and Literary Biography', in Horden, Peregrine (ed.), *Freud and the Humanities* (London, 1985), pp. 58–74

Fish, Stanley, 'Withholding the Missing Portion: Psychoanalysis and Rhetoric', in Meltzer, Françoise (ed.), *The Trial(s) of Psychoanalysis* (Chicago, 1988), pp. 183–209.

Fisher, David James, 'Reading Freud's *Civilization and its Discontents*', in Lacapra, Dominick and Kaplan, Steven L. (eds.), *Modern European Intellectual History* (Ithaca, 1982), pp. 251–78

Galdston, Iago, 'Freud and Romantic Medicine', *Bulletin of the History of Medicine* 30/6 (1956), pp. 489–507

Gedo, John, 'Freud's *Novelas Ejemplares*', in Gedo, John and Pollock, George (eds.), *Freud: The Fusion of Science and Humanism. The Intellectual History of Psychoanalysis* (New York, 1976), pp. 87–111

Gombrich, Ernst H., 'Freud's Aesthetics', in Kurzweil, Edith and Phillips, William (eds.), *Literature and Psychoanalysis* (New York, 1983), pp. 132–45

Grubrich-Simitis, Ilse, 'Reflections on Sigmund Freud's Relationship to the German Language and to some German-speaking Authors of the Enlightenment', *International Journal of Psychoanalysis* 67/3 (1986), pp. 287–94

Hartman, Geoffrey, 'The interpreter's Freud', in Lodge, David (ed.), *Modern Criticism and Theory: A Reader* (London, 1991), pp. 412–24

Holland, Norman N., 'Literary Interpretation and Three Phases of Psychoanalysis', in Roland, Alan (ed.), *Psychoanalysis, Creativity, and Literature: A French-American Inquiry* (New York, 1978), pp. 233–46

Jaffe, Nora Crow, 'A Second Opinion on Delusions and Dreams: A Reading of Freud's Interpretation of Jensen', *Literature and Medicine* 2 (1983), pp. 101–17

Lacan, Jacques, 'Desire and the Interpretation of Desire in *Hamlet*', in Felman, Shoshana (ed.), *Literature and Psychoanalysis. The Question of Reading: Otherwise* (New Haven, 1977), pp. 11–52

— 'The insistence of the letter in the unconscious', in Lodge, David (ed.), *Modern Criticism and Theory: A Reader* (London, 1991), pp. 80–106

— 'Seminar on "The Purloined Letter"', in Berman, Emanuel (ed.), *Essential Papers on Literature and Psychoanalysis* (New York, 1993), pp. 270–99

Mann, Thomas, 'Freud und die Zukunft', in *Schriften und Reden zur Literatur, Kunst und Philosophie* II (Frankfurt, 1968), pp. 213–31

— 'Die Stellung Freuds in der modernen Geistesgeschichte', in *Schriften und Reden zur Literatur, Kunst und Philosophie* I (Frankfurt, 1968), pp. 367–85

Marcuse, Ludwig, 'Die deutsche Literatur im Werke Freuds', *German Quarterly* 29/2 (1956), pp. 85–96

Meltzer, Françoise, 'Partitive Plays, Pipe Dreams', in Meltzer, Françoise (ed.), *The Trial(s) of Psychoanalysis* (Chicago, 1988), pp. 1–7

Muschg, Walter, 'Psychoanalyse und Literaturwissenschaft', in *Pamphlet und Bekenntnis: Aufsätze und Reden* (Olten, 1968), pp. 111–35

Peters, Uwe Henrik, 'Goethe und Freud', *Goethe-Jahrbuch* 103 (1986), pp. 86–105

Robertson, Ritchie, 'Freud's Testament: *Moses and Monotheism*', in Timms, Edward and Segal, Naomi (eds.), *Freud in Exile: Psychoanalysis and its Vicissitudes* (New Haven, 1988), pp. 80–9

Simons, John D., '*In Errato Veritas*: Schiller and Freud on Slips', *The German Quarterly* 56/1 (1983), pp. 14–27

Smith, Joseph H. (ed.), 'Psychoanalysis and Language', *Psychiatry and the Humanities*, whole of volume 3 (1978)

— 'The Literary Freud: Mechanisms of Defense and the Poetic Will', *Psychiatry and the Humanities*, whole of volume 4 (1980)

Starobinski, Jean, 'Acheronta Movebo', in Meltzer, Françoise (ed.), *The Trial(s) of Psychoanalysis* (Chicago, 1988), pp. 273–86

Storr, Anthony, 'Psychoanalysis and Creativity', in Horden, Peregrine (ed.), *Freud and the Humanities* (London, 1985), pp. 38–57

Suleiman, Susan Rubin, 'Nadja, Dora, Lol V. Stein: women, madness and narrative', in Rimmon-Kenan, Shlomith (ed.), *Discourse in Psychoanalysis and Literature* (London, 1987), pp. 124–51

Thomas, Ronald R., '*Traumdeutung* as *Bildungsroman*: Freud's Dream Interpretation and the Novel of His Life', *Michigan Germanic Studies* 13/2 (1987), pp. 182–205

Ticho, Ernst A., 'The Influence of the German-Language Culture on Freud's Thought', *International Journal of Psychoanalysis* 67/2 (1986), pp. 227–34

Timms, Edward, 'Novelle and Case History: Freud in Pursuit of the Falcon', *London German Studies* 2 (1983), pp. 115–34

— 'Freud's Library and His Private Reading', in Timms, Edward and Segal, Naomi (eds.), *Freud in Exile: Psychoanalysis and its Vicissitudes* (New Haven, 1988), pp. 65–79

Trilling, Lionel, 'The Authentic Unconscious', in Bloom, Harold (ed.), *Sigmund Freud* (New York, 1985), pp. 97–109

Trosman, Harry, 'Freud and the Controversy over Shakespearean Authorship', in Gedo, John and Pollock, George (eds.), *Freud: The Fusion of Science and Humanism. The Intellectual History of Psychoanalysis* (New York, 1976), pp. 307–11

— 'Freud's Cultural Background', in Gedo, John and Pollock, George (eds.), *Freud: The Fusion of Science and Humanism. The Intellectual History of Psychoanalysis* (New York, 1976), pp. 46–70
Wittgenstein, Ludwig, 'Conversations on Freud', in Wollheim, Richard and Hopkins, James (eds.), *Philosophical Essays on Freud* (Cambridge, 1982), pp. 1–11
Witzleben, Henry von, 'Goethe und Freud', *Studium Generale* 19/10 (1966), pp. 606–27
Wollheim, Richard, 'Freud and the Understanding of Art', in Bloom, Harold (ed.), *Sigmund Freud* (New York, 1985), pp. 81–95

BOOKS

Adorno, Theodor W., *Aesthetic Theory*, London, 1984
Andreas-Salomé, Lou, *The Freud Journal*, London, 1965
Anzieu, Didier, *Freud's Self-Analysis*, Madison, 1986
Appignanesi, Lisa and Forrester, John, *Freud's Women*, London, 1992
Bellemin-Noël, Jean, *Psychanalyse et littérature*, Paris, 1983
Berman, Emanuel (ed.), *Essential Papers on Literature and Psychoanalysis*, New York, 1993
Bersani, Leo, *The Freudian Body: Psychoanalysis and Art*, New York, 1986
Bettelheim, Bruno, *Freud and Man's Soul*, London, 1985
Bloom, Harold, *The Anxiety of Influence: A Theory of Poetry*, New York, 1973
— *Agon: Towards a Theory of Revisionism*, Oxford, 1982
— *The Western Canon: The Books and Schools of the Ages*, New York, 1994
Bloom, Harold (ed.), *Sigmund Freud*, New York, 1985
— *Sigmund Freud's* The Interpretation of Dreams, New York, 1989
Boothby, Richard, *Death and Desire: Psychoanalytic Theory in Lacan's Return to Freud*, London, 1991
Bowie, Malcolm, *Freud, Proust and Lacan: Theory as Fiction*, Cambridge, 1987
Brandell, Gunnar, *Freud: A Man of His Century*, Brighton, 1979
Breger, Louis, *Freud's Unfinished Journey: Conventional and Critical Perspectives in Psychoanalytical Theory*, London, 1981
Brooks, Peter, *Reading for the Plot: Design and Intention in Narrative*, Oxford, 1984
Brown, Norman O., *Life Against Death: The Psychoanalytical Meaning of History*, London, 1970
Burke, Kenneth, *The Philosophy of Literary Form: Studies in Symbolic Action*, Baton Rouge, 1967
De Certeau, Michel, *Heterologies: Discourse on the Other*, Manchester, 1986
Deleuze, Gilles and Guattari, Félix, *Anti-Oedipus: Capitalism and Schizophrenia*, New York, 1977
Edelson, Marshall, *Language and Interpretation in Psychoanalysis*, New Haven, 1975
Ellenberger, Henri F., *The Discovery of the Unconscious: The History and Evolution of Dynamic Psychiatry*, London, 1970
Empson, William, *Seven Types of Ambiguity*, Harmondsworth, 1973
Eysenck, Hans J., *Decline and Fall of the Freudian Empire*, Harmondsworth, 1986

Felman, Shoshana (ed.), *Literature and Psychoanalysis. The Question of Reading: Otherwise*, New Haven, 1977
Forrester, John, *Language and the Origins of Psychoanalysis*, London, 1980
Fromm, Erich, *Greatness and Limitations of Freud's Thought*, London, 1980
Fuller, Peter, *Art and Psychoanalysis*, London, 1988
Gay, Peter, *Freud, Jews and other Germans: Masters and Victims in Modernist Culture*, New York, 1978
— *A Godless Jew: Freud, Atheism, and the Making of Psychoanalysis*, New Haven, 1987
— *Freud: A Life for Our Time*, London, 1988
Gedo, John E. and Pollock, George H. (eds.), *Freud: The Fusion of Science and Humanism. The Intellectual History of Psychoanalysis*, New York, 1976
Goldberg, Steven E., *Two Patterns of Rationality in Freud's Writings*, Tuscaloosa, 1988
Habermas, Jürgen, *Knowledge and Human Interests*, London, 1972
H.D., *Tribute to Freud*, Manchester, 1985
Hertz, Neil, *The End of the Line: Essays on Psychoanalysis and the Sublime*, New York, 1985
Hoffmann, Frederick J., *Freudianism and the Literary Mind*, Baton Rouge, 1945
Horden, Peregrine (ed.), *Freud and the Humanities*, London, 1985
Hyman, Stanley Edgar, *The Tangled Bank: Darwin, Marx, Frazer and Freud as Imaginative Writers*, New York, 1962
Isbister, J.N., *Freud: An Introduction to His Life and Work*, Cambridge, 1985
Izenberg, Gerald N., *The Existentialist Critique of Freud: The Crisis of Autonomy*, New Jersey, 1976
Jahoda, Marie, *Freud and the Dilemmas of Psychology*, London, 1977
Jones, Ernest, *Sigmund Freud: Life and Work*, 3 volumes, London, 1955–7
Jung, Carl Gustav, *Memories, Dreams, Reflections*, Glasgow, 1980
Kofman, Sarah, *The Childhood of Art: An Interpretation of Freud's Aesthetics*, New York, 1988
— *Freud and Fiction*, Cambridge, 1991
Kris, Ernst, *Psychoanalytic Explorations in Art*, New York, 1971
Kristeva, Julia, *In the Beginning Was Love: Psychoanalysis and Faith*, New York, 1987
Krüll, Marianne, *Freud and His Father*, London, 1987
Kuhn, Thomas S., *The Structure of Scientific Revolutions*, Chicago, 1970
Kurzweil, Edith and Phillips, William (eds.), *Literature and Psychoanalysis*, New York, 1983
Laplanche, Jean and Pontalis, J.-B., *Das Vokabular der Psychoanalyse*, Frankfurt, 1982
Lodge, David (ed.), *Modern Criticism and Theory: A Reader*, London, 1991
Lukacher, Ned, *Primal Scenes: Literature, Philosophy, Psychoanalysis*, Ithaca, 1986
MacCabe, Colin, *The Talking Cure: Essays in Psychoanalysis and Language*, London, 1981
Mahony, Patrick J., *Freud as a Writer*, New Haven, 1987
— *On Defining Freud's Discourse*, New Haven, 1989
Marcus, Steven, *Freud and the Culture of Psychoanalysis: Studies in the Transition from Victorian Humanism to Modernity*, London, 1984

Marcuse, Herbert, *Eros and Civilisation: A Philosophical Inquiry into Freud*, London, 1969

Meisel, Perry (ed.), *Freud: A Collection of Critical Essays*, New Jersey, 1981

Meltzer, Françoise (ed.), *The Trial(s) of Psychoanalysis*, Chicago, 1988

Milner, Max, *Freud et l'interprétation de la littérature*, Paris, 1980

Morrison, Claudia C., *Freud and the Critic: The Early Use of Depth Psychology in Literary Criticism*, Raleigh, 1968

Muschg, Walter, *Die Zerstörung der deutschen Literatur*, Bern, 1956

Orlando, Francesco, *Toward a Freudian Theory of Literature*, Baltimore, 1978

Pfrimmer, Théo, *Freud, lecteur de la Bible*, Paris, 1982

Rank, Otto and Sachs, Hanns (eds.), *Psychoanalysis as an Art and a Science: A Symposium*, Detroit, 1968

Ricoeur, Paul, *Freud and Philosophy: An Essay on Interpretation*, New Haven, 1970

Rieff, Philip, *Freud: The Mind of the Moralist*, London, 1960

Rimmon-Kenan, Shlomith (ed.), *Discourse in Psychoanalysis and Literature*, London, 1987

Robert, Marthe, *The Psychoanalytic Revolution: Sigmund Freud's Life and Achievement*, London, 1966

— *From Oedipus to Moses: Freud's Jewish Identity*, London, 1977

Roland, Alan (ed.), *Psychoanalysis, Creativity, and Literature: A French American Inquiry*, New York, 1978

Rudnytsky, Peter L., *Freud and Oedipus*, New York, 1987

Rycroft, Charles, *Psychoanalysis and Beyond*, London, 1991

— *The Innocence of Dreams*, London, 1991

— *Viewpoints*, London, 1991

Sachs, Hanns, *Freud: Master and Friend*, London, 1945

Santas, Gerasimos, *Plato and Freud: Two Theories of Love*, Oxford, 1988

Schönau, Walter, *Sigmund Freuds Prosa: Literarische Elemente seines Stils*, Stuttgart, 1968

Schorske, Carl E., *Fin-de-siècle Vienna: Politics and Culture*, New York, 1981

Schur, Max, *Freud: Living and Dying*, London, 1972

Simpson, James, *Goethe and Patriarchy: Faust and the Fates of Desire*, Oxford, 1998

Skura, Meredith Anne, *The Literary Use of the Psychoanalytic Process*, New Haven, 1981

Spector, Jack J., *The Aesthetics of Freud: A Study in Psychoanalysis and Art*, New York, 1973

Spence, Donald P., *Narrative Truth and Historical Truth: Meaning and Interpretation in Psychoanalysis*, New York, 1982

— *The Freudian Metaphor: Towards Paradigm Change in Psychoanalysis*, New York, 1987

Sulloway, Frank J., *Freud, Biologist of the Mind: Beyond the Psychoanalytic Legend*, London, 1979

Timms, Edward and Segal, Naomi (eds.), *Freud in Exile: Psychoanalysis and its Vicissitudes*, New Haven, 1988

— *Freud and the Aesthetic of the Dream: The Impact of Psychoanalysis on Modern European Literature*, Cambridge, 1988

Timpanaro, Sebastiano, *The Freudian Slip: Psycho-Analysis and Textual Criticism*, London, 1976

Trilling, Lionel, *Freud and the Crisis of our Culture*, Boston, 1955

— *The Liberal Imagination*, Oxford, 1981

Trosman, Harry, *Freud and the Imaginative World*, New Jersey, 1985

Weber, Samuel, *The Legend of Freud*, Minneapolis, 1982

Webster, Richard, *Why Freud was Wrong: Sin, Science and Psychoanalysis*, London, 1996

Whyte, Lancelot L., *The Unconscious Before Freud*, London, 1962

Wittels, Fritz, *Sigmund Freud: His Personality, His Teaching and His School*, London, 1924

Wollheim, Richard, *Freud*, London, 1982

Wollheim, Richard and Hopkins, James (eds.), *Philosophical Essays on Freud*, Cambridge, 1982

Wright, Elizabeth, *Psychoanalytic Criticism: Theory in Practice*, London, 1984

Zanuso, Billa, *The Young Freud: The Origins of Psychoanalysis in Late Nineteenth-Century Viennese Culture*, Oxford, 1986

Index

DEMCO